CATALYST™
COMIX

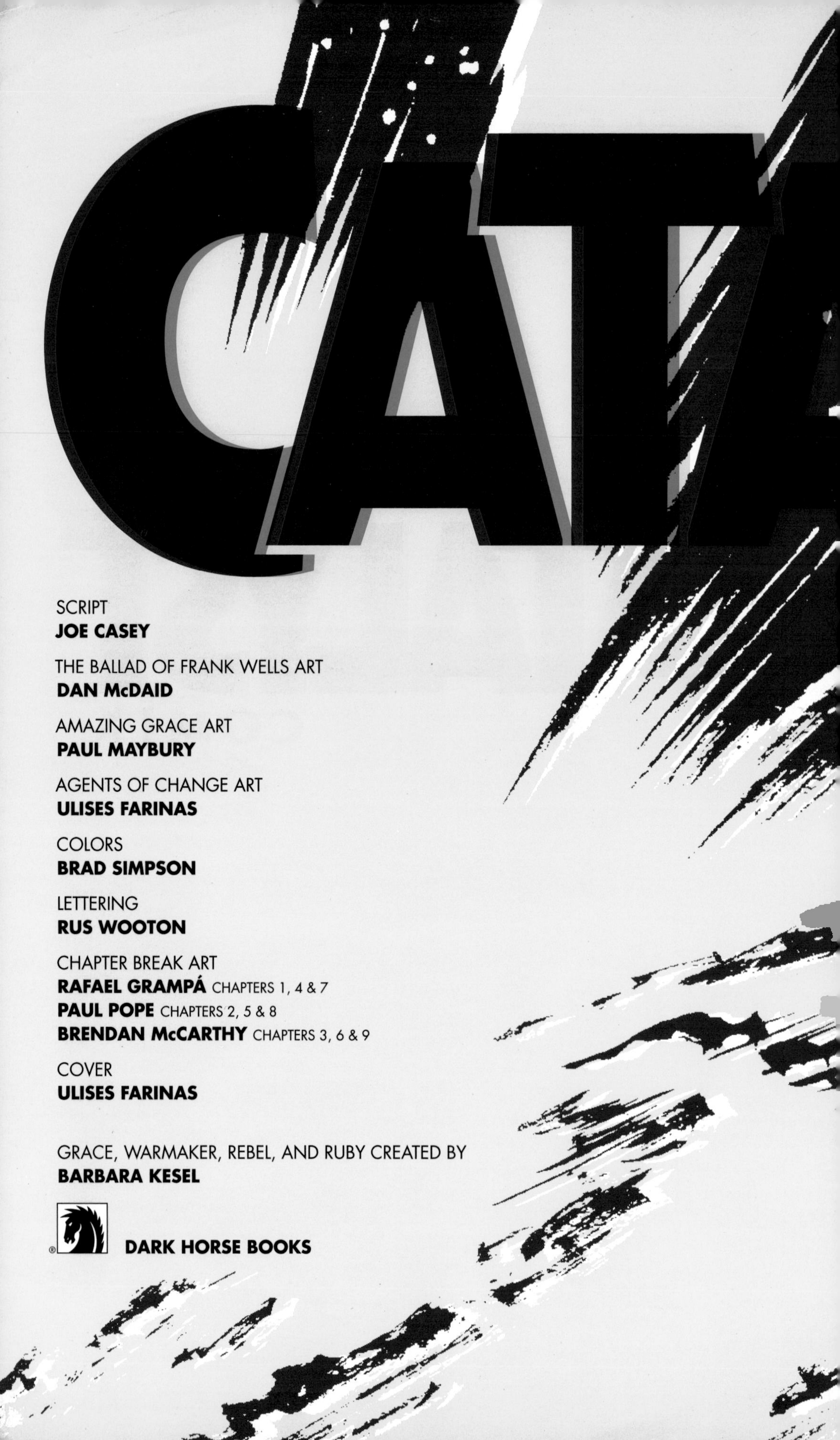

SCRIPT
JOE CASEY

THE BALLAD OF FRANK WELLS ART
DAN McDAID

AMAZING GRACE ART
PAUL MAYBURY

AGENTS OF CHANGE ART
ULISES FARINAS

COLORS
BRAD SIMPSON

LETTERING
RUS WOOTON

CHAPTER BREAK ART
RAFAEL GRAMPÁ CHAPTERS 1, 4 & 7
PAUL POPE CHAPTERS 2, 5 & 8
BRENDAN McCARTHY CHAPTERS 3, 6 & 9

COVER
ULISES FARINAS

GRACE, WARMAKER, REBEL, AND RUBY CREATED BY
BARBARA KESEL

DARK HORSE BOOKS

COMIX

PRESIDENT AND PUBLISHER
MIKE RICHARDSON
EDITOR
BRENDAN WRIGHT
ASSISTANT EDITOR
IAN TUCKER
DESIGNER
JIMMY PRESLER
DIGITAL PRODUCTION
ALLYSON HALLER

This volume collects issues #1–#9 of the Dark Horse comic-book series *Catalyst Comix*.

Published by Dark Horse Books A division of Dark Horse Comics, Inc.
10956 SE Main Street, Milwaukie, OR 97222

DarkHorse.com

International Licensing: (503) 905-2377
To find a comics shop in your area, call the Comic Shop Locator Service toll-free at (888) 266-4226.

First edition: July 2014
Library of Congress Cataloging-in-Publication Data

Casey, Joe.
Catalyst Comix / script, Joe Casey ; illustrated by Dan McDaid, Paul Maybury, Ulises Farinas, Brad Simpson. – First edition.
pages cm.
Summary: "Straight from the glory of Comics' Greatest World, Frank "Titan" Wells, Amazing Grace, and the Agents of Change are back, baby! But you've never seen them like this! Superstar writer Joe Casey–along with the widest array of artistic talent this side of the Renaissance–gives superhero comics a back-alley facelift, as these very different champions confront cosmic threats, personal demons, superheroes' role as global activists, an alien love invasion, and the strangest virtual reality you've ever experienced–but not before they face the end of the world as we know it! Collects Catalyst Comix #1-#9! "– Provided by publisher.
ISBN 978-1-61655-345-6 (paperback)
1. Superhero comic books, strips, etc. I. McDaid, Dan II. Maybury, Paul, 1982- III. Farinas, Ulises IV. Simpson, Brad (Bradley Darwin), 1975- V. Title.
PN6727.C388C38 2014
741.5'973-dc23
2014008661

10 9 8 7 6 5 4 3 2 1
Printed in China

SOMETIMES ALL IT TAKES IS TO KNOCK THAT FIRST DOMINO OVER . . .

Okay, I'll be honest; this book is probably *not* the first domino. But, as a package in and of itself, I'd take bets on whether or not *Catalyst Comix* is somewhere in the domino chain. It holds the torch as high as any book possibly *could* in the name of . . . well, in the name of *something*. I'm not sure what, exactly. All I know for sure is that 1) it's a superhero comic and 2) it's different.

Different than *what*, you might ask. Well, again, that depends on what your particular kink is. But let's just assume that your kink is superheroes. And why wouldn't it be? If there's one thing that comics does better than any other medium . . . it's superheroes. I'm guessing you probably like superheroes just fine. It's a perfectly good kink to have.

And, let's face it, I know my way around superheroes. I've been in this ball game for more than fifteen years, most of them tackling the four-color mythologies that our industry has built itself on since a certain Kryptonian strongman leapt his first tall building in a single bound. I've approached them from just about every angle, from the iconic to the subversive and everything in between. The very concept of the superhero is something that has fascinated me since I was five years old. They're in my blood. They're in my bones. They're in my DNA. Every aspect of their existence—on the page *and* behind the scenes—has helped keep me invested in this art form in what could only be interpreted by an outsider as a deeply depraved way. But you and I know what it's *really* all about, don't we? At their best, they're just so damned *cool*, aren't they?

Now let's get down to it. Just being a longtime *reader* of superhero comicbooks, the patented "revitalization" of otherwise moribund characters is something I've always been a fan of, from Frank Miller on *Daredevil* and Walt Simonson on *Thor* to Alan Moore on *Swamp Thing* and so on . . . to take existing concepts and *try* to make them "work" for the current readership is always a good time, for both reader *and* creator.

So that's where the Comics' Greatest World characters enter the picture. What we've done here is taken some of the cream of that nineties crop and refashioned, repurposed, and regalvanized them for the Tumultuous Two Thousand Teens. Dark Horse Head Honcho Mike Richardson fired the starter pistol and I was off to the races, making a superhero comicbook that set out to be a righteous break from the tedium of the last few years. After picking exactly which characters would be up for the ol' spit 'n' polish . . . we set out to find our spitters. We had to recruit our polishers.

And so we did. Big time.

Dan McDaid draws the Frank Wells strip in atypical apocalyptic fashion. Paul Maybury has climbed right on top of Amazing Grace and ain't gettin' off her. And Ulises Farinas is killing it loudly on Agents of Change.

These are serialized stories. Some of them end up being interconnected—they obviously take place in the same world—and it all builds to something fairly intense. At least, it feels intense to me. And, lemme tell ya, if there's one thing I know when I feel it . . . it's intensity. So we're certainly not holding back in terms of where we're taking these characters. As you'll see, these are superhero comics where *anything* can happen. I'm not sure if I would say these characters have been "updated" as much as we've simply brought out their inherent weirdness and placed it front and center for all to enjoy. And calling it "weirdness" . . . that's not a pejorative, y'know—these are great characters, and we're all getting our collective rocks off using them to make a different kind of comicbook: something a lot more unpredictable than your typical, full-tilt superhero series.

Now, let's talk more about the art (because it's probably the most important part here). These artists—McDaid, Maybury, Farinas—are the future of sequential pop art. They're the next wave of big talent. And these three are just the tip of the iceberg. I could make a huge list of artists that I think are way more accessible as cartoonists than the typical "house style" you'd find in most Marvel and DC books right now. But, y'know, it's the same thing that happened way back in the 1980s, when the independent publishers of the day brought out so many visionary artists that I'd never seen before . . . Bernie Mireault, Dennis Fujitake, the Pander Bros., Mitch O'Connell, Los Bros. Hernandez, Kevin O'Neill, Seth, Ty Templeton, Steve Parkhouse, Chester Brown, Daniel Clowes, Charles Burns, Tim Sale, Peter Bagge, etc. These were not artists that were going to get so-called mainstream Marvel or DC superhero gigs at that time. You weren't going to see them drawing Fantastic Four or Justice League or any of those characters that have morphed into corporate IPs in the last decade. And yet, for me, those artists completely changed everything. Their influence was felt in a big, bad way on my generation and all the ones that came after me. Some of them even went on to prestige gigs at the "Big Two." So, as a tribute to them, it's time to shake things up again, to show that there are other ways to do comics—superhero comics specifically—than what's being forced down our throats by the Big Two.

So obviously I wanted to make sure we pulled in artists that I knew would do soul-cracking work but also happen to draw in individual, idiosyncratic styles that, for some unknown reason, seem to have kept them outside of the mainstream superhero artist loop. I have no idea why that is, because this is how I personally want to see more superheroes depicted. McDaid, Maybury, Farinas . . . these artists are as different from each other as they are from most of the oftentimes interchangeable talents who do get hired to draw the monthly books at Marvel and DC right now, those countless artists who inadvertently promote the dreaded house styles that keep the most well-known superheroes stuck in creative quicksand. At those publishers, these guys would be—and have been—shunted off to the occasional short stories in Marvel's *Strange Tales* anthology or DC's *Bizarro Comics*. I love both of those books—both of them being some early dominoes in the chain—but they were definitely built and marketed as something "other." Or, more specifically, they were not "mainstream" (whatever *that* word means these days). Meanwhile, the artists that fill those books would never be let loose on the monthly, primetime adventures of Captain America or Wonder Woman or the X-Men or whoever. And why not? For my money, the way they depict superheroes is just so much more exciting and individualistic.

But, y'know, it's just a matter of time. It happened before. It'll happen again.

Hey, maybe it *is* happening. Or starting to, at least. I'd be remiss if I didn't point out that, ever since the initial PR for this series hit the streets almost two years ago, and with all my attendant trash talking that went along with it (like the above three paragraphs, but probably even more intense), a keen eye couldn't help but notice that more unique, off-center artists are finally starting to entrench themselves—and their styles—on certain mainstream superhero properties. More dominoes falling, as far as I'm concerned . . .

So, anyway . . . if you like superheroes, you *need* to see this book. You need to momentarily break off from whatever's being spoon fed to you this month by the corporations. I may be talking even more smack here (*hey, sometimes I just can't help myself*), but I know what's *good* when I see it. I also know that times may change, but sometimes you have to do what you can to nudge the times along a little.

And this—*Catalyst Comix*—is how superhero comicbooks can change for the better . . .

. . . one book at a time.

JOE CASEY

Drawing another line in the sand
May 2013 / March 2014

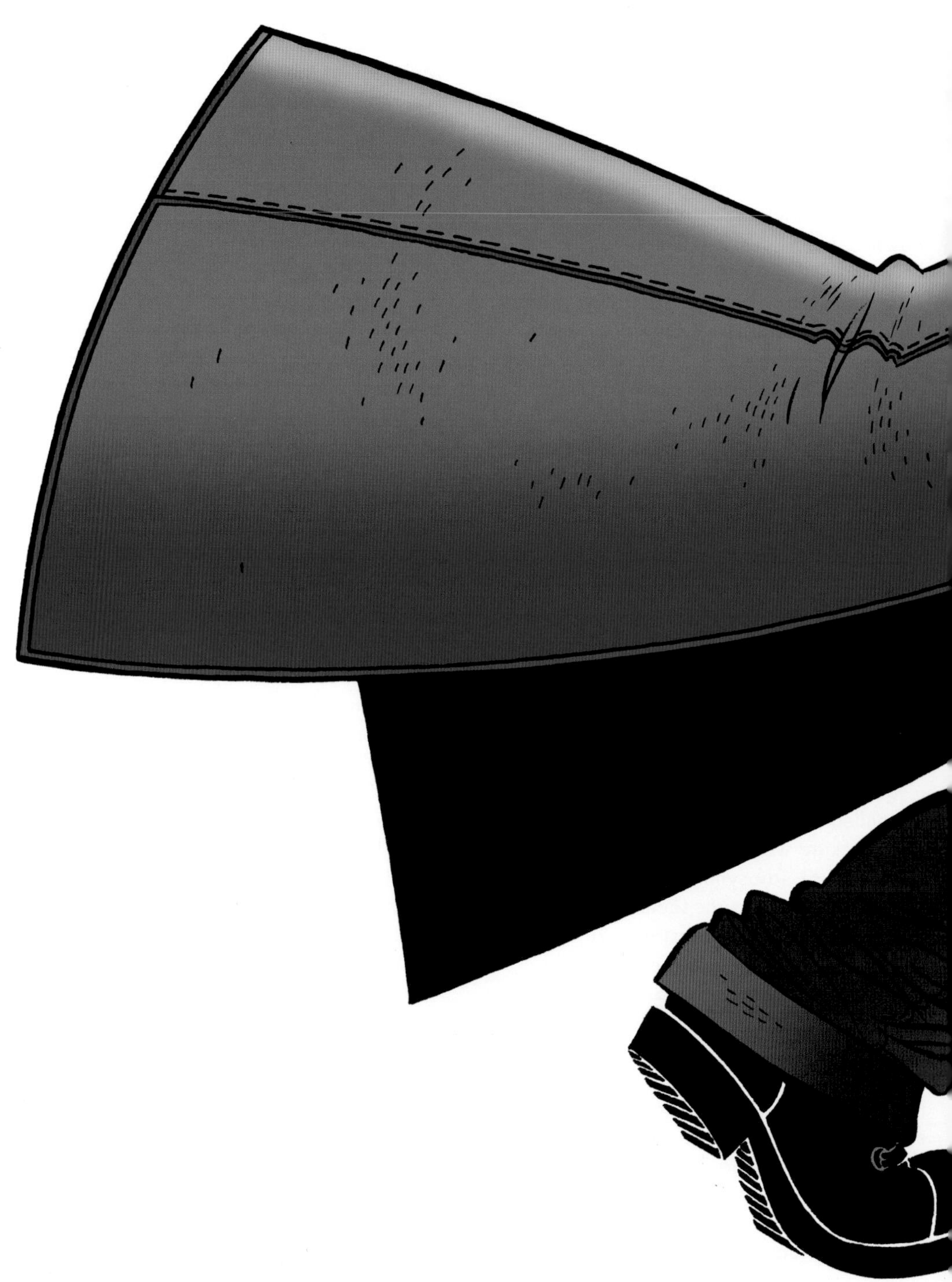

R. GRAMPÁ
12

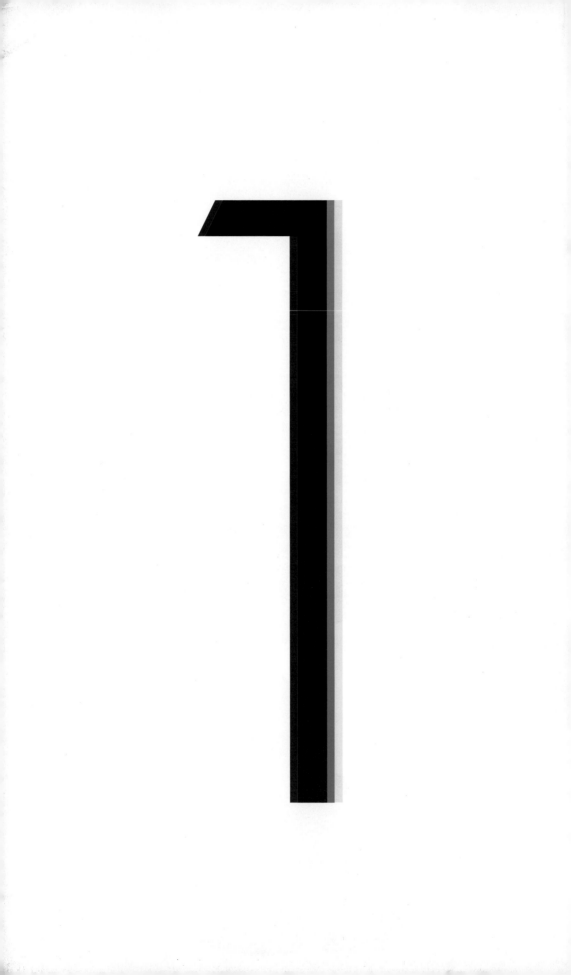

LL OF A SUDDEN...THE INTERNET CAFÉS AND THE JUICE BARS AND THE WHITE NOISE OF THE NEW FALL TELEVISION SEASON WERE RENDERED MEANINGLESS.
THIS WAS THE END OF THE WORLD...AND IT WAS EVERYTHING OUR COLLECTIVE NIGHTMARES PROMISED US IT WOULD BE! AND MORE!
IN A LOT OF WAYS...IT WAS RAPTUROUS (IF YOU'RE INTO THAT SORTA THING). BUT MOST OF US HAD FALLEN HARD FOR THE BIG LIE AND NOW WE WERE PAYING FOR IT THROUGH OUR NOSES...
LUCKILY, SOMEONE HAD THE BIG BALLS TO STAND UP TO TOTAL ANNIHILATION...
...AND HIS NAME WAS FRANK WELLS.
I DON'T...
...WANT TO DIE AGAIN.
12.21.12
THIS IS WHAT WENT DOWN

IT WAS WAY DIFFERENT WHEN THE WORLD CALLED HIM "TITAN"--
HALF OF MANHATTAN IS ALREADY GONE--
--POWER!
--BUT IF THERE'S ONE THING THE END OF THE WORLD PROVIDES, IT'S CLARITY.
--CAN'T LET THIS MONSTER GET ITS MEAT HOOKS IN THE REST OF THE WORLD!
FRANK WELLS IS A GUY WITH A LOT OF THINGS GOING FOR HIM.
MOST IMPORTANTLY--

BUT CLARITY DOESN'T AUTOMATICALLY EQUATE TO INTELLIGENCE, DOES IT...?
DAMN.
SOME KIND OF...FEEDBACK. AND THE SOUND IT MADE...!
MAYBE I ACTUALLY DID MORE DAMAGE THAN I...
...THOUGHT...?

OBVIOUSLY, FRANK WELLS ISN'T A DEEP THINKER. BUT WHO WOULD BE, IN THESE FUNKY CIRCUMSTANCES?
ESPECIALLY WHEN HE'S STARING DOWN MULTIPLE-WARHEAD SLIME HORRORS, EACH ONE WITH THEIR OTHER-DIMENSIONAL SIGHTS SET ON NOTHING LESS THAN COMPLETE HUMAN DEVASTATION!
AVAILABLE FOR ALL OF YOUR END-OF-THE-WORLD-SCENARIO NEEDS!
AT A TIME LIKE THIS, EVEN HIS OWN FLAWED HUMANITY IS GOING TO REAR ITS UGLY HEAD...
ARE...THEY COMING FOR ME...?
AN ACT OF COWARDICE? OR SELF-PRESERVATION? THERE'S NO WAY OF KNOWING...
NO--!
SOME OF THESE BUILDINGS WERE RENOVATED JUST LAST YEAR...!
THE COLLATERAL DAMAGE CANNOT BE IGNORED--

NEVER FACED SOMETHING LIKE THIS BEFORE...
TOO MUCH DEATH...ALL AROUND ME...
SURVIVAL IS AN INSTINCT THAT CAN BECOME AUTOMATIC... EVEN FOR SOMEONE WHO'S BASICALLY INDESTRUCTIBLE.
HEART AND SOUL.
BUT THE HEART IS WHERE THE HURT IS...
MEANWHILE, AT 1600 PENNSYLVANIA AVENUE, ANOTHER HOME--THE GRAND MONUMENT TO METHAMERICA ITSELF--HAS GONE DARK...NO DIFFERENT THAN ANY OTHER HAPLESS HOUSE CURRENTLY ON THE PLANET.
THE FARMERS AND THE PEDDLERS AND THE MINIMUM-WAGE SLAVERS MIGHT ASSUME ALL THE ANSWERS COULD BE FOUND WITHIN--
--IF ONLY THEY COULD ALL BEAR WITNESS TO THIS STRANGE, SORDID SCENE...!
THE ULTIMATE CORRIDOR OF POWER... PARALYZED BY KUMBAYA SYMBOLISM AND USELESS RELIGIOUS FERVOR...
...TO BE ABLE, AT ANY MOMENT, TO SACRIFICE WHAT WE ARE FOR WHAT WE COULD BECOME...
PRESIDENT SANTOS IS DESPERATE, ISN'T HE...?
NORMALLY, HE'D NEVER GET ALL OF HIS VARIOUS ADVISORS IN THE SAME ROOM...
...END OF CIVILIZATION OR NOT, THAT'S JUST BAD POLITICS!

...WE ARE NOT RESPONDING TO THIS INSTANT IF WE ARE JUDGING ANY ASPECT OF IT...
MY APOLOGIES, BELOVED SAGE, BUT I'M NOT SURE ANY OF THIS IS HAVING THE DESIRED EFFECT...
...THE ENTIRE PLANET IS WITHOUT POWER, AND THE SCATTERED REPORTS OUT OF NEW YORK HAVE NOT BEEN OPTIMISTIC.
DO WE NEED TO GET TO THE BUNKER...?
SIR, I DON'T THINK IT'LL DO ANY GOOD FOR US TO--
MR. PRESIDENT!
SIT-ROOM BACKUP SYSTEMS ARE ONLINE!
THE JOINT CHIEFS THINK WE CAN KEY INTO THE SATS AND TRY TO GET A VISUAL!
NO HUMAN TECHNOLOGY COULD EVER MEASURE THE MEGA-THREAT THAT HAS LANDED ON OUR DIMENSIONAL SHORES...
...NOR COULD IT PROPERLY CALCULATE THE TOLL SUFFERED FROM THE ARRIVAL OF SAID MEGA-THREAT.
BUT FRANK WELLS HAS EYES OF HIS OWN...
I DON'T KNOW WHAT TO DO...!
EVERYTHING AROUND ME IS...FALLING APART!
WHY AM I THE ONLY ONE HERE?! THERE'S SUPPOSED TO BE A WHOLE WORLD OF US READY TO STAND AND FIGHT...!
BUT IT'S JUST ME...
ME AGAINST--

To give it a proper NAME is to somehow DIMINISH it. But we're gonna give it one ANYWAY...
It is the ultimate DEATH CONCEPT! It is the FINAL NIGHTMARE made terrifyingly real!
The only word to DESCRIBE it echoes through the universe like a minor metal key, drop D tuned cacophony of chaos!
NIBIRU IS RELEASE!
NIBIRU IS DECAY!
NIBIRU IS EXTINCTION!
NIBIRU IS!
Ignore the PHYSICS. Enjoy the ENTROPY.
IT'S... TOO BIG... I CAN'T--
--HHURRRRMMM--!
A PSYCHIC ATTACK!
A PSYCHOTIC REACTION!
Proximity's a BITCH!

A MOMENT'S HESITATION...
JUST...ONE CHANCE...
...ONE CHOICE...

...AND FRANK WELLS IS ON THE MOVE--
--A HOTSHOT OVERLOAD OF FEAR AND DESIRE!

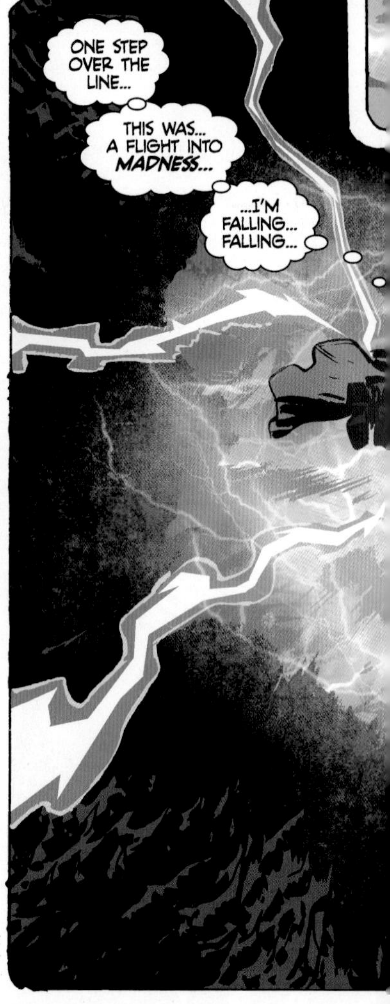
ONE STEP OVER THE LINE...
THIS WAS... A FLIGHT INTO MADNESS...
...I'M FALLING... FALLING...

BOOM
HE SEES THE TARGET...
...A CHOIR OF ANGELS SINGING HIS NAME...A HEAVENLY HOST IN ITS FINAL REFRAIN...
...HE PUSHES THROUGH THE FIERY MEMBRANE.
A SPOONFUL OF SUGAR...
MY MIND--
--IS ON FIRE--!
LOST WITHIN THE CHURN, INHALING THE MOLECULAR CORRUPTION AND GARAGE BAND CLATTER--

--THE PANIC BRINGS OUT EVERY SUBCONSCIOUS DEMON HIDING WITHIN THE SHADOWS OF HIS OWN TWISTED, BROKEN PSYCHE!
ECHOES OF A PAST LIFE... THE TURMOIL OF AN ENTIRE UNIVERSE COLLAPSING IN ON ITSELF...STARING INTO THE AMBIVALENT ABYSS OF THE VORTEX--
--AND BLINKING!
THE DEATH OF TITAN. THE BIRTH OF FRANK WELLS.
HAVING POWER AND CONTROLLING POWER ARE TWO DIFFERENT THINGS--
--AS YOU WILL LEARN!
OR, MORE CONFUSING STILL, HOW FICKLE THE HAND OF FATE CAN BE. WHERE THAT WHICH YOU WERE BORN WITH--THE POWER THAT HAS BEEN YOUR CONSTANT COMPANION ALL YOUR MISERABLE LIFE--IS SUDDENLY GONE.
WHEN POWER IS YOUR IDENTITY... HOW DO YOU COPE? WHEN ITS ABSENCE SUDDENLY LEAVES YOU IN A HORRIBLE, SLOBBERING SORT OF SPASTIC STUPOR...WHAT KIND OF LIFE DO YOU HAVE LEFT?
THIS IS HOW THE FORCES OF ENTROPY WORK ON THE HUMAN MIND...THE COLLAPSE INTO NOTHINGNESS...THE OBLITERATION OF THE SOUL...
I DON'T... UNDERSTAND WHAT'S HAPPENING...
...IS THIS WHAT DE FEELS LIKE...?
ARE YOUR DAYS NOW SPENT SHUFFLING UP AND DOWN A CONCEPTUAL JETTY...PONDERING WHAT'S LEFT OF YOUR IDENTITY WHILE EVERY HIDDEN ORIFICE ABSENTMINDEDLY FILLS THE UNIFORM YOU'D COME TO DEPEND ON...?
AMIDST THE WRECKAGE OF A VERITABLE RAINBOW COALITION OF ESTRANGED HEROISM... WELL-MEANING IDEAS GASPING FOR AIRTIME...THE WINDED MOTHERMISSERS SCATTERED AT HIS FEET...
...ONLY ONE THING IS CERTAIN: DISPLACEMENT IS A DISH BEST SERVED COLD.
NONE OF THIS... IS REAL...
...IS IT...?!
BUT OLD MAN FRANK WON LET GO...THE VIBRATIONS UP AND DOWN HIS SPINE TELLING HIM TO LET IT LOOSE--

--TO UNLEASH THAT LAST, **PRIMAL SCREAM** THAT RISES FROM SOMEWHERE DEEP DOWN INSIDE.

GIMME...

GIMME...

...MORE...!

KILL THE BODY--

--AND THE HEAD WILL DIE!

ALL IT TAKES IS TO EXERT THE NECESSARY **MOJO**--

--AND, FINALLY, THE GLORIOUS **RELEASE!**

THE SOUND IT MAKES IS **INTENSE...** A MIDRANGE **CRUNCH** MIXED WITH THE LOW-END CRACK OF A GALACTIC GLACIER CHIMING ACROSS THE HARMONIC SPECTRUM...

...A **DEATH-RATTLE IMPLOSION** OF MYTHIC PROPORTIONS--

--RIPPLES OF VIOLENT ENERGY BLASTING ACROSS THE CRACKED FACE OF THE WORLD!

BUT THE PARTY'S AT **GROUND ZERO**--

WHAT HAVE I **DONE**--?!

ANYONE HAVE ANY F@¢KING CLUE WHAT'S HAPPENING...?!

I'M SURPRISED OUR SAT ARRAY HASN'T JUST FALLEN RIGHT OUT OF THE SKY...

HEY, IT **STILL** MIGHT...

DAMN...!

SOME KIND OF WEIRD... STATIC ELECTRICITY STILL HANGING IN THE AIR...

TASTES... SWEET ON MY TONGUE...

BUT... DOES THAT MEAN...

...IT'S ACTUALLY **OVER**...?

THERE'S NO REAL **CERTAINTY** IN **THIS** VICTORY.

ONLY THE DISTANT ECHOES OF **PAIN**...THE FADED **SCREAMS** OF THE COUNTLESS CANNON-FODDER CASUALTIES...THE PSYCHIC SUFFERING STILL LINGERING HEAVY AMID THE OXYGEN...

...A COSMIC CARBON **FOOTPRINT** LEFT BEHIND FOR COUNTLESS HISTORIANS TO ANALYZE...

...AND A HERO'S STATE OF CONFUSION.
...I DID IT...!

--KKKKKK--
--APPARENTLY BACK ON THE AIR...
LIVE

...GOT OUR TRAFFIC COPTER UP ABOVE THE CITY NOW...
...SURVEYING THE DAMAGE AND--HOLD ON!--SOMETHING'S EMERGING FROM THE...
...OKAY, THIS CONFIRMS THE GROUND REPORTS THAT WERE COMING IN...
...HUMANITY'S LAST LINE OF DEFENSE WAS THIS MAN!
LIVE

WELL, I DON'T KNOW WHERE HUMANITY EARNED THE KIND OF LUCK WE SEEM TO BE HAVING...
...BUT CONGRATULATIONS, EVERYONE.
WE LIVE TO FIGHT ANOTHER DAY, MR. PRESIDENT...
SIR! NORAD'S GOT ANOTHER UNIDENTIFIED BOGEY MOVING ACROSS THE MIDWESTERN STATES...!
THE NEEDLE DROPS. DIFFERENT VERSE, SAME AS THE FIRST...

...BUT IN THIS JAM, THE ENDING IS ACTUALLY THE BEGINNING.
HMMF.
I GUESS TIMING IS EVERYTHING...

ZIPPING THROUGH THE DAYS AT LIGHTNING SPEED...
FRANK WELLS!
I THINK I'M IN LOVE!
OBEY

DON'T BORE US, GET TO THE CHORUS...
THE SEARCH FOR SELF CAN BEAR BITCHIN' FRUIT.
YIN-YANG... WHAT'S YOUR THANG?

AND THE FINAL FOCUS OF YOUR DISCONTENT...
SO...I SAVED THE WORLD...
...NOW WHAT...?

THE GRAND SOCIAL EXPERIMENT HAS SEEN BETTER DAYS...
ITS ORIGINAL PURPOSE WAS A SIMPLE ONE: TO BE THE HOME OF THE GODS. BUT IN THIS DAY AND AGE, WHO ISN'T A GOD (IN ONE WAY OR ANOTHER)? AREN'T WE ALL "SPECIAL"?
THE VELVET ROPE MENTALITY WORKED FOR A WHILE. FOR YEARS, EVEN. BUT EVERY FAD HAS ITS OWN SHELF LIFE. AND ONCE THE SHINY VENEER HAD WORN OFF WHAT ONE CRITIC CALLED "A SOCIOECONOMIC THEME PARK INCAPABLE OF SUSTAINING ITS MISGUIDED, UTOPIAN IDEALS IN THE GLOBAL VILLAGE OF THE TWENTY-FIRST CENTURY," THE ATTENTION AND THE SCRUTINY OF THE WORLD FINALLY STARTED TO DRIFT AWAY.
BUT THIS WAS EXACTLY WHEN THE REAL WORK COULD BEGIN IN THE FABLED GOLDEN CITY...

...AND THOSE STILL COMMITTED TO ITS CAUSE--THE CITY COUNCIL--HAVE REDOUBLED THEIR EFFORTS TO FORGE A NEW SOCIETY ON THIS MISBEGOTTEN PLANET.
THAT IS, IF THE PLANET ACTUALLY SURVIVES THIS LATEST CRISIS...
...SO SOMEONE DECIDED IT WAS THE END OF THE WORLD AND DIDN'T TELL US?! THE NERVE...!
I HAVE IT ON GOOD AUTHORITY THAT THIS MAY INDEED BE THE REAL THING.
WELL...ARE WE PREPARED FOR THIS IN ANY WAY, SHAPE, OR FORM...?
WHAT DO YOU THINK...?

WORLDWIDE COMMUNICATIONS ARE DOWN...WE'VE SWITCHED THE GRID OVER TO OUR ALTERNATIVE GENERATORS, BUT THEY WON'T LAST FOR LONG...
...ESPECIALLY IF THIS THREAT IS OF, SHALL WE SAY, UNNATURAL ORIGIN.

WHAT ABOUT OUR OWN DETERRENT MEASURE? HAS SHE ACTUALLY--
DON'T WORRY. SHE'S ON IT.
YOU DIDN'T THINK SHE'D JUST SIT AROUND AND WAIT FOR EVERYTHING TO GO TO HELL, DID YOU...?

NAVIGATIONAL ADJUSTMENTS INITIATED///// UTILIZING POINTS OF REFERENCE: ECLIPTIC + CYGNUS OB2/////
ESTABLISHING ANCHOR POINTS/////FIRING RETROTHRUSTERS/////
SOMEONE'S FOUND HERSELF A LONG WAY FROM UTOPIA...

IF YOU HAD THE BALLS TO TRAVEL THREE HUNDRED LIGHT YEARS FROM EARTH...AND FOUND YOURSELF SQUATTING SOMEWHERE BETWEEN OUR OWN SOLAR SYSTEM AND THE SAGITTARIUS ARM OF THE MILKY WAY GALAXY...YOU'D FIND A UNIQUE SERIES OF NONLUMINOUS, MOLECULAR **DUST CLOUDS** EXTENDING OUT FROM THE NUCLEAR BULGE...

...A **DARK RIFT** FROM WHICH EMANATES EVERY **DOOMSDAY SCENARIO** OF BOTH MYTHOLOGY AND SCIENCE. THE BIRTHPLACE OF ALL THINGS BOTH INEXPLICABLE **AND** DEADLY. THE MOUTH OF THE RIVER STYX. THE GAPING MAW OF NOTHINGNESS EXISTING BOTH WITHIN **AND** WITHOUT US. IN **OTHER** WORDS--

--THE **COSMIC MOTHER OF ALL THREATS.**

THE **TRUE** GROUND ZERO FOR THE END OF **EVERYTHING.**

ANYONE NEED TO CHANGE THEIR UNDERWEAR YET...?

12.21.12
THIS IS WHAT REALLY WENT DOWN

ANALYZING MOLECULAR STRUCTURE///// MAPPING M24/////
COUNTING DOWN TO SOLAR ALIGNMENT/////
MEASURING GRAVITATIONAL COMPRESSION/////
STARING INTO THE ABYSS...SHE NEVER THOUGHT IT WOULD BE LIKE THIS. THROUGHOUT THE JOURNEY, SHE QUESTIONED THIS COURSE OF ACTION MANY TIMES.
BUT FINALLY ARRIVING HERE ON THE SHORES OF OBLIVION, SHE REALIZES SHE NEVER HAD A CHOICE...
...SHE HAD BUILT GOLDEN CITY. THE IDEA WAS HERS AND HERS ALONE. SHE LAID THE FIRST BRICK.
WHAT SHE WAS BUILDING WAS MORE THAN A HAVEN FOR THE FORWARD THINKERS OF THIS WORLD...IT WAS A SYMBOL.
AND SYMBOLS STILL MATTER.
IN THE YEARS SINCE ITS INCEPTION...BEYOND THAT INITIAL PERIOD OF SOCIAL TURBULENCE...
...GRACE HAD FOUND HER PEACE.
AND HERE, WHILE MEDITATING DEEP WITHIN HER PERSONAL CITADEL OF SOLACE, SHE FINDS HERSELF ATTUNED TO THE SOUNDS OF THE WORLD.
SOMETIMES WITH TERRIFYING RESULTS--
--IT WAS A QUICK VISION. BUT GRACE KNEW DAMN WELL WHAT IT MEANT.
BUT WAS IT MERELY A WARNING--
--OR WAS IT A MESSAGE?
EITHER WAY, SHE KNEW EXACTLY WHAT TO DO...

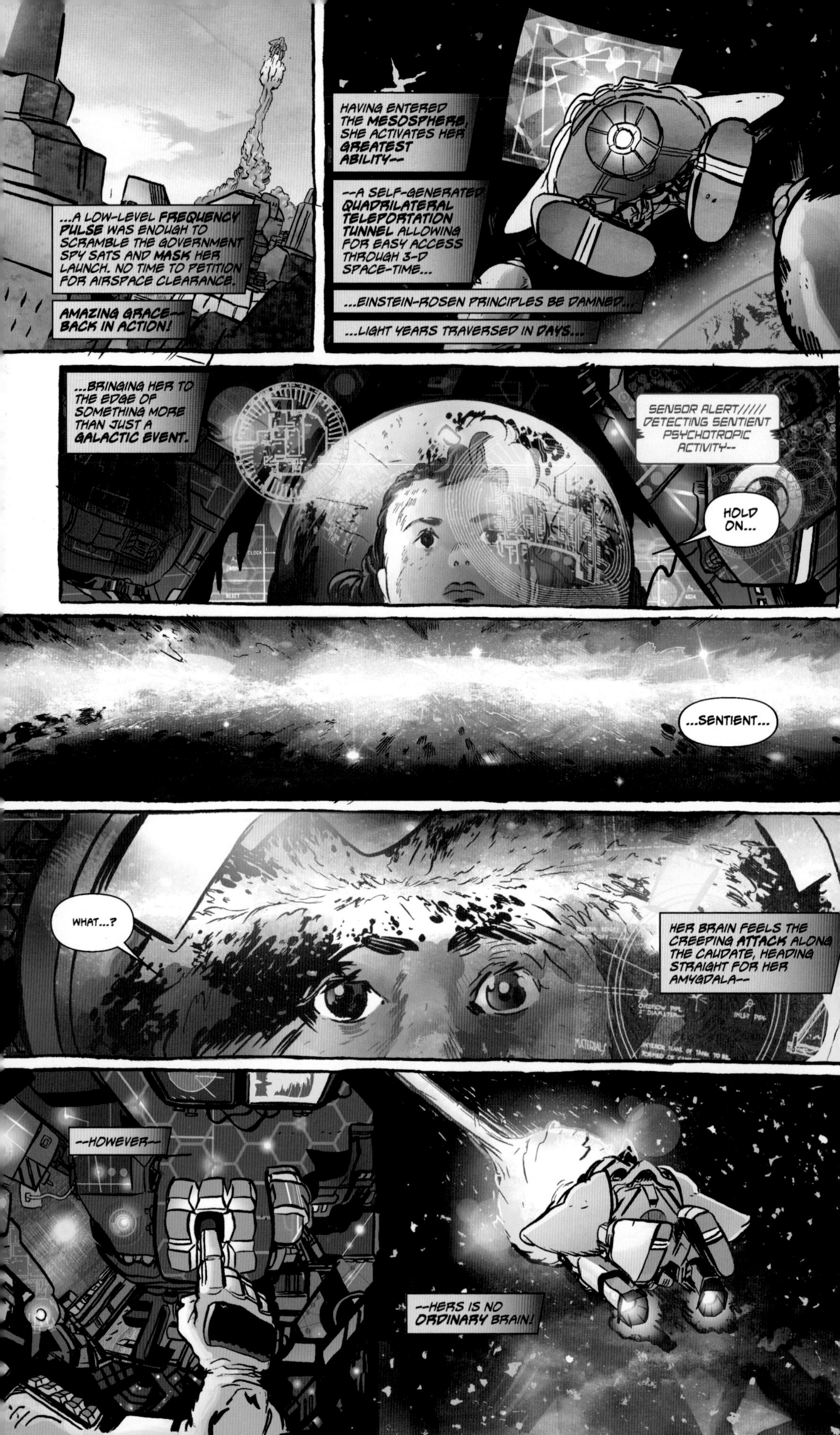
...A LOW-LEVEL FREQUENCY PULSE WAS ENOUGH TO SCRAMBLE THE GOVERNMENT SPY SATS AND MASK HER LAUNCH. NO TIME TO PETITION FOR AIRSPACE CLEARANCE.
AMAZING GRACE-- BACK IN ACTION!
HAVING ENTERED THE MESOSPHERE, SHE ACTIVATES HER GREATEST ABILITY--
--A SELF-GENERATED QUADRILATERAL TELEPORTATION TUNNEL ALLOWING FOR EASY ACCESS THROUGH 3-D SPACE-TIME...
...EINSTEIN-ROSEN PRINCIPLES BE DAMNED...
...LIGHT YEARS TRAVERSED IN DAYS...
...BRINGING HER TO THE EDGE OF SOMETHING MORE THAN JUST A GALACTIC EVENT.
SENSOR ALERT///// DETECTING SENTIENT PSYCHOTROPIC ACTIVITY--
HOLD ON...
...SENTIENT...
WHAT...?
HER BRAIN FEELS THE CREEPING ATTACK ALONG THE CAUDATE, HEADING STRAIGHT FOR HER AMYGDALA--
--HOWEVER--
--HERS IS NO ORDINARY BRAIN!

PHOTONIC CLUSTER PACK.
TIMED RELEASE. SELF-REPLICATING UPON DELIVERY AND DETONATION.
ANOTHER ONE OF HER DAYDREAMS MADE REAL BY THE SCIENTIFIC MINDS OF GOLDEN CITY.
FOR NOW, A MOMENTARY DISTRACTION... THE ONLY KIND THAT WOULD POSSIBLY WORK ON THE DEEPEST DARKNESS.
CLUSTER PACK IS ACTIVE/////UNABLE TO INCREASE SHIELDING///// RADIATION LEVELS RISING///// RECOMMENDATION: INCREASE PERSONAL PROTECTION LAYERS--
NO NEED FOR THAT. I'M FINE.
BESIDES...
...WE'RE NOT GOING TO BE HERE MUCH LONGER.
AND WITH A THOUGHT, ANOTHER QUADRILATERAL TELEPORTATION TUNNEL IS TRIGGERED.
THIS ONE, AS MASSIVE AS SHE'S EVER ATTEMPTED...
...SUDDEN GRAVITATIONAL DISPLACEMENT IS THE FIRST, MOST IMMEDIATE EFFECT.
THE STRUGGLE TO MAINTAIN SANITY IS THE NEXT.
EXOTIC MATTER CASCADES ACROSS THE SHIP'S HULL LIKE WATER ON A WINDSHIELD...NEGATIVE ENERGY DENSITY HELPING TO STABILIZE THIS HOLE AS IT SLIDES THROUGH AT SUPERLUMINAL SPEEDS...
...THE WILDEST RIDE SHE HAS EVER KNOWN.

AND THEN SOMETHING HAPPENS...
SOMETHING DECIDEDLY... UNPREDICTABLE...

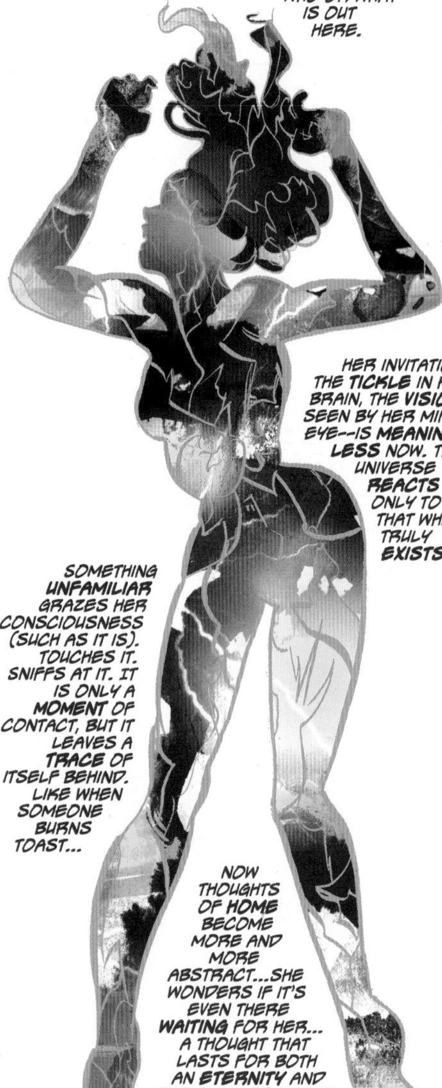
IT WAS A LEAP OF FAITH. NO DOUBT ABOUT IT. TO HURL HER BODY OUT INTO THE VOID...WITH ONLY THE SLIGHTEST INKLING OF WHO OR WHAT IS OUT HERE.
HER INVITATION-- THE TICKLE IN HER BRAIN, THE VISIONS SEEN BY HER MIND'S EYE--IS MEANING-LESS NOW. THE UNIVERSE REACTS ONLY TO THAT WHICH TRULY EXISTS.
SOMETHING UNFAMILIAR GRAZES HER CONSCIOUSNESS (SUCH AS IT IS). TOUCHES IT. SNIFFS AT IT. IT IS ONLY A MOMENT OF CONTACT, BUT IT LEAVES A TRACE OF ITSELF BEHIND. LIKE WHEN SOMEONE BURNS TOAST...
NOW THOUGHTS OF HOME BECOME MORE AND MORE ABSTRACT...SHE WONDERS IF IT'S EVEN THERE WAITING FOR HER... A THOUGHT THAT LASTS FOR BOTH AN ETERNITY AND THE BLINK OF AN EYE.
BUT THAT SAME HOME--SO ALIEN TO HER AT THE MOMENT--IS IN DIRE NEED OF HER TALENTS. IT NEEDS HER IDENTITY. IT NEEDS HER AGONY...HER ECSTASY...

...IT NEEDS A FINAL MEASURE OF GRACE.

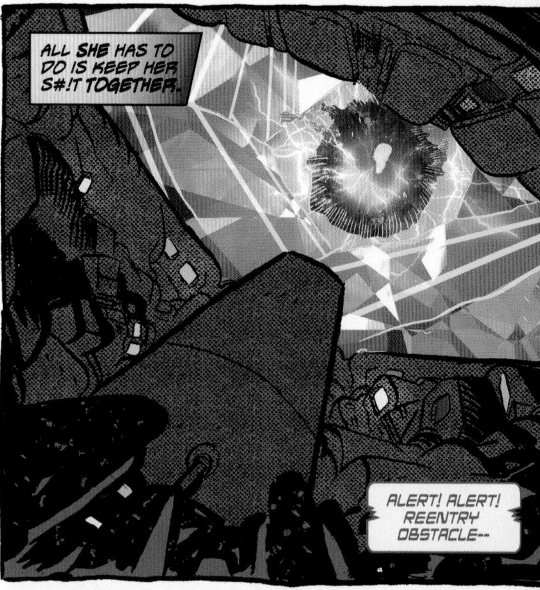
ALL SHE HAS TO DO IS KEEP HER S#!T TOGETHER.
ALERT! ALERT! REENTRY OBSTACLE--

SUDDENLY, A BOTTOMLESS, INSATIABLE HUNGER MATERIALIZES DEEP INSIDE THIS EVER-GROWING NIGHTMARE BEAST!
FOR NIBIRU, EVERY SCREAM TELLS A DIFFERENT STORY...
CLEARLY, GRACE'S ARRIVAL BACK ON EARTH SERVES MORE THAN ONE EXPLOSIVE PURPOSE...

THE FABRIC OF SPACE-TIME RUPTURES--AND THEN INHALES, IN THE DECAY AND THE TUMORS GROWING LOCALLY IN THIS DIMENSION.
GRACE'S SHIP CAN BARELY MAINTAIN ESCAPE VELOCITY--
--AND ANY HOPE OF FLIGHT CONTROL IS A LAUGHABLE CONCEPT.
SUDDEN ALTITUDE LOSS///// HULL INTEGRITY AT SIXTY-FIVE PERCENT AND DROPPING///// BRACE FOR IMPACT--
AND WITHIN THE GOLDEN CITY...
HAVE YOU GOT HER?!
TELEMETRY CONFIRMED! SHE'S COMING IN HARD--
--TRACKING POINT OF IMPACT!
SHE DID IT... SHE ACTUALLY DID IT...!
SOMEONE TRY TO RAISE HER ON THE COMM!
SCRAMBLE MODE, EVERYONE! WE NEED TO GET A FIELD TEAM OUT THERE...
"...BEFORE ANYONE ELSE GETS TO HER!"
SO NOW IT'S COME TO LIGHT...SKIDDING SO CLOSE TO THE END OF THE WORLD...
...AND THE NAME OF ITS TRUE SAVIOR MAY NEVER BE KNOWN...
GRACE? GRACE...!
ARE YOU READING US?!
PLEASE RESPOND!

CW1
REBEL LOVE
TUES 11 PM
HOLLYWOOD
AMERICAN BOY
CONTINENTAL
THERE'S A CERTAIN SMELL IN THE AIR WHEN THE WORLD IS ON THE EDGE OF ANNIHILATION. IT'S NOT THE SMELL OF DEATH, PER SE... MORE LIKE THE PERVASIVE STINK OF EMPTINESS, THE ANTICIPATION OF NOTHINGNESS COME A-CALLIN'...
NOT EASY TO IGNORE, ESPECIALLY WHEN THERE ARE NO OTHER DISTRACTIONS... LIKE ELECTRICITY.
A CONTINENT AWAY, HUMANITY IS GETTING BITCH SLAPPED... BUT HERE ON THE SUNSET STRIP, THERE ARE ACTUALLY OTHER EVENTS AFOOT...

...WALKING THE MEAN STREETS IS NOTHING NEW TO HIM. BUT THEY'VE NEVER BEEN THIS EMPTY BEFORE.
COUNTLESS PAST LIVES HAVE LED HIM TO THIS POINT. EACH ONE LIVED IN THE SHADOW OF THINGS THAT CAN'T BE EXPLAINED.

BUT THIS IS WAY DIFFERENT...

--KKKKKK--
--MASSIVE CASUALTIES IN THE MIDTOWN AREA--
--KKKKKK--
--CAN'T MAINTAIN RADIO SIGNAL--

GUESS WE'VE ALL ENDED UP BACK IN THE STONE AGE FOR A WHILE, HUH...?
SEEMS TO ME TO BE A PERFECT OPPORTUNITY.

ELVIS WARMAKER--

12.21.12 THIS IS WHAT WENT DOWN AND NOBODY CARED (YET)
amazing forest
MOTRO
--YOUR LIFE IS CALLING!
AIN'T MY LIFE YER TALKIN' ABOUT. SOMEONE OUT THERE'S GOT A FUNNY IDEA OF WAR... DOESN'T MAKE ANY SENSE...
AN' YOU LOOK LIKE GOVERNMENT CHEESE T'ME.
NOT THIS TIME. OBVIOUSLY, THE WORLD NEEDS A NEW IDEA...
BY THE WAY, I ASSUME YOU'VE MET WOLFHUNTER IN YOUR TRAVELS?
KIND OF AN ARTIST-FORMERLY-KNOWN-AS TYPE OF THING...
'SUP.

I PLUCKED HIM OUT OF THE GHETTOS OF STEEL HARBOR FOR ONE SIMPLE REASON... HE WAS READY TO STEP UP AND CONTRIBUTE TO THE CAUSE.
ARE YOU...?
FIRST OF ALL, I GOT NO IDEA WHAT "CAUSE" YOU'RE TALKIN' ABOUT. SECOND OF ALL...

...I GOT NO INTEREST IN RUBBIN' ELBOWS WITH NO HAS-BEEN GANGBANGER.
WATCH YOUR MOUTH, FAT ASS...

...THIS ISN'T AN EITHER/OR PROPOSITION, Y'DIG?
TRUST ME, I TRIED TO GET HIM OFF THIS IDEA OF TRACKIN' YOU DOWN...

...TOLD HIM YOU WERE NOTHIN' BUT A BURNT-OUT HAS-BEEN WHO TRADED IN HIS TASTE FOR COMBAT FOR A SAD CASE OF DIPSOMANIA.

WHO YOU CALLING "BURNT OUT"?!
YOU'RE A LONG WAY FROM STEEL HARBOR--
LEMME SHOW YOU WHAT I LEARNED THERE, "ELVIS"!

I WILL BUST YOUR ASS--
ALL RIGHT, ALL RIGHT! ENOUGH POSTURING!
REMEMBER WHAT YEAR IT IS, WOULDJA? THERE'S WORK TO DO!
CHANGES TO BE MADE!

I DON'T "POSTURE," WHOEVER YOU ARE.
EVER HEARD THE EXPRESSION "BETTER TO HAVE A GUN AND NOT NEED IT THAN TO NEED A GUN AND NOT HAVE IT"...?
WORLD CHAMPION
08

YOU'RE GODDAMN RIGHT I HAVE...!
YOU TWO PUT YOUR PISTOLS IN YOUR POCKETS AND GET YOUR MINDS IN THE HERE AND NOW!
SWORDS INTO PLOWSHARES, FOR CHRISSAKES...!

YOU NEED TO ASK YOURSELF, ONCE AND FOR ALL...IS THIS THE LIFE YOU WANTED?!
YOU FELL OFF THE GRID IN A BIG, BAD WAY...SO HOW DOES IT FEEL?
AND WHO THE HELL ARE YOU, ANYWAY?!

ME? I'M THE MAN IN THE SHADOWS. THE GUY BEHIND THE GUY. THE MASTER PLANNER...
AND YOU'VE CLEARLY TURNED INTO A WALKING, TALKING ANACHRONISM.
ARMOR-PLATED IRRELEVANCE.
PATHETIC.

RIGHT.
NICE TRY WITH THE REVERSE PSYCHOLOGY. BUT, JUST FOR GIGGLES...

...LET ME SHOW YOU HOW "IRRELEVANT" I CAN BE.
OH NO...!
C'MON, MAN! DON'T--

A SYMPHONY OF HOT LEAD SPRAYS OUT OF AN INNOCENT STOREFRONT!
AN ORGY OF ORDNANCE ON FULL DISPLAY!
AND WARMAKER STANDS VICTORIOUS!
WELL, YOU SHOWED THAT WINDOW WHO'S BOSS...!
YOUR GUNS MAY HAVE PLENTY OF GIRTH--
--BUT I JUST GET THAT FEELING YOU'VE BEEN LOOKING FOR SOMEWHERE TO AIM THEM... SOMEWHERE THAT'LL ACTUALLY DO SOME GOOD...
"GOOD" IS A RELATIVE TERM.
BESIDES, I'M NOT THAT GUY ANYMORE.
FUNNY.
I'M PRETTY SURE THAT'S WHAT YOU ALL THINK.
YOU'RE NOT THE ONLY ONE I'VE TRACKED DOWN...
...AND YOU'RE SURE AS HELL NOT THE ONLY ONE WHO'S LOST HIS WAY.
CONSIDER YOUR FORMER COLLEAGUE... THE ONE CALLED REBEL. SURE, HE CAN STILL ABSORB ENERGY IN ALL FORMS...HE STILL FLIES...STILL GLOWS WHEN APPROPRIATE... HE JUST CAN'T GET ARRESTED THESE DAYS.
APPARENTLY, THERE'S ONLY ONE THING LEFT TO DO WHEN YOUR PRETTY-BOY POP-STAR-SUPERHERO MOMENT HAS COME AND GONE...MATTHEW AND MARK AREN'T THE KIND OF BROTHERS WHO TURN DOWN AN OPPORTUNITY TO GET BACK IN THE SPOTLIGHT, EVEN IF IT'S REALITY TELEVISION...!
THE FACT THAT WHICHEVER ONE OF THEM ISN'T ENJOYING THE PLEASURES OF BEING REBEL--REMEMBER, THEY TAKE TURNS SHARING THAT POWER--HAS TO SUFFER EXTREME PHYSICAL DEBILITATION ONLY MAKES FOR BETTER TV...
GUYS...I'M SERIOUS...
...THIS MAY BE REALITY T.V.... BUT IT'S STILL T.V....
...C'MON, A LITTLE MAKEUP OVER HERE.
MARK COULD USE A LITTLE, TOO...

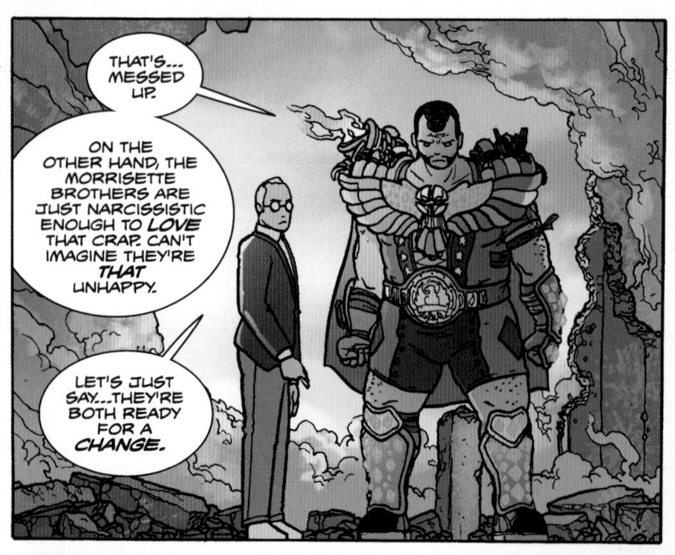

THAT'S... MESSED UP.
ON THE OTHER HAND, THE MORRISETTE BROTHERS ARE JUST NARCISSISTIC ENOUGH TO LOVE THAT CRAP. CAN'T IMAGINE THEY'RE THAT UNHAPPY.
LET'S JUST SAY... THEY'RE BOTH READY FOR A CHANGE.

LEMME TELL YA... I DIDN'T NEED THIS MUCH CONVINCING.
BUT I'VE SEEN THE WRITING ON THE WALL, KNOW WHAT I'M SAYIN'...?
I AIN'T NO SCRATCHER... AND THIS IS THE THANKS I GET...!

SO... WHO ELSE HAVE YOU FOUND...?

...RUBY...?

I FIGURED YOU'D PROBABLY ASK ABOUT HER.

FINDING RUBY WASN'T AS EASY AS YOU MIGHT THINK, CONSIDERING HER RATHER CONSPICUOUS NATURE. SHE'S GOT ENOUGH STREET SAVVY TO KNOW HOW TO GO DEEP UNDERGROUND WHEN SHE WANTS TO.

OHHHH... YEESSSSS...

...AGAIN! AGAIN!

S-SO MUCH... B-BETTER THAN CANDLE WAX!

WHATEVER.

SHE'S NOT QUITE CRASHED OUT ON THE CULTURAL SCRAPHEAP LIKE REBEL, BUT SHE'S DEFINITELY HIT HER OWN KIND OF BOTTOM.

ON THE OTHER HAND, SHE DID FIND A USE FOR HER SPECIFIC TALENTS... BEING ABLE TO INFLICT SIGNIFICANT PAIN THROUGH HER TOUCH.

THERE ARE SOME SAD BASTARDS OUT THERE WHO PAY GOOD MONEY TO EXPERIENCE HER TOUCH... AND THE PAIN THAT GOES WITH IT.

--KKKKK--
ZZZZZTTT--
--GETTING OUR SIGNAL BACK--
--HEARING REPORTS OUT OF MANHATTAN THAT THE THREAT HAS BEEN NEUTRALIZED...

WELL, WELL, WELL.
CHECK THIS OUT...
THINK YOU MIGHT HAVE TIME TO FINISH GETTING THAT TATTOO, ELVIS...
--WE'VE GOT OUR NEWS CHOPPERS IN THE AIR, SO WE'LL BE ON THE SCENE WITH A VISUAL MOMENTARILY...
WARMAKER...!

YOU KNOW I AIN'T MUCH FOR NOSTALGIA.
BESIDES... YOU EVER GONNA TELL ME WHO THE HELL YOU ARE...?!

YOU CAN CALL ME BERT.
I'M HERE BECAUSE I NEED AGENTS. HELL, THE WORLD NEEDS THEM.
SO ARE YOU IN...?

...HUMANITY'S LAST LINE OF DEFENSE WAS THIS MAN!
HUH.
SOMEBODY MADE A GOOD SHOW OF IT.
WHADDYA THINK, B? LOOKS LIKE THE WORLD AIN'T ENDING AFTER ALL...

GUESS NOT...
...BUT AT LEAST NOW OUR WORK CAN FINALLY BEGIN.

2

IT STARTED WITH A HUGE, COLLECTIVE SIGH OF RELIEF. WE HAD COME SO CLOSE...WE COULD ALL TASTE IT LIKE BATTERY ACID ON THE BACKS OF OUR TONGUES.
NOW WE'RE TASTING NOTHING BUT SWEET MAPLE SYRUP.
THE END OF THE WORLD HAD BEEN AVERTED AND WE HAD A BONA FIDE HERO TO THANK FOR IT...
...GOOD OL' FRANK WELLS. THE PEOPLE'S HERO.
WHILE WE COWERED ON THE BRINK... HE WAS THE ONE WHO FLUNG HIMSELF HEADLONG INTO THE VOID, WITH NO THOUGHT OF HIS OWN SAFETY. NO THOUGHT OF HIS OWN LIFE...EXCEPT AS SOMETHING HE WOULD'VE GLADLY SACRIFICED FOR THE REST OF US.
AS IT TURNED OUT, HE DIDN'T HAVE TO. AND NOW WE CELEBRATE HIM FOR IT. WE HONOR HIS COMMITMENT... WE HONOR HIS HEROISM...
...THE WORLD HAS FOUND ITS SAVIOR.
FRANK
HE ACCEPTS THE MANTLE WITH HUMILITY. HE ACCEPTS IT WITH DIGNITY.
FINALLY, HE HAS FOUND HIS PLACE--

--IF ONLY IT WERE REAL.
GUH--!
THIS IS REALITY.
THIS IS THE VILE STINK OF THE WORLD HE SAVED.
AND NO ONE KNOWS.
PING
THE BALLAD OF FRANK WELLS
MISIRLOU
HE CAN HEAR THE SOUNDS OF CIVILIZATION SCURRYING LIKE MICE OUTSIDE THE WALLS OF THIS ABANDONED SQUAT.
THE SOUNDS OF LIFE GOING ON.
WITHOUT HIM.
I DON'T UNDERSTAND... AFTER EVERYTHING I DID...
...WHY AM I STILL SO ALONE?

DEEP INSIDE THE PENTAGON, THERE IS A PURPLE WATER FOUNTAIN.
THE FINAL VESTIGE OF A MILITARY THAT HAD NOT YET FOUND ITS MORAL CENTER...THE FOUNTAIN SURVIVES AS A MINOR MONUMENT TO OUR ALL-TOO-HUMAN FAILINGS.
FITTINGLY, IT NOW SITS JUST INSIDE THE WAR ROOM.
WAR ROOM
GENTLEMEN, IT'S BEEN SIX MONTHS...
...AND WE'VE STILL GOT AN ENORMOUS QUESTION MARK LEFT FROM THE INCIDENT IN NEW YORK.
I CAN'T GET THROUGH A PRESS BRIEFING WITHOUT GETTING INUNDATED...!
AND YOUR DISCRETION IS APPRECIATED, MR. PRESIDENT.
NO NEED TO BUTTER ME UP, GENERAL. I KNOW WHAT'S AT STAKE HERE.
IF WE'RE GOING TO STAY AHEAD OF THIS "END OF THE WORLD" FEVER THAT'S GRIPPED THE ENTIRE GLOBE, WE NEED ALL THE FACTS...
CHIEF
...AND THEY INVOLVE THIS MAN.
I READ THE REPORTS. I READ MY PREDECESSORS' VIEWS ON THE MATTER. ALL THE NONSENSE THAT OCCURRED IN CINNABAR FLATS BACK IN THE DAY...
...WHY HASN'T THIS MAN BEEN FOUND?

WELL, TO BE HONEST, SIR... WE LOOKED UP HIS PSYCHE PROFILE AND, WELL--
IT WASN'T PROMISING, MR. PRESIDENT. TO SAY THE LEAST.
IF I MAY...
...TO PIN THE SALVATION OF OUR SPECIES ON ONE MAN COULD HAVE DEVASTATING PSYCHOLOGICAL RAMIFICATIONS UPON SOCIETY AS A WHOLE.
TO TREAT THIS INCIDENT MORE AS A NATURAL DISASTER...A RANDOM EVENT THAT WE HAVE ENDURED...IS A MUCH MORE POTENT SOLUTION FOR THE MENTAL HEALTH OF THE AVERAGE WORLD CITIZEN...
...IF, IN FACT, THIS IS SOMETHING THAT INTERESTS YOU, SIR.
WELL, OF COURSE IT INTERESTS ME. AND SO FAR, HE HASN'T STEPPED FORWARD TO TAKE THE CREDIT...
...BUT WHAT HAPPENS IF AND WHEN HE CHANGES HIS MIND...?
HE CAN'T REMEMBER THE FIRST TIME HE TOOK FLIGHT.
HE IMAGINES IT WAS QUITE BITCHIN'.
HOW COULD IT NOT BE?

FLIGHT IS AN ESCAPE, BUT UNFORTUNATELY NOT FROM THE THOUGHTS THAT PLAGUE FRANK'S MIND...
...ENDLESS VISIONS OF PARALLEL LIVES...
...STILL-LIFE SCENARIOS THAT SOMEHOW BREATHE AND LIVE WITHIN HIM.
CHOCK FULL OF SYMBOLOGY, BUT MIRED IN THE MUNDANE...
I...I FEEL LIKE I WAS MEANT FOR GREATER THINGS...
QUICK WASH $5
THERE ARE NO EASY ANSWERS... NO BIBLICAL ALLEGORIES TO EXPLAIN HIS STRANGE EXISTENCE...
...NO SCIENCE FICTION FABLES TO MAKE EVERYONE FEEL SECURE ENOUGH TO ACCEPT THE UNEXPLAINABLE.
AND THEN THERE'S ALWAYS THE ABJECT, IRRATIONAL FEARS... THE ONES THAT NEVER LEAVE HIM...
INTERESTING SPECIMEN...
THINK WE'LL FIND A SOUL IN HERE...?
ARE YOU KIDDING?!
MAYBE EVERYONE HARBORS THESE KINDS OF THOUGHTS.
MAYBE NOT.
IN ANY CASE, HE CAN'T LET HIMSELF BE DISTRACTED RIGHT NOW.
THIS IS THE FIRST TIME HE'S BEEN BACK HERE...

...BACK TO THE SCENE OF THE CRIME.

DAMN.

...WHY WOULD ANYONE *WANT* TO REMEMBER?
HOW CLOSE IT ALL CAME TO...
FRANK DOESN'T HAVE TO FINISH THE THOUGHT...

...HIS SENSE MEMORY FINISHES IT FOR HIM.

MAYBE I SHOULDN'T HAVE *COME* HERE--
HEY! WE'RE STILL A FEW MONTHS AWAY FROM *HALLOWEEN,* PAL...!
WHO'RE YOU SUPPOSED TO *BE,* ANYWAY...?
A PERTINENT *QUESTION,* IF YOU ASK ME...

...THE ANSWER, OF COURSE, IS COMPLETELY SUBJECTIVE. IT'S THE JABBERWACKY WE ALL SEEK.
IN ANCIENT TIMES, THE INCANTATION "DURAM BLIP SASSA" WAS USED TO CENTER ONESELF. BUT ALL WORDS BECOME DEVALUED OVER TIME.
NAMASTE.
DID YOU JUST SAY... "JABBERWACKY"?
I DON'T HAVE ANY ANSWERS...
NOT YET, YOU DON'T.
WHAT THE HELL...?
WHO'S HE TALKING TO...?!
BETTER GIVE THIS NUTJOB SOME SPACE, FELLAS...
WAIT... I'M A NUT-JOB...?
WHO SAID THAT? DID WE SAY THAT?
JUST... Y'KNOW... TAKE IT EASY, PAL...
NO WORRIES. I AM RARELY SEEN OR HEARD BY THE SPIRITUALLY UNENLIGHTENED.
BUT ALLOW ME TO INTRODUCE MYSELF...
...I AM THE BABA LAMA.
SORRY... SPIRITUALLY WHAT...?
PERHAPS WE CAN RAISE OUR LEVEL OF DISCOURSE TO SOMETHING SLIGHTLY MORE ELEVATED THAN YOUR SLACK-JAWED DISBELIEF AND MY REITERATIONS OF INTENT.
AFTER ALL THAT YOU'VE SEEN IN YOUR TRAVELS... THE SIGHT OF ONE SUCH AS I REALLY ASTONISHING...?

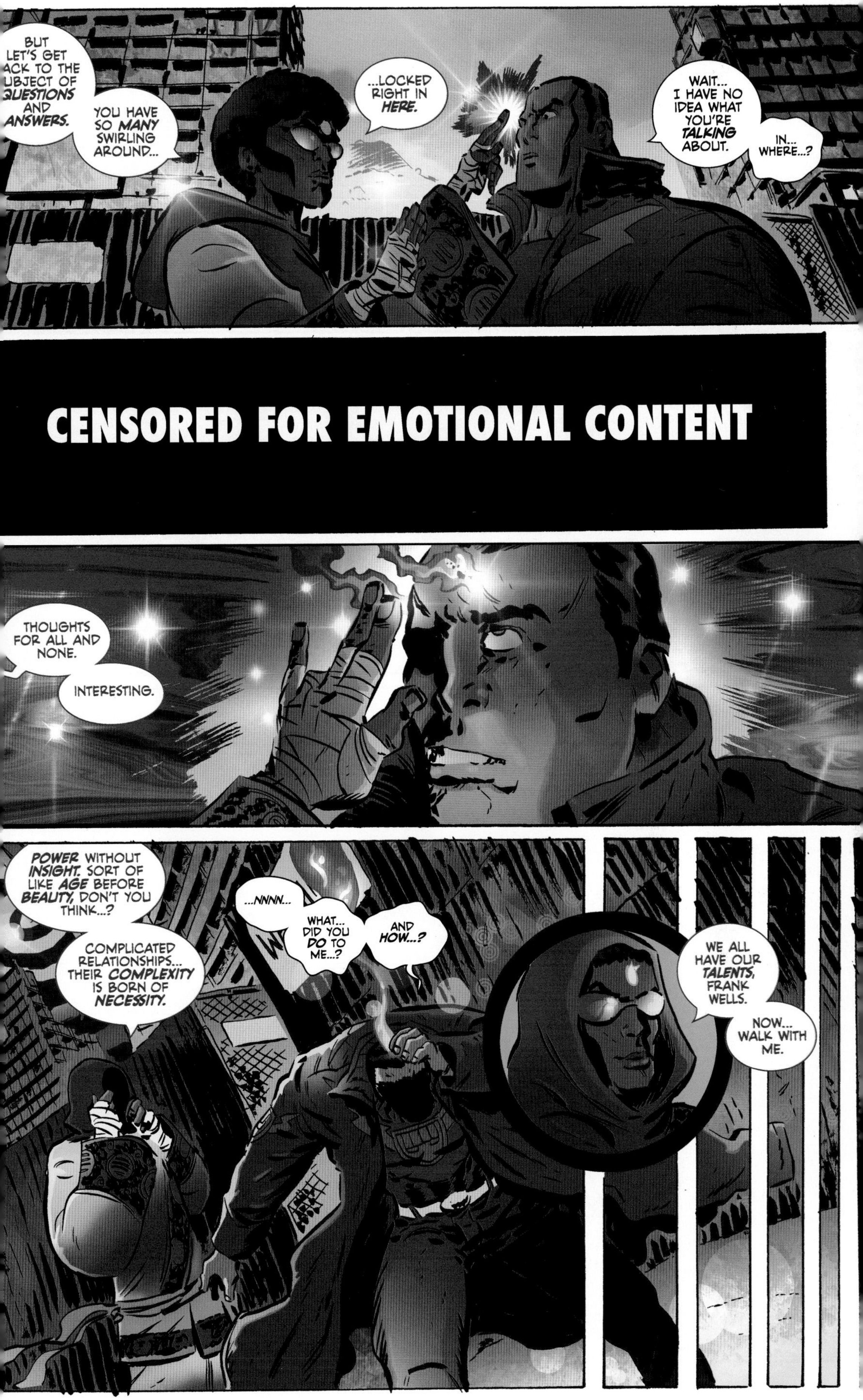

CENSORED FOR EMOTIONAL CONTENT

POWER WITHOUT INSIGHT. SORT OF LIKE AGE BEFORE BEAUTY, DON'T YOU THINK...?

COMPLICATED RELATIONSHIPS... THEIR COMPLEXITY IS BORN OF NECESSITY.

...NNNN...

WHAT... DID YOU DO TO ME...?

AND HOW...?

WE ALL HAVE OUR TALENTS, FRANK WELLS.

NOW... WALK WITH ME.

WHERE...

...WHERE ARE WE *GOING...?*

THE WORLD IS DEEP...DEEPER THAN YOU REALIZE, DESPITE YOUR OBVIOUS PLACE *IN* IT. YOU'VE GOT A FUNKY BUNCH OF *ISSUES* KEEPING YOU DOWN.

BUT LOOK *AROUND* YOU...LOOK WHAT YOU'VE *DONE* HERE. THE STAKES, ULTIMATELY, ARE *MEANINGLESS.* HUMANITY MAY *PISS THEMSELVES* AT REGULAR INTERVALS, EVERY TIME THE SUN SETS. BUT, LET'S BE HONEST...WORLD-THREATENING *CRISES* ARE YOUR STOCK IN TRADE, CORRECT...?

BUT WHEN YOU CONTINU TO ACCEPT THINGS AT *FAC VALUE,* YOU'RE MISSING OUT O *SO MUCH.* EVE THE CONCEPT OF *REALITY ITSELF...*

...CAN BE COMPLETELY *SUBJECTIVE.*

EACH ONE OF US HAS IT *WITHIN* OURSELVES TO *REALIGN* THE FUNDAMENTAL NATURE OF OUR SURROUNDINGS. THE ANCIENT MYSTICS OF CHUMMARA WOULD SIT IN COSMOGEOMETRIC PATTERNS, THEIR HEADZAPOPPIN' FROM THE AROMA OF THEIR SHARED INSIGHTS. DIDN'T *MATTER* WHERE THEY WERE.

YOU ARE A CREATURE OF THE *PHYSICAL* WORLD...AND YOU CANNOT ALLOW YOURSELF TO GET SUCKED INTO THE *CHOICE-VS.-MISERY* DEBATE. NOT *EVERYONE* WEARS THE GRIME OF DYSTOPIA LIKE A SECOND SKIN.

THEN AGAIN...

...IT'S NOT ALL PUFFY WHITE CLOUDS, EITHER. PERHAPS YOU CAN CONVINCE YOURSELF *OTHERWISE,* BUT ULTIMATELY YOU ARE FACED WITH THE *FALSEHOODS* YOU CREATE.

TO THINE OWN SELF BE TRUE. SO *SIMPLE...*YET SO *DECEPTIVE* AN AXIOM. BUT THIS IS THE STUFF OF CHILDREN'S MORALITY TALES. PERSONALLY, I FIND THAT APPROACH TO CONTAIN ITS OWN MEASURE OF *DECAY...*

THE *BOREDOM* SETS IN, AND I FIND MYSELF SLEEPING WHILE STANDING UP. LIKE A BOVINE IN THE FIELD.

AND NEITHER ONE OF US CAN AFFORD TO SLEEP.

AS THE NORTHERN SOOTHSEERS SAY, AN OVERDUB HAS NO CHOICE...AND AN IMAGE CANNOT REJOICE.

HOWEVER... I THINK WE CAN *DO* SOMETHING ABOUT THAT.

OMIGOD...

I DON'T... RECOGNIZE *ANY* OF THIS...

WARNING

--I GOT SOMETHING TO SAY!
THIS WHOLE THING HAS BEEN STAGED BY THE MEDIA!
DO YOU... KNOW HER...?
I DON'T THINK SO...
ALTHOUGH IT'S SUCH A SMALL WORLD... MAYBE I DO...
THERE IS SUPERHEROISM... AND THERE IS SUPERVILLAINY.
AND THEN...THERE ARE ABSTRACT CONCEPTS THAT EXIST IN BETWEEN.
I'VE BEEN SEARCHING FOR SOMETHING TOO! I NEED SOME SATISFACTION! BUT I SEE YOU IN YOUR BRIGHT COLORS, AND IT CALLS OUT TO ME AND MY LADY PARTS!
SO LET'S SEE HOW IT GETS YOU OFF--
--WHEN I TURN ON MY DEADLIGHT...
...AND SHINE IT AT YOU!
THE MOLECULES IN THE AIR STIR AND SHIMMER...
...THERE IS GREAT POWER AND MYSTERY WITHIN THE LIGHT...
...NOT TO MENTION A DREAD INTERLACED WITHIN THE GLOW!
THAT DREAD IS MEANT TO LEAVE YOU BEGGING FOR DEATH!

HOWEVER, IN THIS PARTICULAR CASE...
FEELS A LITTLE FUNNY...
...BUT I'M NOT SURE...
...THINK I'M COMING DOWN WITH A HEAD COLD, MAYBE...?

HEAD COLD?!
I'M IN CONTROL! I CAN TURN IT UP!
YOU WILL SUCCUMB TO THE STENCH OF THE ABYSS!

WAIT... I--
--*
OH... NO...
...MAYBE I SHOULD JUST... LIE DOWN AND DIE...FOR A WHILE...
THAT'S IT, FRANK.
NOW YOU CAN FLOAT IN MY FLUIDS--
--YOU CAN SEE THE WORLD THE WAY I DO!

HOW'S IT LOOK, THEN...?
=SIGH=
LOOKS LIKE I GOT HERE JUST IN TIME...

NOW, LET'S TALK ABOUT US...
...THIS IS THE DYNAMIC THAT WE ESERVE! IT'S ALL OF A PIECE! ON'T YOU GET IT, WELLS?
WE CAN'T CONSORT WITH NORMAL PARTNERS! WE ARE ABOVE THEIR MATING RITUALS! IT'S TIME TO START FASHIONING OUR OWN!
SEX AND DEATH! THEY GO TOGETHER LIKE CHOCOLATE AND PEANUT BUTTER! SO LET'S TAKE ADVANTAGE OF THE CHAOS AND MAKE SOME CANDY!
VANDELAY INDUSTRIES
Y-YOU SEEM...
...VERY... COMMITTED...
WOULD THE TWO OF YOU LIKE SOME PRIVACY...?

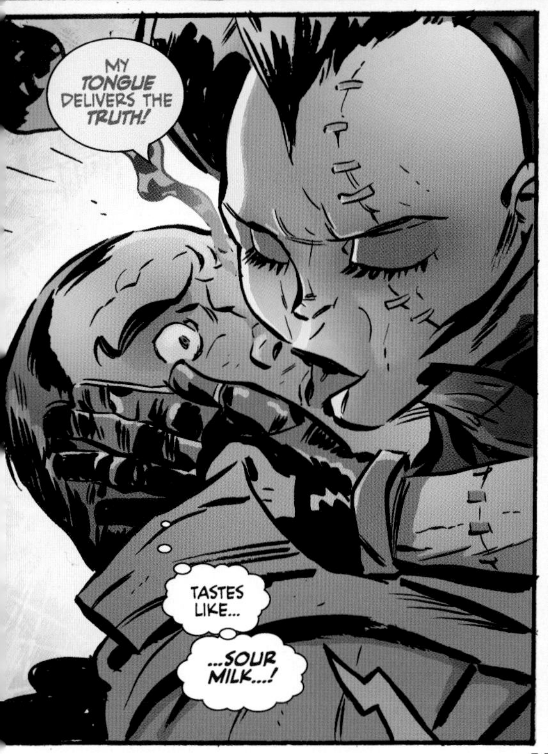
MY TONGUE DELIVERS THE TRUTH!
TASTES LIKE...
...SOUR MILK...!

SORRY... BUT I DON'T SHARE YOUR WORLDVIEW...!
SO, IF YOU DON'T MIND--
NNNF--!

GODDAMN YOU! YOU WOULDN'T KNOW A NEW PARADIGM IF IT HIT YOU OVER THE HEAD!
I NEED THIS!
I CAN SEE THAT...
I HAVE TO LIVE WITHIN MY OWN STORY!
IT'S NEVER BEEN GOOD ENOUGH FOR ME!
DO YOU WANT TO DIE WITHIN YOUR OWN SKIN?!
INTERESTING.
YOU MANIPULATE PSIONIC ENERGY IN SUCH A WAY--THIS "DEADLIGHT" YOU PROJECT--THAT YOUR TARGET IS LEFT UNCERTAIN OF ITS ABILITY TO GENERATE INTERNAL OPTIMISM...
...BUT I'M AFRAID YOU'R WASTING IT ON ME.
THAT'S ENOUGH--!
LOOKS LIKE I MIGHT HAVE TO HAUL YOU TO THE NEAREST PENITENTIARY...!
YOU'D LOVE THAT, WOULDN'T YOU?!
CLICHÉS GET YOU OFF, THEN?!
SHE HAS A POINT, FRANK.
EVEN NOW, YOU ARE LOCKED INTO A MODE OF EXISTENCE THAT HAS HELD YOU BACK YOUR ENTIRE LIFE...
...I THINK IT'S TIME WE BROKE YOU OUT OF THAT.

THEY HAD TO EXTRACT HER FROM THE TWISTED WRECKAGE.
SHE HAS REMAINED UNRESPONSIVE, TO SAY THE LEAST.

BUT HER LEGACY--THE SHINING ACHIEVEMENT THAT IS GOLDEN CITY--ENDURES AS A SYMBOL OF A BYGONE ERA OF POSSIBILITIES.
AMAZING GRACE: THE WEIGHT OF THE NEW WORLD

MEANWHILE, ITS DENIZENS CARRY ON...STRUGGLING TO STEER A SPIRITUALLY RUDDERLESS SHIP.
SO THIS IS A PRESS BLACKOUT... OR SHOULD WE CALL IT A COVER-UP...?
TRY TO TEMPER THE DRAMATICS, TYRONE. WHAT CHOICE DO WE HAVE?
BUT SHE SAVED THE PLANET. ISN'T THIS OUR MOMENT TO--
TO WHAT?

OUR INDEPENDENCE IS OUR STRONGEST ASSET AS A CITY...
...AND PRESIDENT SANTOS PROBABLY HAS HIS OWN THEORIES ON WHY THE WORLD DIDN'T END.
BESIDES...

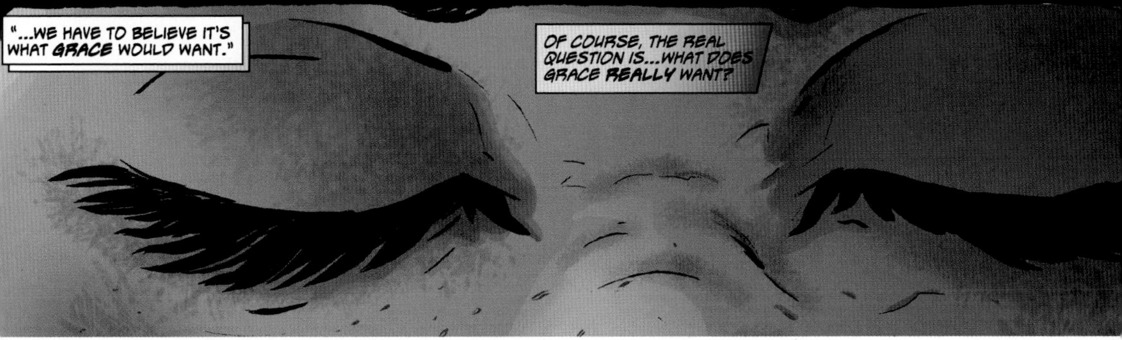
"...WE HAVE TO BELIEVE IT'S WHAT GRACE WOULD WANT."
OF COURSE, THE REAL QUESTION IS...WHAT DOES GRACE REALLY WANT?

ONE THING SHE'S NOT GETTING--EVEN IN THIS STATE--IS PEACE.
SHE LEFT SOMETHING OUT IN THE ENDLESS VOID. HER CONFRONTATION WITH THE ABYSS LEFT A TRAIL OF BREAD CRUMBS...
...THAT LEADS RIGHT BACK HERE.

ONCE AGAIN, THIS IS THE BEACHHEAD. AND THE REALIZATION FEELS LIKE A SMACK TO THE SOUL...
...SHE'S BEEN FOLLOWED.

THE END OF ALL EXISTENCE INSPIRES A CERTAIN KIND OF DREAD. ITS FACE, WHILE INSCRUTABLE, IS A FAMILIAR ONE. NO MATTER WHAT ITS ORIGINS MIGHT BE...THE CONCEPT OF THE FINAL EMPTINESS EXISTS WITHIN US ALL.

BUT THIS IS SOMETHING DIFFERENT. SOMETHING MUCH MORE...ALIEN IN NATURE...

...A STRANGE GREED WITHIN THE ETHER. A BIZARRE LONGING FOR WIDESPREAD POSSESSION PERMEATING ALL OF SPACE-TIME...BEYOND AMBITION...BEYOND PRIMAL NEED. THIS IS CONQUEST IN ITS PUREST FORM.

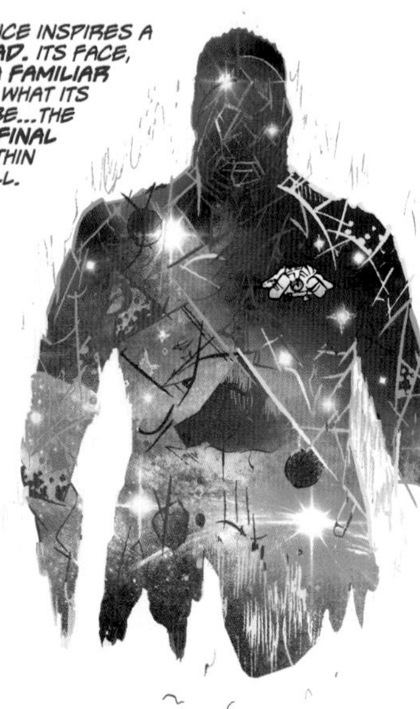

THERE IS A SEDUCTIVENESS TO THIS MOLECULAR VIBRATION. AND ITS ECHOES ARE GROWING LOUDER...AN ATONAL CHORUS OF WHISPERS THAT CALL OUT ACROSS THE EVERLASTING GALACTIC SPAN...

...AND IT CALLS OUT A NAME.

AMAZING GRACE.

HARD TO IMAGINE THE WORLD WITHOUT HER.
THEN LET'S NOT BOTHER...

...SHE'LL SHUFFLE LOOSE THE MORTAL COIL WHEN SHE'S GOOD AND READY. AND, BELIEVE ME, NOW'S NOT THE TIME.
PRETTY SURE ABOUT THAT, AREN'T YOU...?

I HAVE TO BE. IT'S WHAT SHE NEEDS FROM ALL OF US RIGHT NOW.
TOTAL BELIEF.
THINK ABOUT IT. ANY GOD'S POTENTIAL FOR OMNIPOTENCE IS ENTIRELY DEPEN-DENT UPON ONE THING...
AND THAT IS...?

OUR FAITH IN ITS EXISTENCE, OF COURSE.
THERE ARE THOSE TIMES WHEN PERCEPTION IS EVERYTHING.

BUT THERE ARE OTHER TIMES...WHEN PERCEPTION SIMPLY CANNOT BE TRUSTED.

WHAT WE PERCEIVE IS SUBJECT TO THE MOST RANDOM OF INFLUENCES...A BARRAGE OF COSMIC FORCES THAT SERVE PRIMARILY TO TEST ONE'S RESOLVE...NOT TO MENTION ONE'S SENSE OF IDENTITY.
THERE IS A DEMENTED BEAUTY TO BE FOUND IN THE ETERNAL STRUGGLE BETWEEN SURRENDERING TO THE VOID...AND TRANSCENDING IT.
GRACE IS THE STRUGGLE.

THAT STRUGGLE HAS MADE HER A BEACON...AND, BY ASSOCIATION, THE EARTH HAS BECOME A GALACTIC LIGHTHOUSE THAT SHINES ACROSS THE INFINITE EXPANSE OF THE UNIVERSE.
PERHAPS THIS WAS THE GRAND PLAN ALL ALONG--

--PERHAPS IT WAS A DESTINY BUILT RIGHT INTO THE VERY FABRIC OF HER LEGEND.
A HERO FOR OUR TIMES, LIVING BY A CODE EXISTING BEYOND THE CONCEPTS THAT CONSTANTLY DIVIDE AND SEPARATE US...
...POLITICS, RACE, GENDER, RELIGION... THERE ARE GREATER THINGS TO FIGHT FOR.
SHE WILL NEVER LET YOUR SPIRITS DOWN.

THERE ARE DIAMONDS SHINING IN HER EYES.
THEY SEE HUMANITY'S FUTURE.
SHE HAS FOUGHT FOR THAT FUTURE...

...AND WILL CONTINUE TO FIGHT.
PERHAPS EVEN IN DEATH.

MEANWHILE, GOLDEN CITY ABIDES.
ONE OF SEVERAL CITY SQUARES TEEMS WITH LIFE AND SHOPPING AND CONVERSATION.

BUT IT'S NOT JUST THE DARK CLOUD OVER THEIR HEADS THAT OCCUPIES THEIR STRAY THOUGHTS...
OH, WOW...

...IS THAT...?
SHE DOESN'T DARE SPEAK THE NAME OUT LOUD.
JUST IN CASE...

I SEE HER! I DO!
RIGHT THERE!
HOLY CRAP...!
I KNEW SHE HADN'T ABANDONED US...

UHHH.. HOLD ON...
EEE-YIKES!
WHAT THE HELL IS THAT--

NOT A LETHAL EXPLOSION--

--NOT AN OBVIOUS SIGN OF ARMAGEDDON--

--BUT MOST CERTAINLY...
...AN ARRIVAL.

AND FOR THOSE WHO BEAR WITNESS, THE REACTION IS IMMEDIATE...
OMIGOD... IT'S...IT'S...
I... I WANT THAT...
...MMMMMM...
...YEAH...

VERY CLEAN.
I CAN SMELL IT.

PHASE ONE COMPLETE.
THIS IS DEFINITELY THE PLACE TO BE. AND ONCE I MAKE CONTACT, PHASE TWO CAN BEGIN.
NOW... WHERE IS SHE...?

ANYONE ELSE FEEL THAT?!
SOMEONE TELL ME A BOMB DIDN'T JUST DETONATE DOWNTOWN--!

SOME SORT OF TELEPORTATION DELIVERY SYSTEM... THE SIGNAL'S TOO PHASED OUT TO TRACK BACK TO AN ORIGIN POINT...!
NO CASUALTIES YET--BUT THE REPORTS COMING IN ARE A LITTLE CONFUSED...!
CONFUSED?! WHAT IS THAT SUPPOSED TO--
CITY SCANNING ARRAY IS ONLINE... WE'LL HAVE PHYSIOLOGICAL INTEL ON WHATEVER THIS THING IS SOON...

WHEN IT RAINS, IT POURS...
ARE WE REALLY EXPECTED TO DEAL WITH THIS WHEN OUR FIRST AND LAST LINE OF DEFENSE IS STILL LAID UP?! PATCH US THROUGH TO HOSPITAL SECURITY--

"--GET SOMEBODY IN THERE!"
CALL BACK DOWNSTAIRS! WE NEED TO BEEF UP THE MANPOWER UP HERE AS LONG AS SHE'S SO--

--HELPLESS...?
GUESS I DOZED OFF...
...WHAT'D I MISS...?

YOU EVER READ ANY JUAN BAUDRILLARD...?
FORGET THAT. YOU EVER READ "SELF MATTERS"?
POWERFUL STUFF.
THE TAO OF McGRAW NOTWITHSTANDING...

...THIS IS YOUR LIFE, FROM THE INSIDE OUT.
I CAN TELL BY YOUR FACES THAT NO ONE REALLY WANTS TO BE HERE. I TOTALLY UNDERSTAND.
BUT AS LONG AS WE ARE HERE, LET'S TRY TO MAKE THE MOST OF IT...

AGENTS OF CHANGE: TOUCHY-FEELY
...AND REALLY DIG DEEP AND OPEN UP ABOUT OUR FEELINGS.
SUPER HERO SHARE GROUP
ALL WELCOME!

FIRST THINGS FIRST... I SUPPOSE I SHOULD ASK ABOUT EVERYONE'S REACTION TO BEING TOGETHER AGAIN...
WARMAKER...?
PASS.

OKAY, WELL...WOULD ANYONE ELSE LIKE TO CONTRIBUTE TO THE DISCUSSION?
WITHHOLDING EMOTION IS BASICALLY REPRESSION, YOU KNOW...AND WE CERTAINLY FROWN ON REPRESSION HERE.

I NEED ALL OF YOU TO BE PRESENT FOR THIS.

TO WORK TOGETHER--AS A UNIT--YOU MUST BE AWARE OF THE UNIQUE DYNAMIC THAT EXISTS BETWEEN ALL OF YOU.
THAT REQUIRES TRUST...A SENSITIVITY TO EACH OTHER'S NEEDS...
WE NEED TO COMMUNICATE.

WE NEED TO LISTEN TO ONE ANOTHER AND HOPEFULLY...
REBEL--WOULD YOU MIND NOT TEXTING WHILE WE'RE IN GROUP...?
HUH...?
YOU TALKIN' TO ME...?

BLONDIE'S CHECKIN' THE NIELSENS, Y'KNOW...
HANGING HIS SELF-ESTEEM ON HIS Q RATING...
NO DOUBT...
DIDN'T KNOW HIS SHOW WAS EVEN ON THE AIR...

YEAH, IT WAS ON THE AIR! JEALOUS MUCH?
YOU DON'T WANNA FRONT ME, MORRISETTE.
WHICHEVER ONE YOU ARE RIGHT NOW...
LET'S STEER CLEAR OF PERSONAL ATTACKS, PEOPLE...!

OH, YOU'VE BEEN WAITING FOR THIS MOMENT...!
GO AHEAD, ELVIS. UNLOAD ON ME.
YOU'D LOVE THAT, WOULDN'T YOU?
THE NEXT JAMES DEAN, RIGHT HERE IN FRONT OF ME...

OKAY, OKAY...I THINK THE ENERGY IN HERE HAS TURNED SLIGHTLY TOXIC.
LET'S ALL TAKE A DEEP BREATH... MAYBE FIND SOME COMMON GROUND...

FOR INSTANCE: REBEL...DO YOU KNOW WHY YOU'RE HERE?
DO I KNOW?!
I DIDN'T HAVE MUCH OF A CHOICE...

WELL, IT'S ONE OF THOSE THINGS, Y'KNOW...IT'S NOT EASY BEING FAMOUS. IT'S NOT EASY BEING A STAR.
WHY ELSE WOULD I BE DOING THIS? I WANT PEOPLE--MY FANS--TO KNOW WHAT I'M ALL ABOUT. TO GET UP CLOSE AND PERSONAL WITH ME.
REBEL LOVE
REBEL CONFESSIONAL

I MEAN, WE WERE JUST TALKING ABOUT THIS THE OTHER DAY, WEREN'T WE, MATT...?
...
WELL, OKAY...IT WAS KIND OF A ONE-SIDED CONVERSATION...
LOVE
REBEL CONFESSIONAL

LET'S GO, PRETTY BOY!
JEEZUS--!
WHAT THE HELL ARE YOU DOING?!
REBEL CONFESSIONAL

HEY, YOU WANNA TALK ABOUT ENTERTAINMENT... THAT ACTUALLY GAVE FOLKS SOMETHING INTERESTING TO WATCH...
C'MON, YOU'RE TELLING ME YOU THOUGHT YOUR SHOW WAS GOOD...?

...
FAIR POINT.
SEE? PROGRESS...!
LET'S KEEP GOING AROUND THE CIRCLE...

RUBY...?
YOU'VE BEEN REALLY QUIET...

...YOU'RE NO STRANGER TO THIS LIFE. YOU'VE BEEN IN THE TRENCHES, JUST LIKE EVERYONE *ELSE* HERE.
NEVERTHELESS, YOU SEEM VERY... *PENSIVE.*
JEAN M. GIRAUD HIGH SCHOOL FIGHTING ARZACHS

IS THERE ANYTHING IN PARTICULAR YOU FEEL LIKE SHARING WITH--
HEY, SHE'S WELL AWARE OF WHERE SHE WAS *HIDING OUT* BEFORE WE SHOWED UP TO PULL HER BACK IN...

HEY, *RUBY!* YOUR THREE O'CLOCK'S WAITING IN THE LINCOLN BOUDOIR...
...JUST A HEADS-UP: *THIS* POOR SOUL LOOK LIKE HE CA TAKE SOME *PAIN.*
WHATEVER.

OKAY, LET'S GET THE *GROUND RULES* OUT OF THE WAY SO YOU CAN GET WHAT YOU *PAID* FOR WITH NO MISUNDERSTANDINGS.
FIRST RULE: I TOUCH YOU. YOU DON'T TOUCH ME. JUST STAY CALM AND DON'T--

--MOVE...

"YOU SEEMED SURPRISED THAT THEY WOULD ACTUALLY COME LOOKING FOR YOU..."
...BUT YOU MUST KNOW HOW MUCH YOU BELONG HERE.
I DUNNO.
MAYBE I DO... MAYBE I DON'T.
THINK THE JURY'S STILL OUT...
EXIT
OKAY... WELL, WE CAN EXPLORE THAT.
IN THE MEANTIME, MAYBE YOU SHOULD ALL TAKE A MOMENT TO CONSIDER YOUR PLACE IN THIS UNIQUE MICROCOSM.
YOU'RE ALL SPECIAL. EACH AND EVERY ONE OF YOU.
YO.
YOU'RE INVADING MY PERSONAL SPACE...
I CAN'T BE THE ONLY ONE HERE WHO THINKS THIS IS A MASSIVE WASTE OF...
?
ANYBODY ELSE FEEL THAT...?
BET YO' ASS I DID...!
I-IS IT AN EARTHQUAKE, OR DID SOMETHING ACTUALLY--

--WHOA!
MECHA--?!
I THOUGHT THOMASON WAS ON OUR SIDE--!
DAMN! MAYBE HE IS--!
HUUHHHNNT--!
OR MAYBE -HNG- HE AIN'T--!
HEY, IF WE GOTTA WASTE HIM--IT'S ALL IN THE NAME OF SELF-DEFENSE!
MELT HIM DOWN TO SLAG, KID!
THIS IS HOW WE GET IN TOUCH WITH OUR FEELINGS!
OKAY, I GIVE THEM POINTS FOR TENACITY.
I THINK WE'VE LEARNED EVERYTHING WE WANTED TO LEARN FROM THIS EXERCISE...

...START BRINGING THEM BACK.
OKAY, HERE WE GO. START PULLING THE PSYCHOTROPIC LEVELS DOWN...KEEP IT ALL EVEN STEVEN...
SHIFTING FROM VIRTUAL-REALITY SCENARIO INTO NORMAL R.E.M. STATE...

...CONTINUING TO MONITOR VITALS.

I.D. SUBJECTS: WARMAKER... RUBY...REBEL... WOLFHUNTER...

...RELOADING CONSCIOUSNESS PLATFORMS...ENTRAINMENT SYSTEMS...SPATIAL-AWARENESS RATIOS...MAPPING NEUROTRANSMITTERS...

HOLDING STASIS PATTERNS AT DELTA 1-4 HZ...HORMONE BALANCING...

PRESENTING THE PROTOTYPE BINAURAL BEAT BOX, INDUSTRIAL SIZE...GUARANTEED TO PROVIDE **LIFELIKE** EXPERIENCES WITHIN THE MIND'S EYE.

HE SUIT KNOWN ONLY AS HERBERT ALKS LIKE A MAN WITH A PLAN.

WE DON'T HAVE TIME TO WASTE ON EMOTIONAL **BONDING...**

...THIS ISN'T ABOUT **FRIENDSHIP.** IT'S ABOUT **CHANGE.**

ALL THINGS CONSIDERED, THEY DID **JUST FINE...**

..NOW THEY'RE READY FOR THE **NEXT** EVOLUTIONARY STEP."

STYLISH SUPERHERO STORYTELLING AT ITS BEST--GUTSY MORALITY WITH ACTION, MOOD, AND SOUL. IT ALL STARTS NOW--AND IT DOESN'T STOP 'TIL THE END. SO COME ON--!!
FRANK WELLS'S SUPERHERO BONA FIDES ARE TITANIC IN NATURE. HE CAN FLY! HE CAN FIGHT! HE CAN CROW! AS THE WORLD FACED UNHOLY ARMAGEDDON, IT WAS FRANK WHO STOOD, UNFLINCHING, IN ITS PATH--AND YET THE AFTERMATH OF THIS SELFLESS ACT HAS LEFT HIM CONFOUNDED AND CONFUSED!
EVERY MAN, AT SOME POINT IN HIS LIFE, REACHES A CROSSROADS... AND, FOR FRANK WELLS, THIS IS IT! THIS IS HIS MOMENT OF DECISION! FROM THIS POINT ON, EVERYTHING IS ON THE TABLE!
THIS IS THE UNIVERSE THAT DEMANDS YOUR ATTENTION NOW! THIS IS THE WORLD THAT COULD MIRROR YOUR OWN--BUT ONLY IF YOU DARE VIEW IT THROUGH A FOUR-COLOR PRISM BUILT SPECIFICALLY TO OBLITERATE YOUR NOTIONS OF NOSTALGIA AND FIRE YOU HEADLONG INTO THE FUTURE!
YOU HEAR THAT, FRANK?! THIS IS YOUR FUTURE CALLING!
THE BALLAD OF FRANK WELLS:
SCHIZOPOLITICS
(or: $#!% GETS REAL)
Nastie's CRACK BAR

THE TIBETAN PLATEAU IS THE LARGEST, HIGHEST AREA ON EARTH...THE RESULT OF INTENSE TECTONIC ACTIVITY FOLLOWING THE BREAKUP OF THE ORIGINAL SUPERCONTINENT ONE HUNDRED MILLION YEARS AGO.
BUT ENOUGH ABOUT GEOLOGY...
THOSE WHO CHOOSE TO COME HERE DO SO FOR A REASON...

...FRANK WELLS IS JUST WAITING FOR SOMEONE TO TELL HIM WHAT THE HELL IT IS.
BABA LAMA... WE'RE A LONG WAY FROM GERZE...
OH, YOU HAVE NO IDEA.

IS THIS SOME KIND OF... EXISTENTIAL THING? I MEAN, THERE'S NOTHING OUT HERE!
OR IS THAT THE POINT? AM I HERE TO CONFRONT THE NOTHINGNESS...?

PUT AWAY YOUR PHILOSO CLIFFS NOTES. WE DO W IS NECESSARY TO EVOLVE.
EVEN THE MOST EXTRAORDINAR CHIMP MUST EA HIS BANANA.

WHAT IS GREAT IN MAN IS THAT HE IS A BRIDGE AND NOT AN END --
WAIT.
YOU FEEL THAT? THE GROUND...

...IS THIS AN EARTHQUAKE...?!
LOOK OUT--!
THE MOUNTAIN ERUP LIKE TEENAGED ACNE

AND AN ANCIENT CRET **REVEALS** ELF!
MBERING AND RRIFYING!
RIGHT.
TIME TO GET TO WORK--
BELAY THAT "UP AND AWAY"!
THE ***GUARDIAN AT THE GATE*** IS NO MERE ANTAGONIST! NO SIMPLE ENTRY IN YOUR ROGUES HANDBOOK!
OBVIOUSLY, THIS IS ***STRENGTH VS. STRENGTH...*** AND IN ***MY*** EXPERIENCE, ***MIGHT*** MAKES ***RIGHT!***
YOUR ***"EXPERIENCE"*** IS SEVERELY ***LIMITED!***
THINK ***ILLUMINATION*** OVER ***OBLITERATION.***
A WISE MAN NAMED LARRY MOREY ONCE SAID, "WHISTLE WHILE YOU WORK..."
...FOR WHAT ***SAVAGE BEASTS*** ABOUND...?
SHAMA-LAMA DING-DONG.

A NEAR MISS! BUT THE EARTH SHUDDERS UPON SUCH FIERCE IMPACT!
I'M NOT SPEAKING IN CODE, FRANK...

THIS IS THE DYNAMIC THAT HE RECOGNIZES. AND YET...
...THE WORDS OF THE BABA LAMA HAVE THE RING OF ETERNAL TRUTH...

...AND, PERHAPS, A WAY FORWARD.
♪
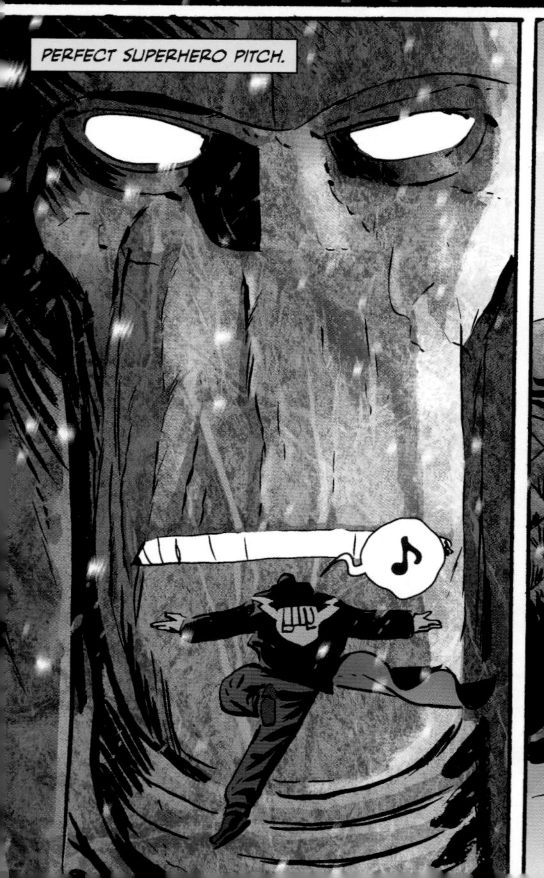
PERFECT SUPERHERO PITCH.
♪

PERFECT SUPERHERO RESULT.
ZZZZ
WELL, THAT WAS EFFECTIVE...
INDEED. THANKS TO YOU, THE GUARDIAN HAS SLIPPED INTO THE TRANQUILITY OF A WONDER SLUMBER.
AND THE DREAMS THAT LIE WITHIN...

...PERHAPS
KIND WHICH
S TO SPIRITUAL
IGHTENMENT.
DO I USE THAT WORD TOO OFTEN...?
WHERE ARE WE...?

FORTUNATELY, I DON'T POSSESS THE ARROGANCE TO CLAIM THIS SPACE AS MY OWN. I AM MERELY A HUMBLE STEWARD.
BUT THE ENERGIES TO BE FOUND WITHIN THIS ANCIENT STRUCTURE...YOU'D BE SURPRISED AT THE AMOUNT OF MOJO CONTAINED HEREIN...

OF COURSE, I DO HAVE CERTAIN PRIVILEGES.
SNAP
THE AIR SPARKS...

...AND THERE IS LIGHT.
THE PATTERN OF CANDLES SUGGESTS WARMTH AND BELONGING...AND OTHER NEW AGE NONSENSE...

LET NOT YOUR MIND BE BURDENED WITH SKEPTICISM, FRANK.
STEP INTO THE SWIRL AND BE CERTAIN OF FOOT.

I'M...NOT SURE I'M CERTAIN OF ANYTHING RIGHT NOW...

THAT'S GOOD.
THE FEWER PRECONCEIVED NOTIONS, THE BETTER. YOU'VE BEEN BURDENED WITH THOSE FOR FAR TOO LONG.
HOW... HOW DO YOU KNOW THAT...?

SORRY, I CAN SMELL IT ON YOU. IT'S JUST ONE OF THOSE THINGS.
NOW CLOSE YOUR EYES...

...AND OPEN YOUR MIND'S EYE.
AH, THAT OL' CHESTNUT...THE "MIND'S EYE": THE CAPACITY TO SEE WITHOUT SEEING. TO VISUALIZE THAT WHICH IS WITHIN YOU.

THAT MEANS... CERTAIN NEURONS ARE ACTIVATING WITHIN THE BRAIN. VISUAL PATHWAYS ARE OPENING...

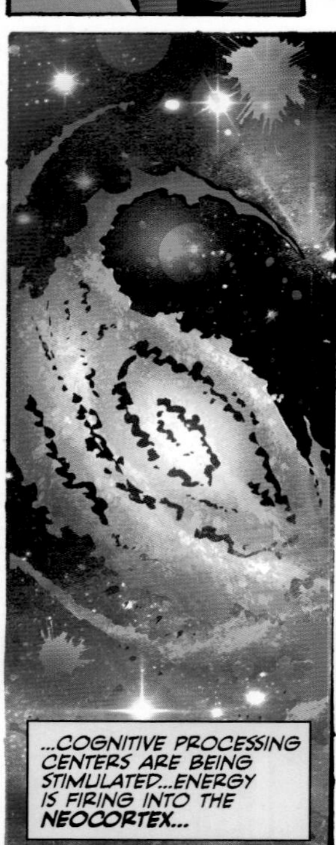
...COGNITIVE PROCESSING CENTERS ARE BEING STIMULATED...ENERGY IS FIRING INTO THE NEOCORTEX...

...DRAWING UPON MEMORIES... EMOTIONS...FEARS...

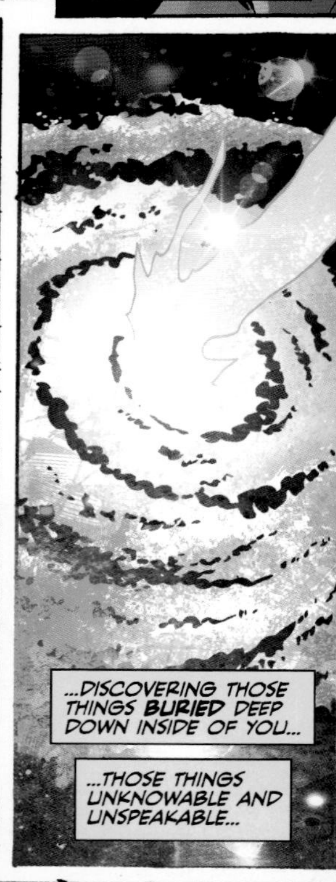
...DISCOVERING THOSE THINGS BURIED DEEP DOWN INSIDE OF YOU...
...THOSE THINGS UNKNOWABLE AND UNSPEAKABLE...

NCLUDING YOUR MOST ARSOME **NIGHTMARES**--

--THAT WHICH IS **WITHIN** YOU.

NO--!

SOME SAY THE WORLD IS DIVIDED BETWEEN MASTERS AND MONGRELS. A CLASS OF SUPREMACY AND A CLASS OF OPPRESSED.
THEY OPERATE ON THAT BASIS, STRIVING TO BE ONE WHILE SUBJUGATING THE OTHER.
CASE IN POINT...
WAIT.
WHERE... ARE WE?!
THE UNIVERSAL DECLARATION OF HUMAN RIGHTS STATES, "NO ONE SHALL BE HELD IN SLAVERY OR SERVITUDE; SLAVERY AND THE SLAVE TRADE SHALL BE PROHIBITED IN ALL THEIR FORMS."
CLEARLY, NO ONE TOLD THESE POOR SOULS...
TO ANSWER YOUR QUESTION...WE ARE ON THE IVORY COAST OF AFRICA. THESE COCOA FIELDS SPECIALIZE IN EXPLOITING A CERTAIN TYPE OF WORKER.
THE WORKERS ARE CHILDREN... BROUGHT HERE AS SLAVES.
AS THE NORTHERN REBELS ACT ILLEGALLY TO EXPORT--OF ALL THINGS--CHOCOLATE TO THE WORLD, THE IVORIAN GOVERNMENT TURNS A BLIND EYE TO THE TORTURE, RAPE, AND MURDER THAT OCCURS HERE...
SURELY, THIS BRUTALITY CANNOT STAND...
...CAN IT?
FRANK FEELS IT. MAYBE FOR THE FIRST TIME...
...THAT CERTAIN INNER TURMO THAT CHURNS WITHIN THE MOS CONFLICTED OF HEARTS WHE FACED WITH THE INHUMANITY OF MAN...

CONVERSELY, THE WHITE HOUSE 2 A.M. IS A FAR MORE SERENE ONUMENT TO MANKIND'S OLUTIONARY POTENTIAL.
EN AT THIS LATE HOUR, ERE IS STILL PROPER ECUTIVE PROTOCOL...
THIS PRESIDENT NEVER RAIDS THE FRIDGE IN THE SECOND-FLOOR FAMILY KITCHEN...
...NOT WHEN ALL THE GOOD GRUB IS DOWN IN THE MAIN KITCHEN.
YOU SHOULD TRY THE CHOCOLATE ROOM...
HUH--?!
WHO'S THERE?!
...THAT'S WHERE THEY MAKE THE MORE...SINFUL CONFECTIONS.
FOOD'S BEEN TASTING BETTER LATELY, HASN'T IT...?
MILK
I...DON'T KNOW WHAT YOU MEAN, SIR.
OH, YES YOU DO.
THE WORLD ON THE BRINK...I WAS THERE--I WATCHED YOU SCRAMBLE FOR SOLUTIONS. BUT NONE WERE FORTHCOMING.
I... SUPPOSE I GOT LUCKY.
WE ALL DID.
AND SO NOW YOU COMMENT ON EVENTS, AS OPPOSED TO SHAPING THEM?
NOT QUITE AS PRESIDENTIAL AS YOU'D HOPED TO BE, EH...?

IN MY DAY, CHOICES WERE MUCH CLEARER. I SAW A SITUATION...I DEALT WITH IT. IN WHATEVER MANNER I FELT WAS APPROPRIATE.
HE'S STILL OUT THERE, ISN'T HE? THE REAL SAVIOR...

...LIKE A TICKING TIME BOMB. IT'S GETTING EMBARRASSING, DON'T YOU THINK?
I WAS ADVISED... IT WOULD BE DETRIMENTAL TO... SOMETHING OR OTHER...I'M NOT SURE...
BUT YOU MAKE A GOOD POINT...

AHHH, MR. PRESIDENT, ARE YOU SURE YOU'D RATHER NOT GIVE IT SOME MORE TIME...?
AFTER ALL, WE ALL AGREED THAT DISCRETION IN THIS MATTER WAS THE BEST WAY TO PROCEED.
SIR, IF YOU INSIST ON WARMING UP THE SILOS NOW--
I DON'T WANT TO HEAR IT, GENERAL--

--YOU HAVE YOUR ORDERS AND I EXPECT YOU TO FOLLOW THEM!
NOW-- GET THEM IN THE AIR!
YES, SIR...

"...DEPLOYING REDLINE SQUADRON!"
SOMEWHERE IN MIDDLE AMERICA...
...A LONG-DORMANT FACILITY SUDDENLY COMES TO LIFE.

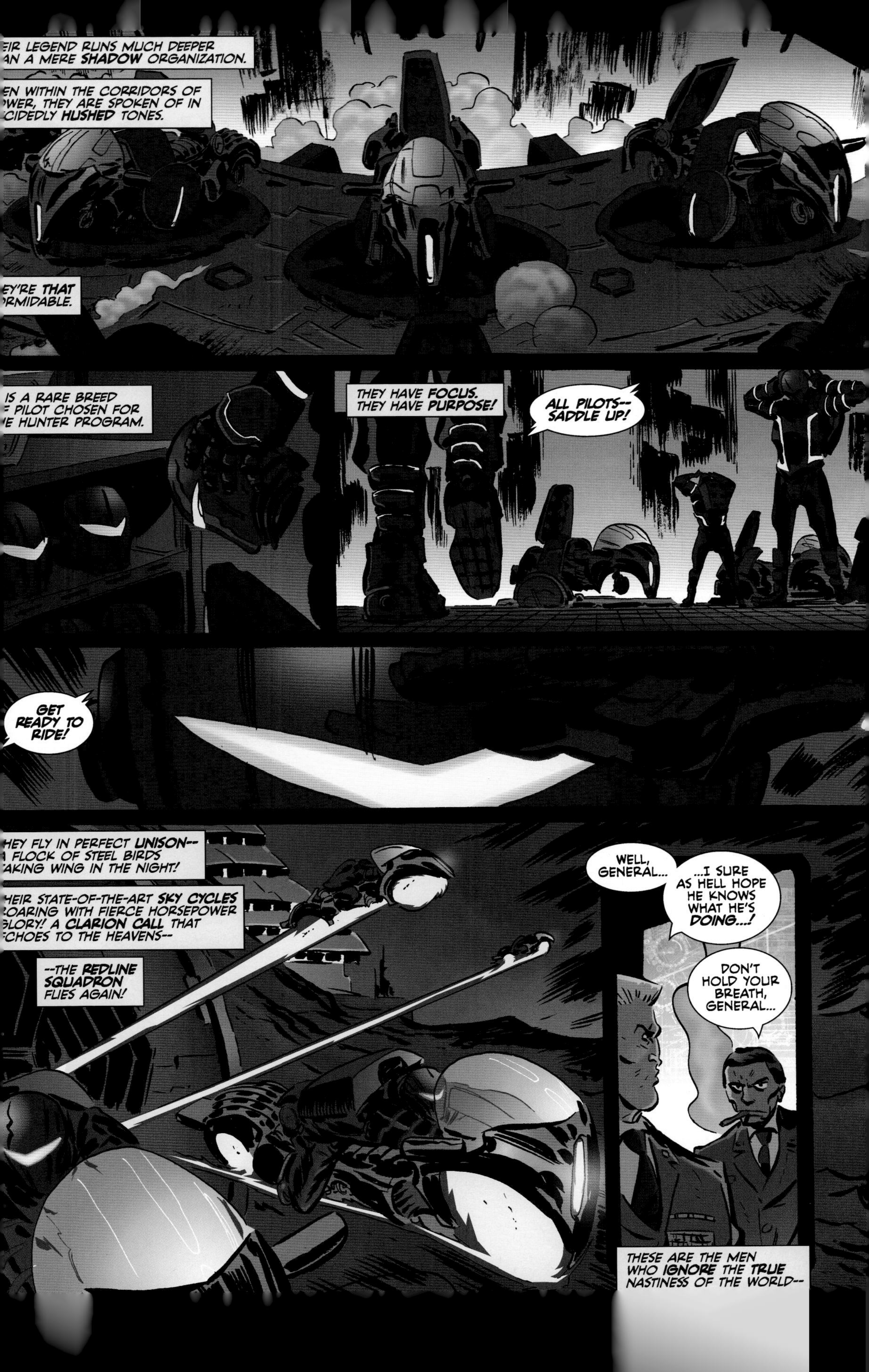
EIR LEGEND RUNS MUCH DEEPER
AN A MERE SHADOW ORGANIZATION.
EN WITHIN THE CORRIDORS OF
OWER, THEY ARE SPOKEN OF IN
CIDEDLY HUSHED TONES.
EY'RE THAT
ORMIDABLE.
IS A RARE BREED
F PILOT CHOSEN FOR
E HUNTER PROGRAM.
THEY HAVE FOCUS. THEY HAVE PURPOSE!
ALL PILOTS-- SADDLE UP!
GET READY TO RIDE!
HEY FLY IN PERFECT UNISON-- A FLOCK OF STEEL BIRDS AKING WING IN THE NIGHT!
HEIR STATE-OF-THE-ART SKY CYCLES ROARING WITH FIERCE HORSEPOWER LORY! A CLARION CALL THAT CHOES TO THE HEAVENS--
--THE REDLINE SQUADRON FLIES AGAIN!
WELL, GENERAL...
...I SURE AS HELL HOPE HE KNOWS WHAT HE'S DOING...!
DON'T HOLD YOUR BREATH, GENERAL...
THESE ARE THE MEN WHO IGNORE THE TRUE NASTINESS OF THE WORLD--

--THAT WHICH IS TOO UGLY TO ACKNOWLEDGE!
<YOU NEVER STOP WORKING, WHELP!>
<YOUR ASS BELONGS TO US!>
<TRANSLATED FROM BAOULÉ>
I DON'T THINK SO.
THESE KIDS HAVE NEVER SEEN A SUPERHERO IN ACTION BEFORE.
IT'S WAY MORE BRUTAL THAN THEY EVER COULD'VE IMAGINED...
...BUT THIS IS A SPECIAL CASE.
...UUUHHHH...
THE RESPONSE IS IMMEDIATE AND EFFUSIVE. WHEN CHILDREN LIVING IN THE DARK SEE A LIGHT...THEY RUSH TOWARD IT.
FRANK FEELS THE DIFFERENCE. THE GRATITUDE EXPRESSED FROM SOMEONE TEMPORARILY RELEASED FROM HIS PAIN--LIKE A DIAMOND BULLET SHOT STRAIGHT THROUGH HIS HEART.
THIS SURE AS HELL AIN'T WHAT HE'S USED TO.

MADNESS... MEET METHOD.
SO YOU SEE WHAT AN EFFECT A TRUE HERO CAN HAVE?
THERE'S THE DANCE... AND THEN THERE'S THE SHOW.
YOU MAY NEVER WIN THE COSPLAY SWEEPSTAKES-- WHERE YOU AND YOUR KIND DISPLAY YOUR COLORS LIKE A WALTER HILL FANTASY--BUT YOU CAN STILL HAVE A REASON FOR BEING.
ALL YOU HAVE TO DO... IS LOOK OUTSIDE YOURSELF.
THEN YOU MUST DECIDE... JUST HOW FAR ARE YOU WILLING TO GO...?
IN THE BLINK OF THE MIND'S EYE...
TWELVE MILES SOUTH. THE MAIN SLAVE CAMP.
THERE IS NO HESITATION.
NOT THIS TIME.
FOR THOSE OF YOU PAYING ATTENTION...
NOT TO GET ALL SCHOOLHOUSE ROCK ON YOU...BUT TO LIVE IS TO LEARN, OR WHAT'S A SOUL FOR...?
THERE ARE STEPS BELOW...AND THERE ARE STEPS BEYOND. AND THEN THERE'S GOOD OL' FRANK WELLS...WHO ALWAYS HAD TROUBLE TAKING ANY STEPS AT ALL...

SURELY, YOU SEE HOW IT IS.
SO WHAT CAN BE DONE? IN A WORLD SO OPPRESSED BY THE EVIL MEN CAN DO...TO WATCH FRANK AND THE REST OF HIS ILK WRESTLING AROUND LIKE IGNORANT PIGS IN THE MUD, IT GETS A LITTLE TEDIOUS, DON'T YOU THINK?
THAT... I CANNOT DIG.
BUT THERE IS ANOTHER WAY. IT GOES ALL THE WAY BACK TO THE BEGINNING.
IDENTIFYING THE TRUE VILLAINS... THE REAL EVIL... AND THEN TAKING REAL ACTION...
ACTION...LEADING TO RIGHTEOUS RESULT.
NOW THIS IS A VICTORY. HE FEELS IT... WAY DOWN DEEP INSIDE HIS BONES. THE PREVIOUS NONSENSE OF HIS LIFE SEEMS TO BURN AWAY WITHIN THE FIRES OF THIS SINGLE ACT OF LIBERATION.
IT'S LIKE A DRUG... THE BUZZ IS INCREDIBLE...
...IT FEEDS HIM. A HUNGER HE NEVER KNEW.
IT FUELS HIM. MAKES HIM EVEN STRONGER.
HE WANTS MORE...

ARRIVAL WAS DRAMATIC...
N FOR GOLDEN CITY.

NY OTHER DAY,
WOULD'VE PLAYED
QUITE DIFFERENTLY.
NOT TODAY.

AY...THE GOLDEN CITY
NCIL MUST ENDURE THE
KIEST OF FILIBUSTERING...

I HAVE COME TO PLANT MY FLAG...

...SO TO SPEAK.

I'VE NEVER BEEN HERE BEFORE, SO MY VERNACULAR MIGHT BE A BIT OFF. APOLOGIES.

BUT...IT'S THE MOTH THAT'S DRAWN TO FLAME, CORRECT...?

MY NAME IS SEAVER.

THIS IS YOUR CIVILIZATION'S ACKNOWLEDGED SEAT OF POWER, IS IT NOT...?

THAT... DEPENDS.

YOU'RE SURE... YOU WOULDN'T PREFER TO HAVE A SEAT...?

...Y-YES... ON MY LAP, MAYBE...

SORRY, MA'AM. WE THOUGHT YOU WERE STILL COMATOSE.
AN UNKNOWN LIFE FORM TOUCHED DOWN IN THE NORTH CITY SQUARE. WITNESSES ON THE SCENE CLAIM--
FORGET IT.

I'LL SEE FOR MYSELF. THE NORTH CITY SQUARE...?
NOBODY INVADES MY HOMETOWN AND GETS AWAY WITH IT.

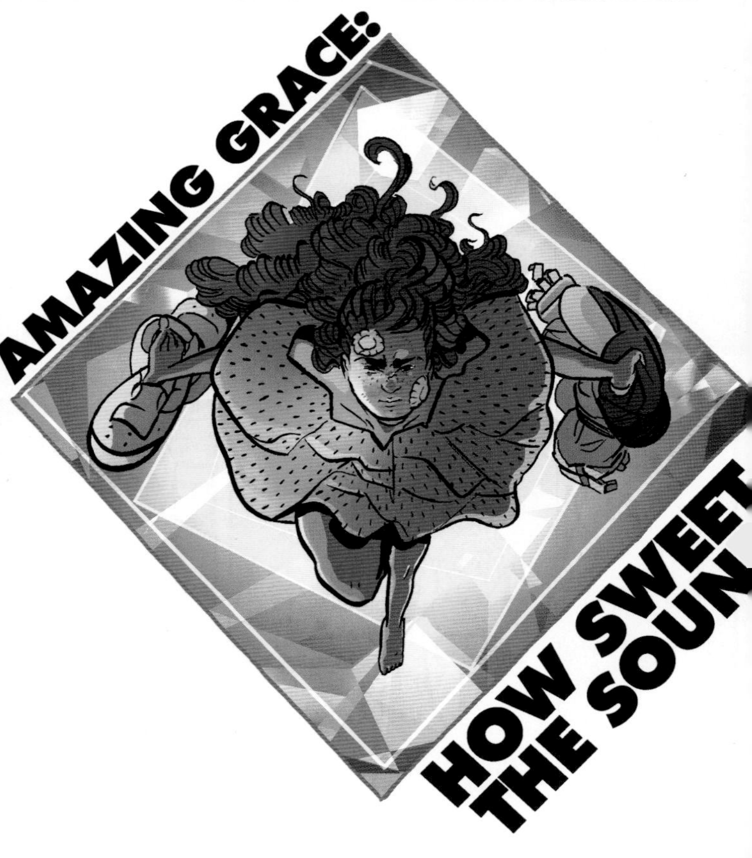
AMAZING GRACE:
HOW SWEET THE SOUN

CVX
SHE OFTEN RUSHES IN WHERE ANGELS FEAR TO TREAD. THAT'S THE STINK OF HEROISM.
UNFORTUNATELY, HER LITTLE TIME-OUT HAS COST HER DEARLY. HER CAPACITY TO ENDURE...HAS BEEN TEMPORARILY DIMINISHED.
HER CONTROL OF THE QUADRILATERAL TELEPORTATION TUNNELS SHE IS ABLE TO SELF-GENERATE...IS TENUOUS AT BEST...

...AND **AWKWARD** AT WORST.
WONDERS IF SHE ACTED **TOO SOON.** WONDERS IF SHE'S ABLE TO FACE TEVER **CHALLENGE** LIES AHEAD.

HUNNDDT

WOW...
...THAT WAS **AMAZING.**
YOU READY TO KICK SOME ASS, MA'AM?

LET NOT YOUR HEART BE TROUBLED, HUMANS.
I MAY **APPEAR** AS ONE OF YOU, BUT REST ASSURED--
HOLD IT RIGHT THERE!

DON'T! MOVE! A! MUSCLE!
YOU'RE **SURROUNDED...** SO LET'S AVOID A **MESS,** Y'HEAR ME?

I AM AS CLEAN AS AN IDIOT'S SOUL.
IF **THIS** IS THE DRAMA THAT MUST BE PLAYED OUT TO CONFIRM A SENSE OF GRAVITAS, THEN SO BE IT.
DO YOUR WORST... BUT WATCH THE HAIR.

GOLDEN CITY SECURITY ISN'T KNOWN FOR THEIR ITCHY TRIGGER FINGERS. BUT THEY DO ENJOY A GOOD SHOOTOUT.
THIS TARGET IS LIKE DUCKS ON THE POND. HOWEVER...
I THOUGHT YOU WANTED TO AVOID A MESS...
...AND YET YOUR WEAPONS LEAVE SO MANY REMNANTS BEHIND.
THEY CANN REMEMBER TIME WHEN FELT SO LI HOPE...
...BUT THEY DON'T KNOW EVERYTHING.
THIS IS HER CITADEL OF SOLACE. THE CENTER OF TRANQUILITY FOR ONE WHO HAS SEEN SO MUCH.
THIS IS WHERE SHE WILL MAKE HER STAND.
GUH--!
OKAY... WHATEVER YOU ARE...
COME AND GET ME...
WELL, CAN I SAY HOW ENJOYABLE IT'S BEEN TO SPEND THIS TIME WITH YOU...?
BUT SHE TASKS ME, AND I SHALL HAVE HER.
SO IF YOU'LL EXCUSE ME...

"...I HAVE A DATE WITH DESTINY."

VERY NICE IN HERE. LOTS OF SPACE.
OKAY, OKAY... I CAN ADMIT IT NOW...
...I'M NOT FROM AROUND HERE.

BUT, LET'S FACE IT, WHAT HUMAN COULD POSSIBLY BE GOOD ENOUGH FOR YOU?
THAT'S WHY I'VE COME.
YOU ARE A MAGNIFICENT SPECIMEN. AND, OF COURSE--

AH, YES. THIS IS EXCITING. YOU'RE DISPLAYING YOUR PLUMAGE...

...WELL, I CERTAINLY ACCEPT YOUR GRACIOUS INVITATION.
TO WHEREVER IT IS YOU'VE BROUGHT ME.
IT DOESN'T MATTER WHERE YOU ARE NOW--
EH...?
--AS LONG AS YOU'RE OUT OF MY CITY.
NOW, I DON'T KNOW WHO YOU ARE OR WHAT YOU WANT.
BUT YOU'RE CLEARLY AN UNINVITED GUE
ON THIS PLANET
SO I'M GOING T
TREAT YOU LIK
ONE.

UNINVITED?! ARE YOU NOT OPENING WIDE THE GATES TO ME NOW?
CAN'T YOU FEEL THE IMMEDIATE CHEMISTRY THAT EXISTS BETWEEN US?
I CERTAINLY CAN.
YOU WANT TO FEEL SOMETHING? I'LL BE HAPPY TO OBLIGE...
YOU ARE A FIERY ONE. I LIKE THAT.
CALL ME SEAVER. LOCAL CUSTOMS DEMAND THAT I BREAK BREAD WITH YOU...
E'S GIVING OFF A VIBE... LIKE A PHEROMONE EQUENCY WITH DEFINITE ALIEN OVERTONES. IT IS CHEMICAL.
ANY NORMAL WOMAN WOULD OBABLY JUMP INTO D WITH HIM BEFORE HEY EVEN KNEW WHY.
BETTER HUMOR HIM FOR NOW...
OKAY, MR. SEAVER.
YOU WANT TO TAKE ME OUT? I'M NOT A CHEAP DATE...
EXCELLENT.
I PREDICT AN EPIC INTERACTION.
GOOD FOR YOU. I PREDICT PAIN.
BEGIN PHASE TWO.

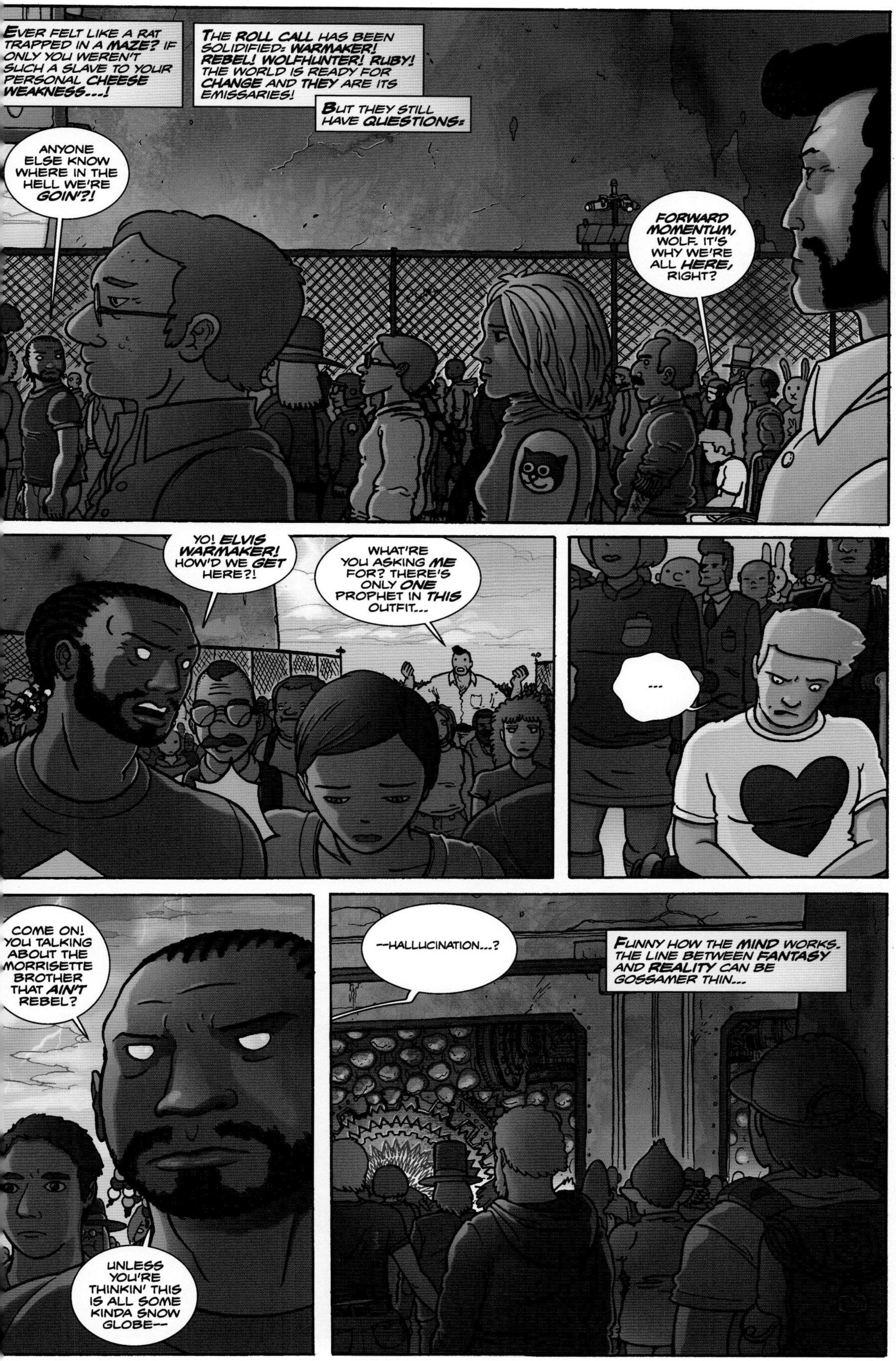

EVER FELT LIKE A RAT TRAPPED IN A **MAZE?** IF ONLY YOU WEREN'T SUCH A SLAVE TO YOUR PERSONAL **CHEESE WEAKNESS...!**

THE **ROLL CALL** HAS BEEN SOLIDIFIED: **WARMAKER! REBEL! WOLFHUNTER! RUBY!** THE WORLD IS READY FOR **CHANGE** AND **THEY** ARE ITS EMISSARIES!

BUT THEY STILL HAVE **QUESTIONS:**

ANYONE ELSE KNOW WHERE IN THE HELL WE'RE ***GOIN'?!***

FORWARD MOMENTUM, WOLF. IT'S WHY WE'RE ALL ***HERE,*** RIGHT?

YO! ELVIS WARMAKER! HOW'D WE GET HERE?!
WHAT'RE YOU ASKING ME FOR? THERE'S ONLY ONE PROPHET IN THIS OUTFIT...

...

COME ON! YOU TALKING ABOUT THE MORRISETTE BROTHER THAT AIN'T REBEL?
UNLESS YOU'RE THINKIN' THIS IS ALL SOME KINDA SNOW GLOBE--

--HALLUCINATION...?
FUNNY HOW THE MIND WORKS. THE LINE BETWEEN FANTASY AND REALITY CAN BE GOSSAMER THIN...

...IT ALL COMES DOWN TO EXACTLY WHAT YOU'RE LOOKING FOR!
AGENTS OF CHANGE: TURN AND FACE THE STRAIN
CAN YOU HEAR IT--THE GEARS GRINDING INSIDE? THE HELPLESS MEAT GETTING TORN APART...?

WHOA! I DON'T WANT NO PART A THAT--!
WHAT'S THE MATTER WITH YOU PEOPLE?! OUTTA MY WAY!

I DIDN'T SIGN UP FOR THIS!
NOOOOOOO..

GUH--!

OH DAMN... THAT WAS ONE FUGGIN' REVERIE...
SO WHILE WOLFHUNTER TRIES TO SORT IT ALL OUT...
IF THAT'S... REALLY WHAT IT WAS...

...WARMAKER IS ON THE PROWL, CRUISING IN HIS '74 CADILLAC COUPE DEVILLE.
"FOUR CORNERED ROOM" BLASTING ON THE 8-TRACK!
BEEN A WHILE SINCE I'VE CHECKED IN...

"...IT'D BETTER STILL BE HERE."
1864

OL' BERT MAY HAVE HIS IDEAS ABOUT WHAT'S REAL AND WHAT'S NOT...
...BUT I'VE GOT MINE.

NOT ENOUGH REAL TO GO AROUND THESE DAYS--
ELVIS! YOU CALL THIS A SAFE HOUSE?!

STILL PINCHING YOURSELF OVER THERE...?
DON'T EVEN TRY TO TELL ME IT'S AN ANALOG VERSUS DIGITAL THING, BERT...

...THAT'S CRAP AND YOU KNOW IT.
IF WE HAD TIME TO SIT AROUND--HOLDING HANDS AND GETTING TO KNOW EACH OTHER--WE WOULD. BUT I THINK LAST DECEMBER PROVED SOMETHING...
...CHANGE IS A DISH THAT IS BEST SERVED COLD.

I THINK I HEARD THAT IN A MOVIE ONCE.
HERBERT'S SECRET AGENDA WARMS HIS OWN HEART...JUST LIKE THE CAMELS THAT FEED HIS ORAL FIXATION.
IF EVER A WIZ THERE WAS...

ONLY ONE WITH A FEW TRICKS UP HIS SLEEVE.
RUBY CAN BE SNEAKY AS HELL, WHEN SHE WANTS TO BE.
BUT FOLLOWING WARMAKER HERE IS ONE THING--
MADNESS OF HIS POP LIFE IS SOMETHING ELSE ENTIRELY!
SOMEONE'S SAFE HOUSE AIN'T SO SAFE!
DEATHCARD! ANARCHISTIC ASSASSIN TO THE STARS! HE DOESN'T NEED A REASON TO KILL!
RUBY?!
WHAT THE HELL ARE YOU DOING HERE?!
GOOD QUESTION! WHAT'RE YOU DOING HERE?!
PERSONAL BUSINESS!
NOW BUZZ OFF SO I CAN DEAL WITH THIS BULLET HEAD!

WELL, OOKIE WHAT E HAVE ERE--!
ANOTHER TARGET! ANOTHER NOTCH ON MY BED-POST!
LISTEN, THE T.V. SHOW PAID FOR MY MEDICAL INSURANCE. FOR GUYS IN OUR SITUATION, THAT'S A BIG DEAL...
IS THAT HOW A HERO TALKS?
HEY, IF YOU HAD TO DO THE PATENTED TAG-TEAM BIT WITH YOUR BROTHER, YOU'D KNOW WHAT I WAS TALKING ABOUT!
YOU THINK IT'S EASY TO HAVE TO GIVE THIS UP...
...JUST SO I CAN BE JUST LIKE HIM?!
HEY, DEATHCREEP--
--YOU'RE MY TARGET!

IMAGINE THE SOUND OF YOUR LIFE EXPLODING--
--AND YET, THAT LIFE GOES ON IN ALL ITS FIERY SPLENDOR!
WOO-HA! I DO LOVE A GOOD, LOCALIZED APOCALYPSE--
WELL, THEN YOU'LL LOVE THIS--
--GIVE ME A FEW SECONDS, AND I'LL DISINTEGRATE YOUR FACE!
THAT'S WHAT I DO.
YEEAARRRGGH..
HE'S GONNA FEEL THAT IN THE MORNING...
YOU STILL GOT GOOD TIMING, HON.
DON'T PRETEND IT WAS THE INSURANCE THAT KEPT YOU ON THAT STUPID SHOW.
YOU'RE A FAME WHORE, AND WE BOTH KNOW IT.
BUT YOU'RE HERE BECAUSE YOU KNOW THERE'S SOMETHING BEYOND THAT. YOU JUST DON'T KNOW WHAT.

AND YOU DO...?
YOU REALLY THINK YOU'RE THE ONE HOLDING THE KEYS TO THE FUTURE...?

LEMME TELL YOU SOMETHING, REBEL...NOT ONLY AM I HOLDING THE KEYS...
...I OWN THE CAR.

EANWHILE, THINGS HAVE OTTEN A LITTLE SAFER IN ARMAKER'S SAFE HOUSE.
ALL THIS VIDEO GAME VIOLENCE-- FOR WHAT...?
HAD TO COME BACK AND GET SOMETHING...

ARE YOU SERIOUS...?!

I DON'T THINK IT GOES WITH YOUR ARMOR, ELVIS.
AIN'T ABOUT STYLE, BELIEVE ME.
I DON'T KNOW IF BERT'S ON SOME NOSTALGIA KICK, GETTING THE OLD BAND BACK TOGETHER...OR IF IT ACTUALLY MATTERS FOR WHATEVER'S COMING NEXT.
HANG IN THERE

EITHER WAY...
...IT'S ALWAYS GOOD TO KNOW WHAT TIME IT IS.

R.GRAMPÁ
2013

Amazing Grace
SOMETHING ABOUT HIM...HE'S IRRESISTIBLE TO WOMEN!
BUT HIS CHARMS DON'T WORK ON ME--
--OR DO THEY...?
XOXO
HE TRAVERSED THE GALAXY TO BE WITH HER! HE WAS SUAVE! HE WAS SOPHISTICATED! BUT COULD SHE TRUST HIM? COULD LOVE BE IN THE AIR WHEN SHE KEEPS ASKING HERSELF, "WHO'S THAT KNOCKING ON MY SECRET DOOR?"

IT LOOKS SO PEACEFUL FROM THIS DISTANCE. NOT AT ALL LIKE THE BEACHHEAD IT'S TARGETED TO BE...

...MAYBE ONLY IN GOLDEN CITY ARE THEY FEELING THE HEAT!
IT'S OBVIOUS-- WE'RE BEING INVADED!
OUR OWN SATS CAN'T GET AN ACCURATE SCAN ON THIS GUY!
THIS IS AN ODD KIND OF DIPLOMACY YOU'RE PRACTICING...!
YOU CAN'T POSSIBLY THINK THAT--
EVERYONE NEEDS TO CALM DOWN--

--I KNOW I WAS CHECKED OUT FOR A WHILE THERE, BUT I'M BACK NOW.
AND YOU HAVE TO TRUST THAT I KNOW WHAT I'M DOING.

IT'S NOT THAT, GRACE...WE'VE ALL SEEN WHAT THIS INDIVIDUAL CAN DO...!
AND, FRANKLY, YOUR REACTION IS A BIT--
VEXING, PERHAPS? WELL, THAT'S TO BE EXPECTED...

...AFTER ALL, THERE'S DESTINY IN THE AIR.
I CAN TASTE IT... CAN'T YOU...?
HE CALLS HIMSELF MR. SEAVER AND HE'S GOT A CERTAIN SPRING IN HIS STEP...

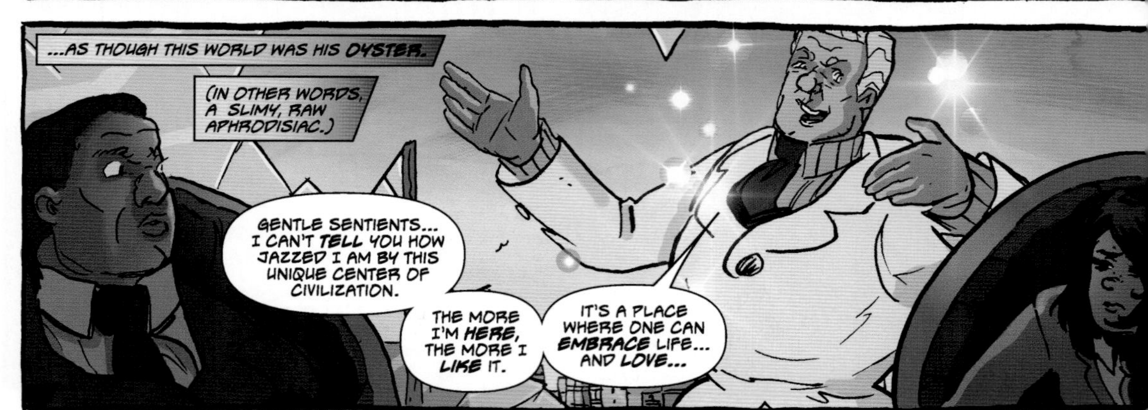
...AS THOUGH THIS WORLD WAS HIS OYSTER.
(IN OTHER WORDS, A SLIMY, RAW APHRODISIAC.)
GENTLE SENTIENTS... I CAN'T TELL YOU HOW JAZZED I AM BY THIS UNIQUE CENTER OF CIVILIZATION.
THE MORE I'M HERE, THE MORE I LIKE IT.
IT'S A PLACE WHERE ONE CAN EMBRACE LIFE... AND LOVE...

...AND EVERYTHING ELSE TO BE FOUND WITHIN THE EMOTIONAL SPECTRUM.
NEW AGE RHETORIC...
...I MAY VOMIT.

FROM THE HOUSES OF THE HOLY...TO PURPLE MOUNTAINS' MAJESTY...LOOK AROUND YOU...
THE WILL TO INDULGE IS STRONG. AND WHY NOT? IT'S A BEAUTIFUL THING, WHEN YOU DIG DEEP ENOUGH...

...IT'S JUST A LITTLE HUMAN NATURE.
AM I RIGHT...?

OOOOHHH...
WHAT THE HELL--?!
SOMEBODY GRAB HER--

MY GOD! IS SHE ALL RIGHT...?
SHE'S BARELY CONSCIOUS...
GET HER TO THE MED CENTER, RIGHT AWAY.
AND TELL THE TECHS TO DO A FULL WORKUP AND CALL ME WITH THE RESULTS--WHATEVER THEY FIND...!

OKAY, SEAVER... IF YOU'RE DONE MAKING SPEECHES, I'M STILL WILLING...
...YOU WANT A NIGHT OUT WITH ME?
FOR STARTERS.
SHALL WE...?

GOLDEN CITY AT SUNSET! NOT MUCH ON THIS EARTH CAN MATCH THE BEAUTY ON DISPLAY HERE...
...THEN AGAIN, THESE THINGS ARE ALL IN THE EYE OF THE BEHOLDER.

MEANWHILE, GRACE IS FEELING THE PINCH...
THIS IS THE PAYOFF FOR THE POWER YOU WIELD...

...A GRAND MONUMENT TO ALL THAT YOU REPRESENT. A FITTING TRIBUTE TO WHAT YOU HAVE ACHIEVED.
YOU ARE TRULY AMAZING, GRACE...

HE'S DROPPING LINES LEFT AND RIGHT. THIS REALLY IS SOME KIND OF SEDUCTION.
I'M JUST NOT FEELING THE CHEMICAL REACTION...

I'M STILL QUITE CURIOUS ABOUT THIS WORLD OF YOURS. THERE IS SO MUCH TO SEE.
WOULD YOU BE MY GUIDE? I CAN THINK OF NO ONE BETTER...
YOUR "GUIDE," HUH...?

WELL, SOMEONE HAS TO LEAD IN THIS DANCE...
...DON'T YOU THINK...?

I SUPPOSE YOU'RE RIGHT.
WE CAN DECIDE WHICH ONE OF US WILL LATER...

...KNOW WHAT I MEAN?
HA.
YOUR WIT IS INCENDIARY, GRACE.

SO LET'S LOOK AT THE WORLD FROM AN APPROPRIATE VANTAGE POINT...
...A GOD'S VANTAGE POINT.
THEY LEAVE THE GROUND FAR BELOW. TWO HEARTS IN FULL FLIGHT.
HIS...FULL OF PROMISE.
HERS...FULL OF SUSPICION.

SOMEWHERE IN THE UNIVERSE, MORE COMPONENTS OF A COSMIC WAS-PASSIERT-DANN-MASCHINE CLICK INTO PLACE...

...BUT DO THEY GO UNHEARD...?
HE'S MAKING ALL THE TYPICAL ALPHA MOVES...

...LET'S SEE HOW HE LIKES IT WHEN A FEW ARE MADE ON HIM...!
NG--!
YOU POSSESS... GREAT ENTHUSIASM...!
THIS WILL COME IN... QUITE HANDY, I THINK.
WE'LL SEE.
THE HIMALAYAS. DURING THE LAST WORLD WAR...PILOTS NICKNAMED THIS TITANIC MOUNTAIN RANGE "THE HUMP."
THE ROOFTOP OF THE WORLD...
...A PLACE WHERE DESTINIES ARE DISCUSSED.
NOT A BAD VIEW HERE, EITHER...

NATURAL BEAUTY ABOUNDS.
ALL AROUND ME. AND RIGHT IN FRONT OF ME...

...I THINK WE'RE HAVING A MOMENT, DON'T YOU?
DEPENDS ON WHAT KIND OF "MOMENT" YOU'RE REFERRING TO.

GRACE... I THINK YOU KNOW EXACTLY WHAT I'M REFERRING TO. WE BOTH FEEL IT.
IT'S UNDENIABLE... AND ITS EFFECTS ARE INSTANTANEOUS.

THE ENERGY BETWEEN US...
TOGETHER, WE CAN DO ANYTHING...

...GO ANYWHERE...
HE MAY BE RIGHT. BECAUSE SOMETHING IS HAPPENING BETWEEN THE AUSPICIOUS COUPLE...
...A SHIFT IN THE FABRIC OF SPACE-TIME...

...SOME NEW DOORWAY OPENING...

...AND EVEN AMAZING GRACE IS NOT IMMUNE TO MR. SEAVER'S SO-CALLED "EFFECTS"...

...AT LEAST IT HAPPENS QUICK.
!

AND WHILE THE VENUE MAY CHANGE... THE SONG REMAINS THE SAME...

INCREDIBLE... THE PLACES YOUR HEART CAN TAKE YOU...

OF COURSE, I'VE ALWAYS BEEN A ROMANTIC AT HEART.

WELL, WE ALL HAVE OUR WEAK POINTS...
...YOU COME HERE OFTEN, THEN...?

I'VE DINED HERE ON OCCASION, YES.
BUT NEVER WITH SOMEONE SO... UNIQUE. IT REALLY MAKES A DIFFERENCE. BUT MAKE NO MISTAKE...

...ALL OF THIS IS FOR YOU.

WHAT DO YOU WANT, SEAVER?
WHAT DOES ANY MAN WANT?
A GOOD WOMAN AT HIS SIDE. THE CHANCE TO SIGN HIS NAME IN THE GREAT COSMIC GUEST BOOK...
...TO FULFILL HIS OWN SENSE OF PURPOSE.

AS YOU MAY KNOW, THE UNIVERSE IS VAST. JUST LOOK AROUND...
...SO MANY DIFFERENT LIFE FORMS. SO MANY VARIED CIVILIZATIONS. YET, SO MUCH CONFUSION...

I TAKE IT YOU'RE NOT CONFUSED ABOUT--
I AM SOMEONE WHO POSSESSES THE WIDEST POSSIBLE VIEW OF THE COSMIC LANDSCAPE.

IT IS HARD-WON KNOWLEDGE, TO BE SURE. BUT I HAVE MY OWN MANDATE...

...AS YOU CAN IMAGINE.

I GIVE YOU CREDIT, GRACE. I FEEL LIKE YOU ACTUALLY KNOW THE SCORE...

...YOU'RE BEYOND THE GAMES I'VE BEEN FORCED TO PLAY SO MANY TIMES BEFORE.
FOR THE FIRST TIME, SHE THINKS SHE FEELS SOMETHING...

...BUT THAT FEELING IS SHORT LIVED.

HOLD ON.

SOMETHING'S JUST HAPPENED AT HOME...

A MILD UNDERSTATEMENT.

THE MULTINATIONAL SPACE STATION. LOCATED IN LOW EARTH ORBIT. A JOINT PROJECT BETWEEN THE FIVE LARGEST SPACE AGENCIES. BUILT PRIMARILY FOR ZERO GRAVITY SCIENTIFIC STUDY AND AS A STAGING AREA FOR VARIOUS MOBILE SPACE MISSIONS.

RIGHT NOW...IT'S JUST ANOTHER VICTIM OF APATHETIC GOVERNMENT BUREAUCRACIES AND A BUDGETARY-BASED LACK OF SERVICE INSPECTIONS.

--THIS IS WHAT I DO.
THERE IS NO HESITATION. THERE IS ONLY ACTION.

SWIFT AND EFFECTIVE.

THAT'S...
...IMPRESSIVE.

NEED TO SEPARATE THE DAMAGED MODULES FROM THE INTACT ONES...
THAT SHOULD DO IT.

EVERYONE STILL ALIVE IN HERE?
DON'T WORRY, FOLKS. I'LL HAVE YOU DOWN ON THE GROUND, SAFE AND SOUND, IN A MOMENT...

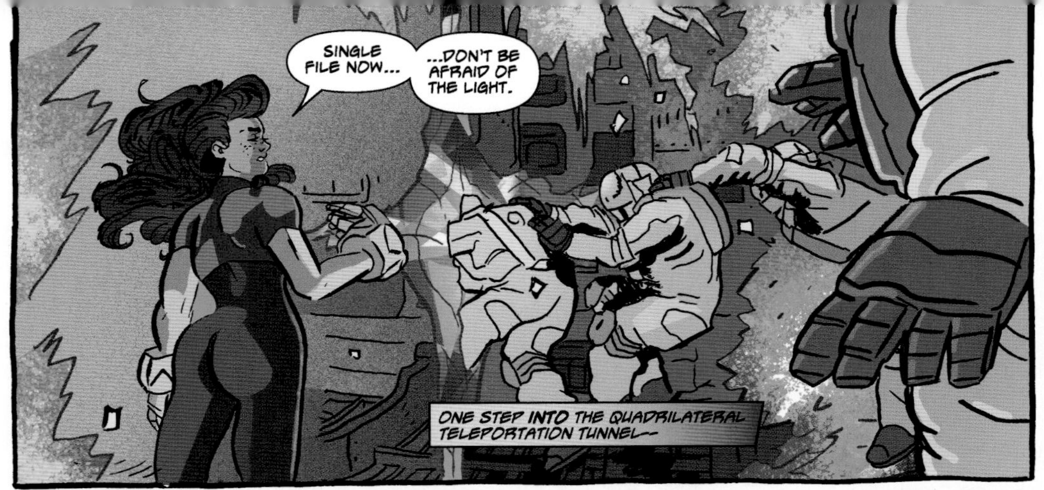
SINGLE FILE NOW...
...DON'T BE AFRAID OF THE LIGHT.
ONE STEP INTO THE QUADRILATERAL TELEPORTATION TUNNEL--

--ONE STEP OUT... INTO MISSION CONTROL!
GAH--!
JEEZ... SO THAT'S HOW IT WORKS...

AH, THERE YOU ARE.
YOUR SUBTLETY... YOUR FINESSE... I'M EVEN MORE CHARMED BY YOUR LIMITLESS POTENTIAL.

I USED TO BE MUCH MORE TERRITORIAL... BUT I SUPPOSE I'VE WIDENED A FEW OF MY OWN VIEWS LATELY.
POTENTIAL FOR WHAT, BY THE WAY...?
WON'T THE REST OF THIS WRECKAGE RAIN HELL DOWN UPON THE PLANET BELOW...?

NOT MY FIRST RODEO, SEAVER...
...I KNOW EXACTLY WHERE TO PUT THIS.

THE GREAT BASIN DESERT. LARGEST EMPTY SPACE IN NORTH AMERICA...

...PERFECT SPOT TO DUMP THIS UNTIL THE SCIENTISTS CAN DO THEIR TECHNICAL AUTOPSY.
YOU FEEL SOME SENSE OF RESPONSIBILITY TO THIS WORLD, DON'T YOU...?

IT'S ADMIRABLE.
SOMETHING ABOUT THE WAY YOU SAY THAT... I DON'T KNOW...
I'M STILL NOT SURE WHAT YOU'RE ACTUALLY TRYING TO ACCOMPLISH HERE.

BUT MY GUT TELLS ME THAT IT'S PROBABLY NOT--
HOLD ON. CALL COMING IN...
GOTTA TAKE THIS.

YOU'VE GOT GRACE. WHAT'VE YOU FOUND OUT...?

WE'VE GIVEN COUNCILWOMAN HUDSON THE FULL ANALYSIS AND WE'VE UNCOVERED SOME **INTERESTING** RESULTS...

...WHILE **DEFINITELY** NOT OF THIS EARTH, IT'S SPECIFICALLY DESIGNED TO **WORK** ON HUMAN FEMALE PHYSIOLOGY.

WAIT. **WHAT'S** DESIGNED TO WORK...?

I'LL GET THERE. SO, HER **GONADOTROPIN RELEASE** IS OFF THE CHARTS, SO THAT WAS OUR **FIRST** CLUE...

...FROM THERE, WE WERE ABLE TO SEPARATE AND ISOLATE SPECIFIC **MOLECULAR** TRACE ACTIVITY.

OKAY, KEEP GOING. I THINK I FOLLOW...

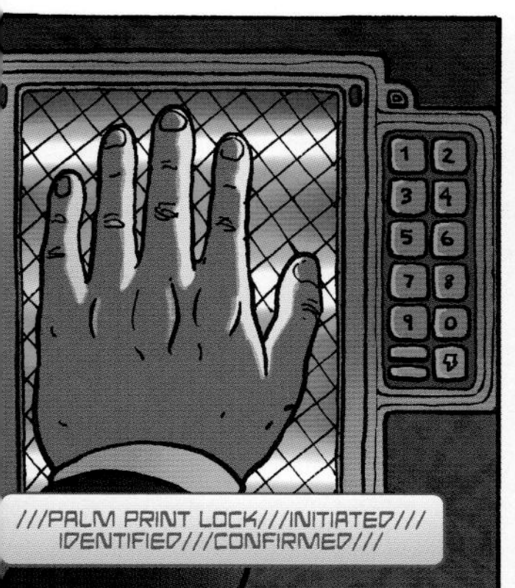

HAT WOULD **YOU** DO IF YOU WERE AGGED AS AN "AGENT OF CHANGE"? F YOU WERE PEGGED AS SOMEONE HO POSSESSED THE NECESSARY KILLS TO SOMEHOW **EFFECT** THAT HANGE? IF YOU WERE IDENTIFIED S SOMEONE WHO COULD ACTUALLY **ANDLE** SUCH RESPONSIBILITY?

DOESN'T SOUND QUITE **RIGHT**, DOES IT...?

IT BEGS THE QUESTION: WOULD **YOU** WANT TO JOIN A CLUB THAT WOULD ACTUALLY ACCEPT **YOU** AS A MEMBER?

MAKES YOU THINK... THERE MIGHT BE **BETTER** WAYS TO WASTE YOUR TIME...

AGENTS OF CHANGE: BURN, BABY, BURN

2001 ODYSSEY

UNITED ICEE CORP

THE MUSIC IS A HEARTBEAT. IT PUSHES THE BLOOD THROUGH ALL THE NECESSARY TUBES.
THE SMELL OF SWEAT AND ALCOHOL IN THE AIR IS AN INVITATION...
...BUT AN INVITATION TO WHAT...?

ELVIS WARMAKER! RUBY!
ALOHA, FELLOW AGENTS!
NICE TO SEE YOU FOUND THE PLACE.
I'VE GOT BUILT-IN G.P.S.
MADE IT EASY.

THERE ARE NO THOUGHTS OF CHANGE OCCURRING ON THE DANCE FLOOR...
...ONLY THOUGHTS OF INSTANT GRATIFICATION.

HEY, IF WE'RE REALLY GONNA TALK... THIS AIN'T A BAD PLACE. THEIR CHOICE OF SPINS NOTWITHSTANDING.
IT CAN'T ALL BE SLY AND THE FAMILY STONE, WOLFHUNTER.

WELL, WHAT'S THEN IS NOW. WELCOME TO MODERN MEDIA.
READY TO TALK CHANGE, MATTY-BOY...?
...

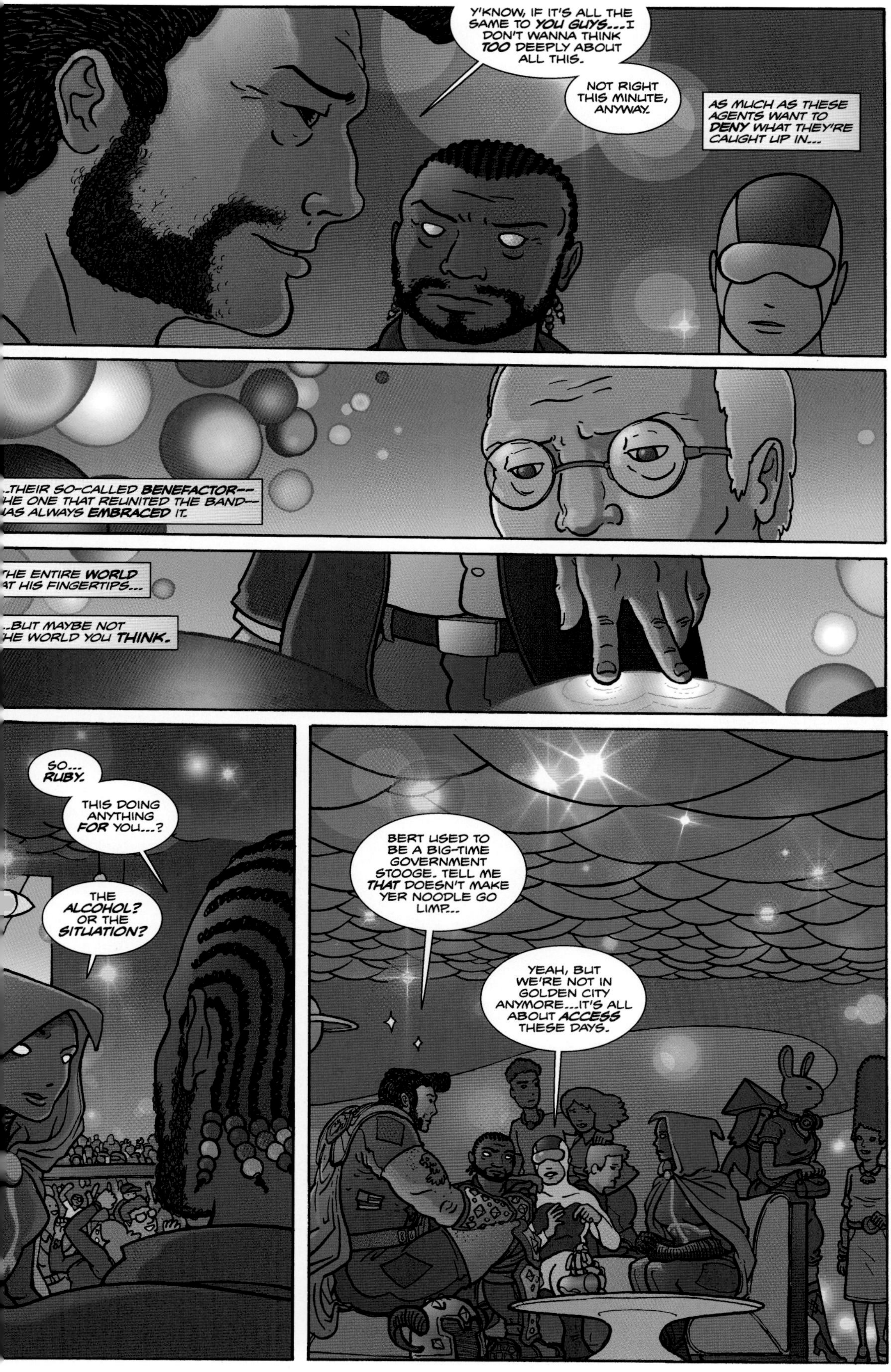

Y'KNOW, IF IT'S ALL THE SAME TO *YOU GUYS*... I DON'T WANNA THINK *TOO* DEEPLY ABOUT ALL THIS.

NOT RIGHT THIS MINUTE, ANYWAY.

AS MUCH AS THESE AGENTS WANT TO **DENY** WHAT THEY'RE CAUGHT UP IN...

..THEIR SO-CALLED **BENEFACTOR**-- HE ONE THAT REUNITED THE BAND-- HAS ALWAYS **EMBRACED** IT.

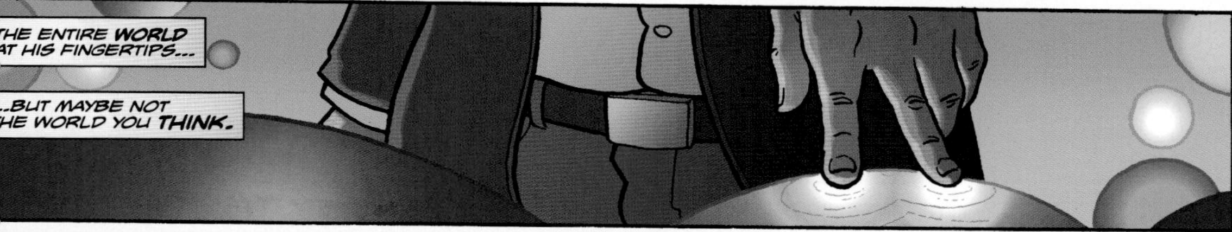

HOW MUCH "ACCESS" DO YOU THINK YOU NEED, REBEL?!
WE'RE THE SUPERHEROES HERE...!
AN' WHEN A WHITE MAN'S PULLIN' THE STRINGS, YOU KNOW IT'S NOT--
OKAY, BEFORE WE GET TOO DRUNK UP IN HERE--
--LET'S MAKE SURE WE KNOW WHERE WE STAND...!
WHO THE HELL KNOWS IF WE'LL EVER GET ANOTHER CHANCE?!
EVERYBODY! LISTEN UP!
WHAT THE HELL ARE YOU DOING, E...?!
HOLD OFF ON YOUR FOREPLAY BOOGIE FOR A SEC AND CHECK THIS OUT! YOU KNOW YOU'RE IN THE PRESENCE OF GREATNESS, DON'T YOU?!
APES + BABES
THE AGENTS OF CHANGE HAVE BEEN TAKEN OFF THE BLOCKS AND PUT BACK ON THE RACETRACK!
FULL SPEED AHEAD!
THING IS...WE HAVE NO IDEA WHY! BUT I'LL BETCHA IT'S GONNA BE BIG-- WHATEVER IT IS!
MAYBE WE'LL SEE YA ON THE OTHER SIDE! BUT IN CASE WE DON'T, REMEMBER THIS--

--WE'LL BE RIGHT THERE ON THE FRONT-LINES, FIGHTIN' FOR YA!
AWWWW YEAH!
GET YOUR FREAK ON, YOU FREAK!
'BOUT TIME SOMEONE TOOK IT TO THE MOUNTAIN!

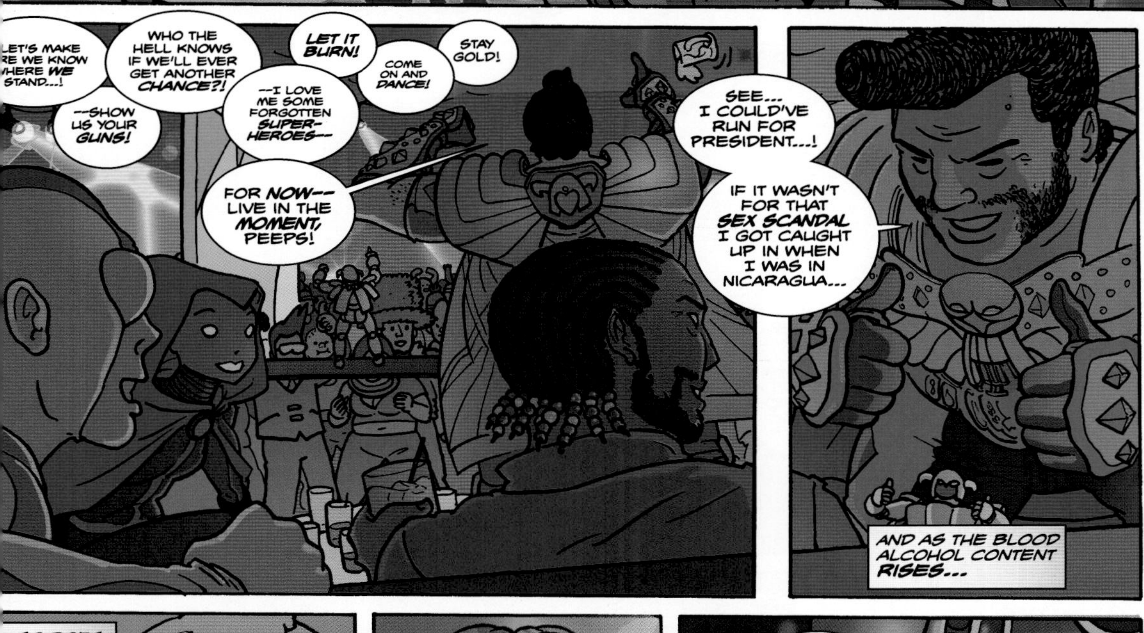
LET'S MAKE RE WE KNOW HERE WE STAND...!
--SHOW US YOUR GUNS!
WHO THE HELL KNOWS IF WE'LL EVER GET ANOTHER CHANCE?!
--I LOVE ME SOME FORGOTTEN SUPER-HEROES--
LET IT BURN!
COME ON AND DANCE!
STAY GOLD!
FOR NOW-- LIVE IN THE MOMENT, PEEPS!
SEE... I COULD'VE RUN FOR PRESIDENT...!
IF IT WASN'T FOR THAT SEX SCANDAL I GOT CAUGHT UP IN WHEN I WAS IN NICARAGUA...
AND AS THE BLOOD ALCOHOL CONTENT RISES...

...SO DOES BERT'S AMBITION.
WE'RE ALMOST THERE, VERYONE.
PRETTY EXCITING, HUH?

FROM A SINGLE MAN'S DREAM OF IMMORTALITY...
...TO THE COLLECTIVE CONSCIOUSNESS THAT SEEKS TO ACHIEVE AN EVEN HIGHER LEVEL OF BEING.

I'VE DONE WHAT YOU ASKED. FROM JAPAN...TO FRANCE... TURKEY AND MADRID...I'VE GATHERED THE NECESSARY INTEL.
NOW WE'RE STANDING ON THE EDGE OF THE CLIFF...

...AND I THINK THE WORLD IS READY TO JUMP.
IF THAT NEAR MISS LAST YEAR PROVED ANYTHING, IT'S THAT WE REALLY ARE TRYING TO BEAT THE CLOCK.
WE'VE OVERSTAYED OUR WELCOME... AND SINCE SPACE FLIGHT DIDN'T QUITE PAN OUT FOR MANKIND, WE'VE EMBRACED ANOTHER SURVIVAL OPTION.
AND THIS WORLD NEVER HAS TO END.
MEANWHILE, I'M PREPPING OUR AGENTS IN EVERY WAY I KNOW HOW. WHEN THE TIME COMES FOR OUR MASS EXODUS...
"...THEY'LL BE MORE THAN READY."

POST TIME!
ONE SHOT-- KNOCK IT BACK!
BUT I HATE THE TASTE...!

NG! OH YEAH...!
THAT'S WHY YOU DRINK IT FAST, RUBY...
YOU DON'T WANNA HAVE TO THINK ABOUT IT TOO MUCH...RIGHT, MATTY?
...

WELL, I CAN'T THINK OF A BETTER WAY TO WASTE TIME WHEN IT COMES TO--
HOLD UP. WHERE THE HELL'S EVERYBODY RUNNING OFF TO...?

IT COULDN'T HAVE BEEN MY SPEECH--
ATTENTION, "HEROES"--

--YOU ARE PARTICIPATING IN AN UNAUTHORIZED METAGATHERING! YOU ARE TO DISPERSE IMMEDIATELY!
DO NOT TEST OUR RESOLVE! AS OFFICERS OF THE COUNTERSTRIKE SECURITY FIRM, WE ARE FULLY PREPARED TO FORCE THE ISSUE!

N YOUR NEXT VACATION, TRAVEL SCENIC MARRAKESH! FROM E MOUASSINE MOSQUE TO THE VEN SAINTS' TOMBS--IT'S L HAPPENING RIGHT HERE, GHT NOW!
EVER READ GIBSON'S "NEW ROSE HOTEL"? THEN MAYBE YOU ALREADY KNOW WHAT'S UP!
REGARDLESS, A PLACE LIKE THIS IS PERFECT FOR ENLIGHTENED SOULS TO RENDEVOUS AND COMPARE NOTES ON THE PROGRESS OF HUMANITY...
...OR SOMETHING QUITE LIKE IT.
HARVEY! YOU OLD SALT! THANKS FOR MEETING ME...
THIS IS BECOMING A RARE OCCURRENCE, BABA. HOW COULD I REFUSE YOUR INVITE?
WHAT IS RARE IS OUR BREED, SIR. AND THE SPACE BETWEEN US CAN BE LIMITLESS...
TEN-FOUR ON THAT, GOOD BUDDY. THE HEALTH OF THE HERE AND THE HEREAFTER ARE OUR JURISDICTION. NOTHING TO SNEEZE AT.
SO... PULLING ANY GOOD STRINGS LATELY...?
A FEW, HERE AND THERE.
ONE IN PARTICULAR HAS BEEN QUITE THE CHALLENGE. HE DIDN'T START OUT WITH MUCH, BUT I'VE BEEN LEADING HIM SLOWLY THROUGH THE GARDEN.
HIS NAME IS FRANK WELLS...
...AND HE'S HAVING A HELL OF A TIME FINDING HIMSELF."

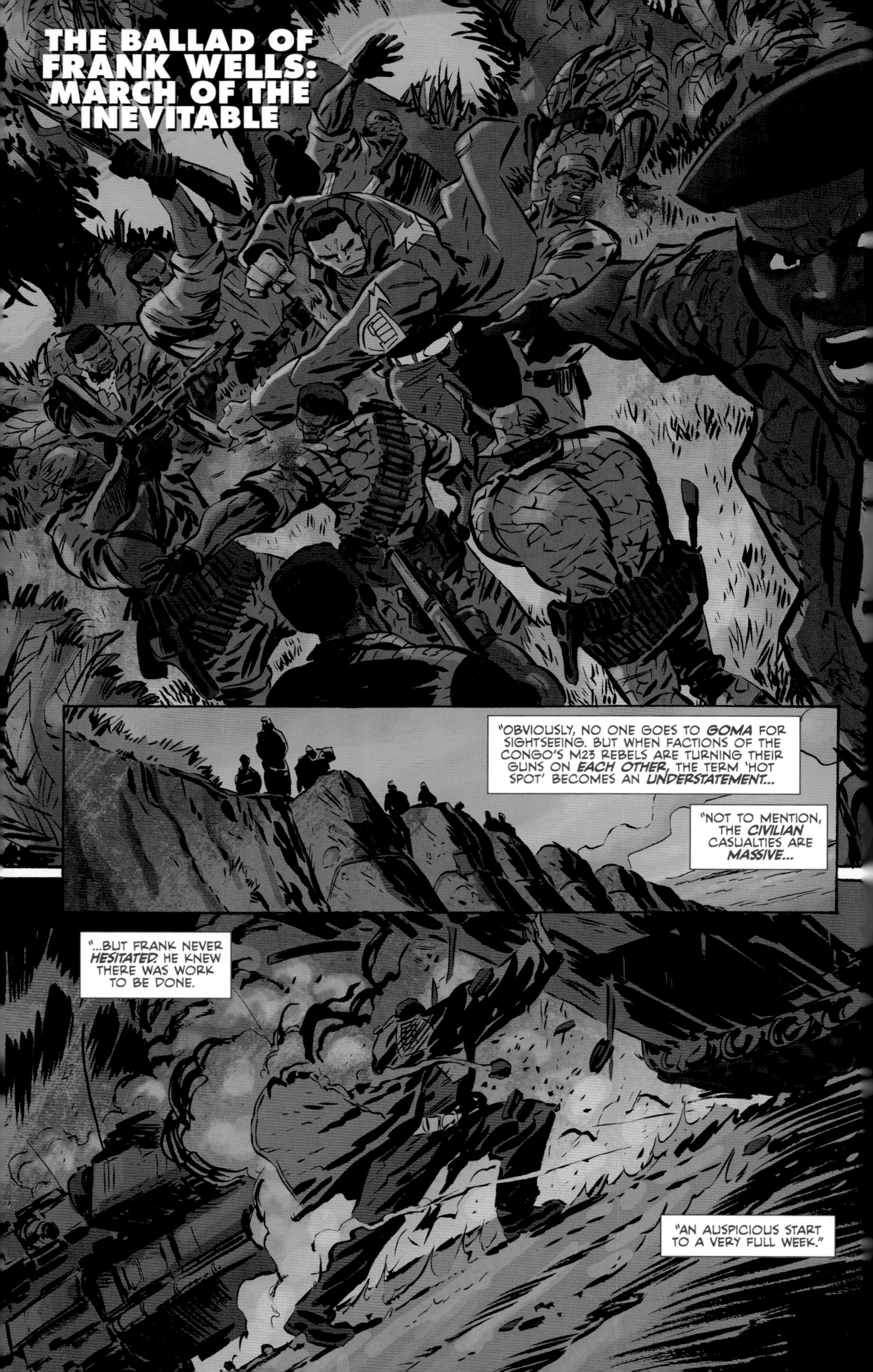
THE BALLAD OF FRANK WELLS: MARCH OF THE INEVITABLE
"OBVIOUSLY, NO ONE GOES TO GOMA FOR SIGHTSEEING. BUT WHEN FACTIONS OF THE CONGO'S M23 REBELS ARE TURNING THEIR GUNS ON EACH OTHER, THE TERM 'HOT SPOT' BECOMES AN UNDERSTATEMENT...
"NOT TO MENTION, THE CIVILIAN CASUALTIES ARE MASSIVE...
"...BUT FRANK NEVER HESITATED. HE KNEW THERE WAS WORK TO BE DONE.
"AN AUSPICIOUS START TO A VERY FULL WEEK."

THE CONGO? ONE OF *MANY* PLACES WHERE SUPERHEROES FEAR TO TREAD...

WELL, THAT'S THE *POINT,* ISN'T IT? HE WANTED TO MAKE A REAL *DIFFERENCE* IN THE WORLD...

"...SO WE BEGAN LOOKING FOR PLACES WHERE HE *COULD.*

"A *COLLAPSED MINESHAFT* N ROMANIA, FOR INSTANCE. WENTY-THREE COAL MINERS *TRAPPED* FOR EIGHT DAYS... RESCUE EFFORTS HAD BEEN *FUTILE...*

"...UNTIL *FRANK* SHOWED UP.

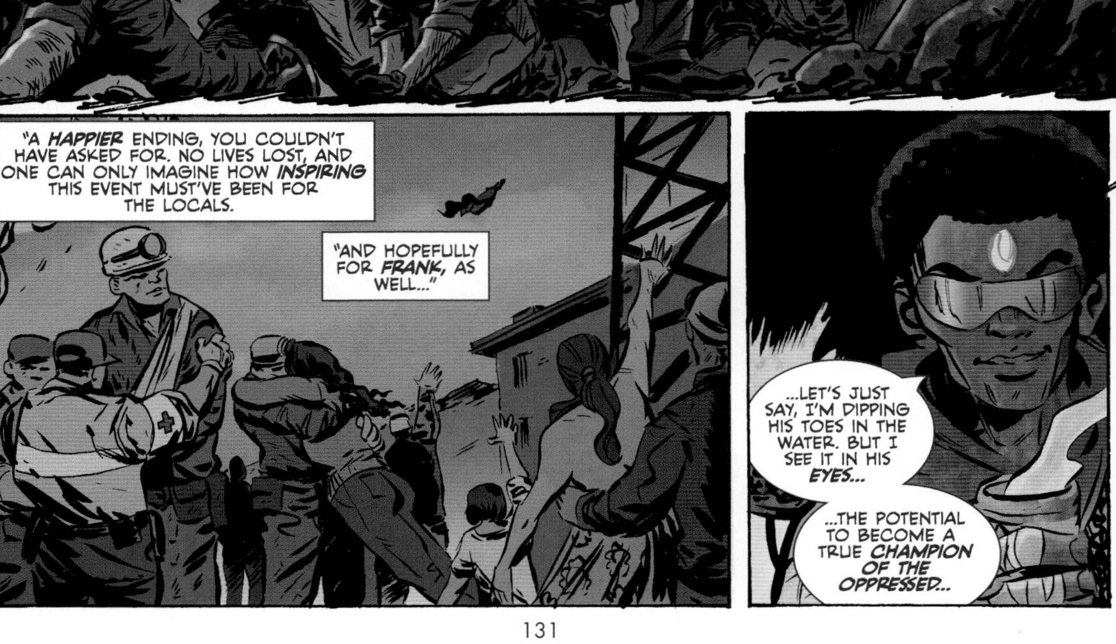

"...AND YOU KNOW THAT KIND OF AMBITION TAKES YOU TO SOME INTERESTING LOCALES. LIKE PUEBLA, MEXICO.
"LABOR DISPUTE AT A TEXTILE PLANT. TYPICAL STORY. SOMEONE FINALLY TOLD THEM THAT WORKING FOURTEEN-HOUR SHIFTS WITHOUT OVERTIME PAY WAS INHUMANE...
"...AND MANAGEMEN DIDN'T AGREE.
IGUAL
SOLIDARIDAD
PAGO JUSTA
"BUT FRANK WAS RIGHT ON IT.
"HE KNEW WHICH SIDE HE WAS FIGHTING FOR.
PAGO JUSTA
JUSTA
"NOT MUCH OF A CHALLENGE...
LE BALADA DE FRANCISCO WELLS...
"...BUT THE CELEBRATION THAT FOLLOWED WAS ONE FOR THE AGES.
"THEY CHEERED HIS NAME.. THEY WORSHIPED AT HIS FEE THE KIND OF ADULATION EVE SUPERHERO DREAMS OF...
"...BUT HE WAS STARTING TO WONDER WHAT THE LONG GAME WAS SUPPOSED TO BE."

HOWEVER, THINGS HAPPEN FAST WHEN IT COMES TO TACKLING WORLDWIDE INJUSTICES. NOT A LOT OF TIME TO SIT AND PONDER.
THE NUBA MOUNTAINS OF SUDAN DEMANDED IMMEDIATE ATTENTION...
"...IT'S THE BORDER REGION BETWEEN SUDAN AND SOUTH SUDAN, WHERE CIVILIAN POPULATIONS ARE BEING TARGETED TO GET AT THE REBEL MILITIAS.
"IT'S BASICALLY THE SUDANESE GOVERNMENT VERSUS THE DEFENSELESS NUBA FAMILIES WHO LIVE IN FEAR OF CONSTANT AERIAL ATTACK.
"THE SUDANESE AIR FORCE HAVE BEEN USING ANTONOV AN-26 AIRCRAFT AS MAKESHIFT BOMBERS, THE NEWEST VERSION OF ETHNIC CLEANSING TO CLEAR THE AREA OF A PEACEFUL, INDIGENOUS POPULATION THAT ARE NO LONGER WELCOME.
"FRANK QUICKLY PUT A STOP TO THAT.
"HE ESTABLISHED A NO-FLY ZONE, AND NO ONE--INCLUDING OMAR AL-BASHIR--WAS GOING TO ARGUE WITH HIM.
"FOR THE NUBA... WELL, THEY DON'T HAVE TO LIVE IN CAVES ANYMORE.
"FOR THE CELEBRITY ACTIVISTS WHO HAPPENED TO BE THERE... I'M SURE THEY'LL SPREAD THE WORD...
"...THERE'S A NEW WORLD SHERIFF IN TOWN."

NOW, SPEAKING OF LAW ENFORCEMENT...
...THE FABLED (AND FORMIDABLE) REDLINE SQUADRON WRAPS UP TRAINING MANEUVERS IN THE EMPTY AIRSPACE ABOVE MONTANA.
REDLINE FIVE TO REDLINE LEADER--
--RECEIVING FINAL UPLOADS ON OUR TARGET.
I SEE IT, REDLINE FIVE.
HE'S MOVING AROUND A LOT. LOOKS LIKE WE'RE IN FOR A BIT OF A CHASE...
IN CASE YOU DIDN'T KNOW, NORTH KOREA HAS AN ACTIVE NUCLEAR PROGRAM. THIS IS FRIGHTENING FOR MULTIPLE REASONS.
THE ACCEPTED TIMELINE HAS PUT THEM DEEP INTO "PHASE FOUR"...
...CLEARLY, THIS IS THREE PHASES TOO FAR.
HUH...GUESS THEY WERE FURTHER ALONG THAN EVEN C.I.A. INTEL HAD THEM...!
BUT MAYBE SOMEBODY CAN TELL ME WHY I'M--
A DIFFERENT KIND OF TREADMILL, ISN'T IT...?

CERTAINLY NOBLE, BUT I CAN ALREADY FEEL YOUR GROWING FRUSTRATION, FRANK.
NAMASTE, BY THE WAY.
THERE YOU ARE!

Y'KNOW, I CAN STILL SMELL THE NOBILITY OF MY RECENT ACTIONS, BUT--
NG!
--DAMMIT!

THESE GUYS DON'T KNOW WHEN TO QUIT--!

AM I REALLY MAKING ANY DIFFERENCE HERE? I COULD SPEND A LIFETIME DEALING WITH THESE HOT SPOTS...
IT'S A LONG ROAD TO WISDOM, FRANK WELLS. THESE ARE MERELY THE FIRST STEPS.
YOU REALLY HAVE NO IDEA HOW BIG THE WORLD IS...

"...DO YOU?"
REMEMBER ME?
LOST IN THE FLOOD...?

SHARE THE SECRETS OF...
Amazing Grace
A STORY THAT DARES TO TELL... "THE TRUTH ABOUT MR. SEAVER!"
I CAME HERE LOOKING FOR LOVE! GRACE AND I ARE DESTINED TO BE TOGETHER! OUR UNION WAS WRITTEN IN THE STARS!
BUT I CAN NEVER LET HER FIND OUT ABOUT--
--MY SECRET LIFE!

A SUPERHERO'S WORK IS NEVER DONE!
PERHAPS THE ABILITY TO MULTITASK IS GRACE'S GREATEST STRENGTH!
SHE GOES WHERE SHE IS NEEDED. WITHOUT QUESTION. WITHOUT HESITATION.
TIME AFTER TIME, SHE DEMONSTRATES HOW ESSENTIAL SHE IS TO THE QUALITY OF LIFE ON EARTH.
BUT GRACE'S MIND IS ELSEWHERE...
...ANY BREAK IN THE ACTION BRINGS HER BACK HOME.
GOLDEN CITY. THE ULTIMATE SOCIAL EXPERIMENT IN URBAN DEVELOPMENT. A CULTURAL MECCA OF TECHNOLOGY AND PHILOSOPHY...
...TRULY THE GLEAMING EPICENTER OF HUMAN CIVILIZATION.
THE TRAVEL BROCHURES AREN'T LYING--IT'S THE PLACE TO BE!

THE STERILE HUM OF PROPRIETARY GOLDEN CITY TECHNOLOGY IS A COMFORTING SOUND...

...AND, LIKE SO MANY OF US, HE HAS SOMEONE HE MUST ANSWER TO.

LOOKS LIKE HE STOPPED SOMEWHERE...
PROBABLY SOME UNCHARTED ISLAND LANDMASS. MAYBE HE WANTS A LITTLE PRIVACY...
FOR WHAT?

YOU HAVEN'T ACTUALLY... I MEAN...THE TWO OF YOU--
DON'T BE STUPID.
BESIDES, I DON'T THINK THIS BIOLOGICAL IMPERATIVE HAS MUCH TO DO WITH ME...

ON THIS LONELY, ISOLATED BEACH...HE FEELS THE TROPICAL BREEZE AGAINST HIS FACE... HE FEELS THE CALM WITHIN HIMSELF...
...THIS IS EXACTLY WHAT HE NEEDED...

...TO FIND HIS CENTER...
...AND TO REACH OUT...

MAYBE NOT. BUT THE FACT THAT YOU SEEM TO BE MOSTLY IMMUNE TO HIS...
...WELL, HIS CHARMS...
...WE THINK THAT'S INDICATIVE OF... SOMETHING.
UH-HUH... RIGHT...

HOLD ON--
--HIS SIGNAL'S FLUCTUATING...

BOOST THE INTERPRETIVE SYSTEM. MEASURE THE FLUCTUATION. FIND OUT WHAT'S HAPPENING...
AND WHAT DID SHE MEAN BY "MOSTLY IMMUNE"...?!

HIS BODY CONSTRUCT HAS BECOME UNCANNILY CALM...ALLOWING HIS MIND CONSTRUCT TO HURL ITSELF ACROSS THE GRAND COSMIC CONSCIOUSNESS--

--AND INTO THE BELLY OF HIS UNHOLY ALIEN MASTERS!

WHOA...WHATEVER HE'S DOING, IT'S ACCESSING SOME NEW SIGNAL FREQUENCY THAT OUR INSTRUMENTS CAN'T IDENTIFY...!
INITIATE SPECTRAL ANALYSIS NOW--!
DON'T BOTHER. I DOUBT HE'S COMMUNING WITH ANY EARTHBOUND NATURE...

SUE THAT! WITHIN THE STRAL STEW LOCATED THE OTHER SIDE OF E UNIVERSE--
THAT WHICH APPEARS AS MR. SEAVER" ON ARTH REVEALS BOTH ITS WN TRUE NATURE...
...AND THAT OF ITS MASTERS, AS WELL!

AND THEY ARE NOT HAPPY!

THAT WHICH DEFINES HIM IS DISSECTED AND DISSEMINATED FOR THE PURPOSES OF TOTAL COMMUNICATION!

AND THIS DOES NOT GO UNNOTICED--

HOLY JEEZ! SENSORS JUST PICKED UP A WICKED ENERGY SPIKE-- LIKE SOMETHING JUST STABBED HIM IN THE BRAIN!

THAT'S IT--

--THIS COULD BE OUR ONLY CHANCE TO PEEL THIS ONION!

I'M BETTING HE'S OTHERWISE ENGAGED AT THE MOMENT...HIS DEFENSES MIGHT BE DOWN...

...AT LEAST ENOUGH FOR ME TO SEE WHAT'S WHAT.
WHAT IS SHE DOING...?
DON'T ASK. SHE'S OPERATING ON A LEVEL WE'LL NEVER UNDERSTAND...!
LET'S SEE IF I CAN DO A BIT OF LONG-DISTANCE EAVESDROPPING HERE...
AMAZING GRACE FINDS HER CENTER!

WHILE MR. SEAVER IS LOST WITHIN A PSYCHOGALACTIC REPRIMAND FROM THAT WHICH SPAWNED HIM--
--MORE OF AN IDEA THAN AN ACTUAL ENTITY, ITS GOALS ARE STILL BORNE ON THE BLOODY VISCERA LEFT OVER FROM THE BIG BANG...!
NEVERTHELESS... THEY ARE IN CHARGE, AND HE IS THEIR BITCH!

...HER PENCHANT FOR QUADRILATERAL TELEPORTATION, USING DIAMOND TUNNEL TECHNOLOGY TO CROSS 3-D SPACE-TIME...

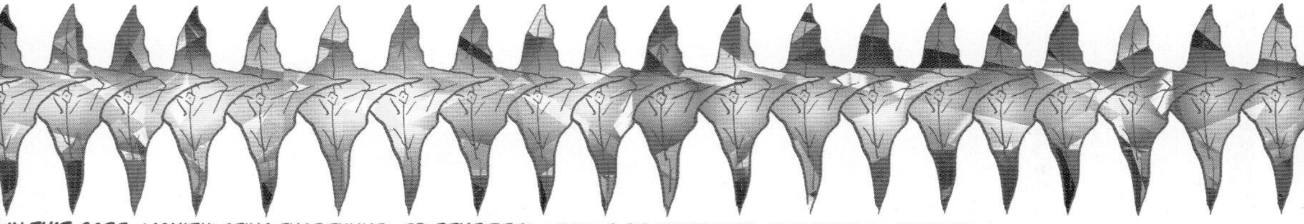

.IN THIS CASE, MANIPULATING THAT TUNNEL TO ETHEREAL LEVELS OF EXISTENCE, CREATING A MODIFIED 'SYCHIC CONNECTION THAT CAN REACH THROUGH THE SURREALOSPHERE--FROM ONE MIND TO ANOTHER!

THE CONNECTION IS TENUOUS...CUTTING IN AND OUT LIKE A SHORTWAVE TRANSMISSION...

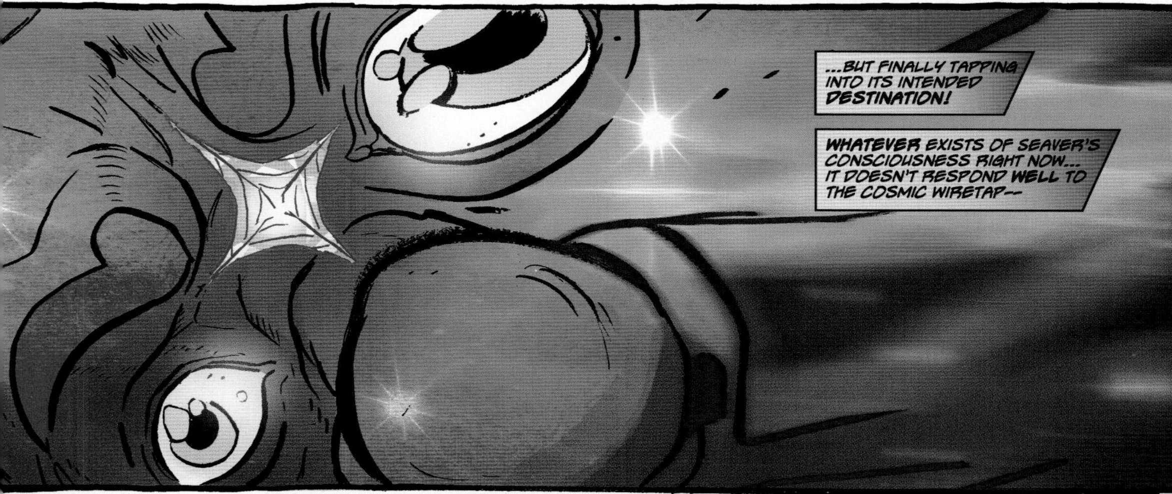

CAN YOU FEEL THAT?! HER WHOLE BODY'S BUZZING...!
JUST GET HER UP HERE!
UUUHHH...

...THERE'S... DATA...BANGING AROUND IN... MY HEAD...
...TRACK IT... RUN IT THROUGH THE OPTIMIZER...

I'M ON IT!
SORTING THROUGH THE RANDOM PATTERN FIELD...COLLATING THE SIGNAL RATIOS...
HURRY UP! THE RESIDUAL FEEDBACK IS FADING...!

...WOW... OKAY...
...THAT WAS... INTERESTING...

I'VE GOTTA GO TO HIM-- RIGHT NOW!
HOLD ON! WHAT DID YOU GET FROM THAT...?
ANYTHING USEFUL?

ONLY FAINT IMPRESSIONS... FEELINGS...EMOTIONS... EXPECTATIONS...
...HE'S DEFINITELY HERE FOR A REASON... BUT IT'S NOT GOING ACCORDING TO PLAN...
BUT THERE'S A LOT AT STAKE... THERE'S A LOT ON THE LINE FOR HIM PERSONALLY...

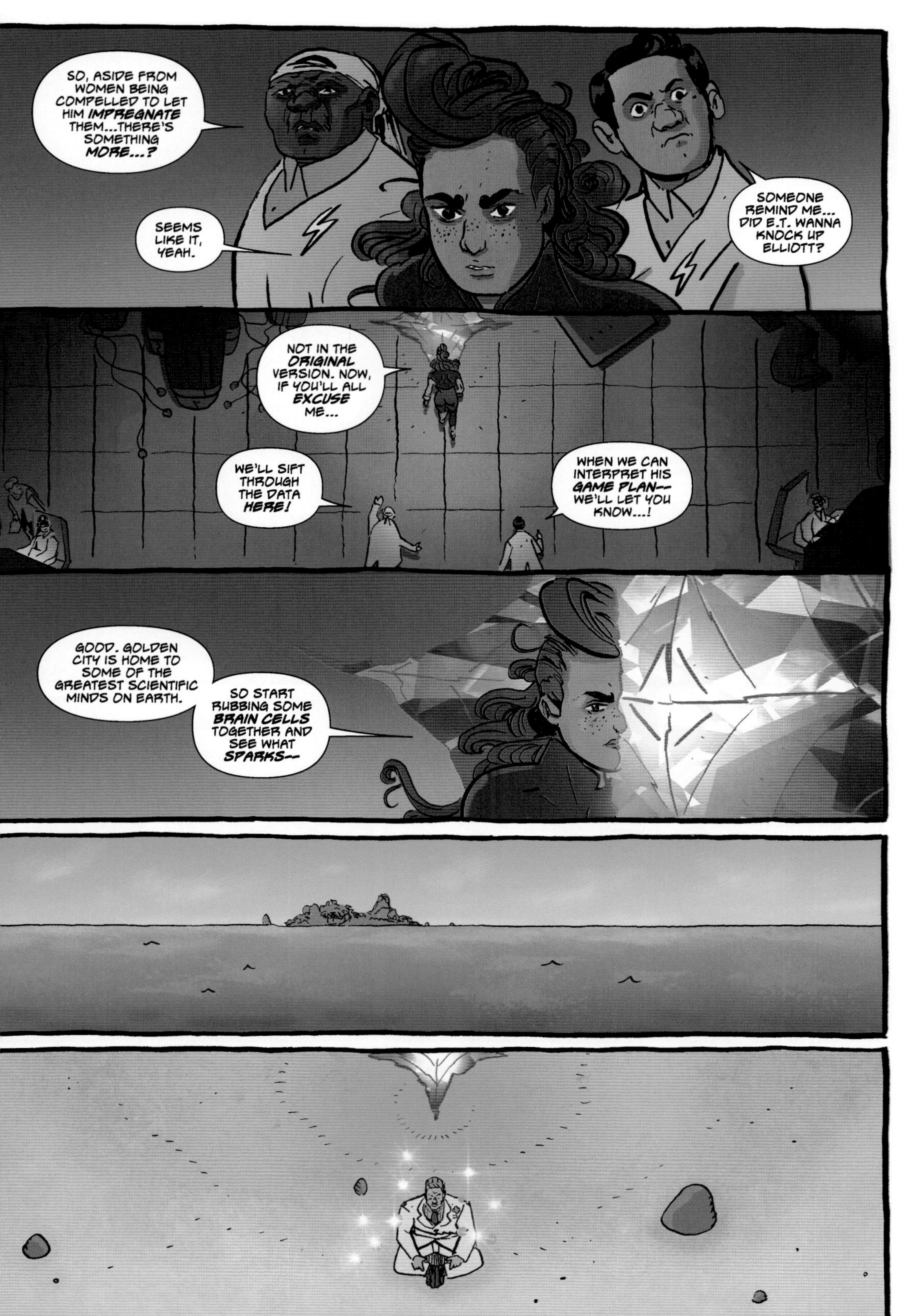
SO, ASIDE FROM WOMEN BEING COMPELLED TO LET HIM IMPREGNATE THEM...THERE'S SOMETHING MORE...?
SEEMS LIKE IT, YEAH.
SOMEONE REMIND ME... DID E.T. WANNA KNOCK UP ELLIOTT?
NOT IN THE ORIGINAL VERSION. NOW, IF YOU'LL ALL EXCUSE ME...
WE'LL SIFT THROUGH THE DATA HERE!
WHEN WE CAN INTERPRET HIS GAME PLAN-- WE'LL LET YOU KNOW...!
GOOD. GOLDEN CITY IS HOME TO SOME OF THE GREATEST SCIENTIFIC MINDS ON EARTH.
SO START RUBBING SOME BRAIN CELLS TOGETHER AND SEE WHAT SPARKS--

AHA...
...AND SHE ARRIVES, AS IF ON CUE.
LIKE A VISION... THE ANTIDOTE TO THE ETERNAL LONGING WITHIN EVERY CONFLICTED HEART...
...WITH EACH AND EVERY GESTURE, SHE--
THAT'S ENOUGH, SEAVER.
YOU'RE EMBARRASSING YOURSELF.
AM I...?
OR AM I FINALLY EXPRESSING MYSELF IN A MANNER THAT YOU CANNOT COMPREHEND...?
NOW...
...CAN YOU GUESS WHAT I'M THINKING...?
BACK IN THE LAB, THE SPARKS ARE DEFINITELY FLYING...
...RIGHT, SO HERE'S WHAT WE'VE PUT TOGETHER, BASED ON THE INFORMATION THAT GRACE WAS ABLE TO DOWNLOAD PLUS COUNCILWOMAN HUDSON'S POSTTRAUMA ANALYSIS.
THIS HOLOGRAPHIC MODEL REPRESENTS A POSSIBLE D.N.A. MOLECULE...
...A RECONSTRUCTION OF MR. SEAVER'S D.N.A.

FIRST, THE OBVIOUS...THIS IS AN ALIEN LIFE FORM PRETENDING TO BE A HUMAN MALE.
BUT NOT JUST ANY OL' HUMAN MALE, CORRECT?

DON'T YOU GET IT? YOU'VE COME TO ME NOW...
...AND I SEE GREAT SIGNIFICANCE THERE.
I'M SURE YOU DO. YOU'VE CLEARLY REPLICATED HUMAN EGO TO A NEAR-PERFECT DEGREE.

GRACE... IT'S NOT EGO THAT DRIVES ME.
IT'S DESTINY.
THAT'S WHAT HAS BROUGHT US TOGETHER.

CLEARLY, WE'VE ESTABLISHED THAT HIS PHEROMONES DELIVER A POWERFUL PUNCH--
THAT'S...AN UNDERSTATEMENT...!

I'VE NEVER EEN SO... EAK IN THE KNEES.
COUNCILWOMAN HUDSON... GLAD YOU COULD JOIN US.
YOUR FIRSTHAND INSIGHTS ARE INVALUABLE. YOU WERE READY, WILLING, AND ABLE...

BUT A COSMIC LOTHARIO COMING HERE TO ENJOY SOME SORT OF SHORE LEAVE MAKES NO SENSE.
THE CHEMICAL DATA MIGHT GIVE US THE "HOW"... BUT NOT THE "WHY"...!

THINK OF THE UNIVERSE, GRACE... IN ALL ITS VASTNESS...
...ONE CAN FEEL SO OVERWHELMED IN THE FACE OF IT.

HELPLESS... DEFENSELESS...
SORRY, SEAVER.
THOSE ARE FEELINGS I'M NOT OVERLY FAMILIAR WITH.

WHAT KIND OF STRATEGY INVOLVES FEMALE SEDUCTION...?
AND COULD ANY WOMAN RESIST HIS INFLUENCE...?
I...I DOUBT IT.
IT WAS... PURE LUST, GENTLEMEN.

ANY THOUGHTS OF LOYALTY TO THE HUMAN RACE...SIMPLY WEREN'T A CONCERN...
I JUST WANTED HIM...
...INSIDE OF ME...

YOU DON'T GIVE UP, DO YOU?
NO, I DON'T.
EVEN IF I HAD A CHOICE IN THE MATTER...

WHAT IF... GRACE WERE SIMPLY THE FIRST TARGET...?
WHAT IF HE MEANT TO IMPREGNATE THE ENTIRE FEMALE POPULATION OF THE PLANET WITH ALIEN OFFSPRING...?

HELL OF A WAY TO MOUNT AN INVASION, ISN'T IT...?
I GUESS THEY WANTED TO START AT THE TOP...
...WITH THE PREEMINENT FEMALE ON EARTH...!

IT'S ALWAYS BEEN ABOUT YOU, GRACE...
...YOU AND ME TOGETHER...

...AND OUR PROGENY SHALL BE THE BEGINNING...

...YOU WILL BE UNABLE TO RESIST ME--

GHUUHD--!

WANNA BET?
YOUR GAME IS WEAK, SEAVER.

THIS IS... NO GAME.
THIS IS NATURE IN ITS PUREST FORM. THE COSMIC FOOD CHAIN IN ALL ITS TRUTH.

I HAVE COME HERE TO PLANT THE FIRST SEED...ONE THAT WILL GROW INTO A NEW TOMORROW.
IT'S AN INEVITABILITY.
BUT IF YOU WILL NOT SUBMIT TO ME THROUGH CIVILIZED MEANS...

...THEN I HAVE NO CHOICE BUT TO FORCE THE ISSUE.

FINE.
LET'S DANCE.

OL' HERBERT'S BEEN AROUND. HE'S SEEN IT ALL. AND YET, THIS IS A CONCEPT THAT HUMBLES HIM.
A WICKED NOTION OF PURE SALVATION...
YOU HAVE NO IDEA HOW CURIOUS I AM TO KNOW WHAT IT'S LIKE FOR ALL OF YOU...
...PIONEERS IN THE PROMISED LAND.
THE BRAVE NEW WORLD OPEN WIDE FOR THE REST OF US.
WE'VE TAKEN IT AS FAR AS WE CAN WITHIN THIS REALITY.
BUT WE'RE ENTERING THE FINAL PHASES NOW, AND ONCE WE WRAP A FEW MINOR DETAILS IN OUR PREPARATIONS, THERE'S NO DOUBT IN MY MIND...
...WE CAN REALLY CHANGE THINGS.
THAT'S SOME FANCY TALK FOR A GUY WHO DOESN'T EVEN WEAR A UNIFORM...
...ESPECIALLY WHEN THE REAL QUESTION EVERYONE SHOULD BE ASKING IS, WHEN IT COMES TO "US" AND "THEM"--
--WHO'S GOT THE BETTER DANCE MOVES?
ONLY WAY TO FIND OUT THE ANSWER TO THAT QUESTION...IS A GOOD, OLD-FASHIONED DANCE-OFF! THAT KIND OF CONTEST IS A REAL CROWD PLEASER TOO...
...SO, WHY THE HELL ARE THESE PEOPLE RUNNING SCARED?!
AGENTS OF CHANGE: WINDOW PAIN

THIS IS AN UNLAWFUL ASSEMBLY AND IT WILL NOT BE TOLERATED!
YOUR BLATANT DISREGARD FOR SOCIAL CONVENTIONS--THE GALL TO DRESS LIKE THAT IN PUBLIC SITUATIONS--IS CAUSE FOR IMMEDIATE ACTION!
AS DULY APPOINTED OFFICERS OF THE COUNTERSTRIKE SECURITY FIRM, WE ARE AUTHORIZED TO--
--TWO SIDES DRAWN AND LOCKED INTO THEIR OWN IDEOLOGIES!
STAND DOWN, "SUPERHEROES"!
WE ARE CAPABLE OF DOING TERRIBLE DAMAGE TO YOUR GENERAL PERSONS!
YOU SURE AS HELL TALK LIKE THE MAN!
IS THIS WHAT WE SIGNED UP FOR, Y'ALL?!
HELL, NO!

YEAH, YEAH, YEAH...SO YOU SAID! AND I KNOW EXACTLY WHAT THE WORDS "SECURITY FIRM" MEAN...!
THE MAN IS CRACKIN' DOWN!
IS THIS HOW YOU TREAT A FAMOUS PERSON?!
I MEAN, DON'T I HAVE SOME KIND OF...CELEBRITY DIPLOMATIC IMMUNITY OR SOMETHING?!
THEY ARE ELVIS WARMAKER! REBEL! WOLFHUNTER! RUBY! EACH ONE OF THEM--AN AGENT OF CHANGE!
FACING A SHOWDOWN IN FULL SWING--
WE WILL ISSUE NO MORE WARNINGS!
THIS IS YOUR LAST CHANCE!
SEE-- THIS IS THE PROBLEM WITH CORPORATE-SPONSORED HEAVIES--
--TOO MANY WARNINGS!
TOO MUCH YAMMERING!
IT DOESN'T TAKE MUCH TO BRING OUT THE "WAR" IN WARMAKER!

AGGRESSIVE POSTURING!
COUNTERSTRIKE AGENTS-- ENGAGE!
THE ORDER IS GIVEN! THE ACTION IS TAKEN--
--AND THE RESPONSE IS EXPLOSIVE!
THEY BLINKED!
I JUST NEEDED A REASON, YO--!
RIGHT ON! LET'S...
...THINK... I'VE REACHED... MY LIMIT...
...OOOOHHHHH DAAMNNN...!
THE PAIN IS SUDDEN AND INTENSE...THE SIGNAL THAT REBEL NEEDS TO MAKE THE SWITCH...!
I DON'T GET IT-- BERT NEVER SAID ANYTHING ABOUT THIS--!
IS THIS ANOTHER TEST?!
GYEEAAHH--!
MAYBE NOT SO MUCH ANOTHER TEST...
...AS SIMPLY ANOTHER STEP.
YOU'RE ONE OF THE SPECIAL ONES, AREN'T YOU?
YOU CAN DO CERTAIN THINGS...

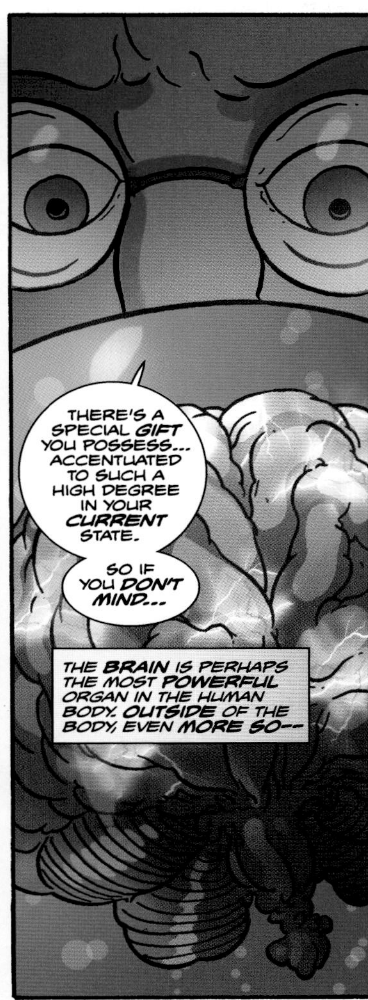

--CASE IN POINT:

HEADS UP! THESE GUYS ARE ***GENETICALLY ENGINEERED!*** THEY ACTUALLY ***GAIN*** FROM ***PAIN!***

AT LEAST IT'S NOT OL' ***EMMIT*** BACK IN THESE--

--CLOWN SUITS...?

H-HEY--!

WHAT JUST ***HAPPENED?!***

WHERE THE HELL ***AM*** I--?!

ONLY $99

IT'S A **FINE LINE** BETWEEN **REALITY** AND **FANTASY...**

...WHO'S REALLY QUALIFIED TO SAY WHICH IS WHICH?
MAN DOWN!
ALTHOUGH I HAVE NO IDEA HOW!

NO WORRIES, E!
YOU GOT ME BACK ON THE FRONT-LINES!

IT'S ABOUT TIME, REBEL!
LUCKILY, THERE'S A WAY TO DEAL WITH THESE CHEESE HEADS!
HUUHHNN--!

AND SO THE DANCE CONTINUES... IN ALL ITS VIOLENT GLORY...
...WITH WOLFHUNTER TAKEN OFF THE FIELD--

--IN MORE WAYS THAN ONE!
DO YOU KNOW WHERE YOU ARE, PUNK?!
OH, COME ON...!

YOU IN THE *JUNGLE*, BAY-BEE!
THE ALLEYWAYS OF THE *MIND*, YO--!
AIN'T NO *BEAT DOWN* LIKE THE ONE YOU GIVES *Y'SELF!*
DON'T HATE ON THE *GAME*, PLAYA!
MAYBE NOT A *VIRTUAL* REALITY, BUT A WHOLLY CREATED *MINDSCAPE* CAN STILL BE PRETTY DAMNED *CONVINCING...*

...EVEN FOR ITS *CREATOR.*

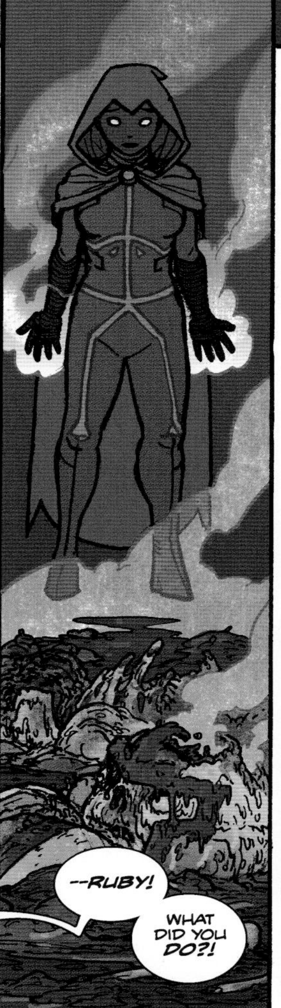

HE QUEEN ELIZABETH HOTEL! LOCATED IN MONTREAL, CANADA! SUDDENLY THE EPICENTER OF MODERN HERO CULTURE!
NOT SINCE THE OCTOBER CRISIS HAS THE GRAND OLD BUILDING SEEN THIS KIND OF EXCITEMENT--
ZABETH
--AND, TYPICAL OF THAT SELFSAME CULTURE, THE INTERNATIONAL MEDIA IS OUT IN FULL FORCE!
OKAY, INFORMAL POLL--WHO HERE THINKS THIS IS ALL JUST A STUNT...?
WELL, IF IT IS, IT'S CERTAINLY WORKED. WE'RE ALL HERE...
...AND IF HE'S UP THERE AND HE'S WILLING TO TALK, THEN WHY NOT?
DAMN STRAIGHT HE'LL TALK...!
SO HE'S GOT SOME MESSAGE HE'S TRYING TO GET ACROSS...?
WHO KNOWS? SINCE WHEN DID ANY SUPERHERO HAVE ANYTHING TO SAY...ABOUT ANYTHING?!
OKAY! RIGHT THIS WAY, FOLKS--
--REMEMBER THE WAIVERS YOU'VE ALL SIGNED. MR. WELLS CANNOT BE HELD LEGALLY RESPONSIBLE FOR YOUR PERSONAL SAFETY IN THIS ENVIRONMENT.
WE'RE ROTATING PRESS IN AND OUT EVERY FIFTEEN MINUTES, SO HAVE YOUR QUESTIONS READY...

...NO ONE WANTS THIS TURNING INTO SOME SORT OF *CIRCUS.*

SAVING THE WORLD... ONE HOTSPOT AT A TIME

TITAN

FAMOUS LAST WORDS, BRYN.

BUT SO FAR, SO GOOD.

POWER

WILL TO POWER

THE BALLAD OF FRANK WELLS: WHO BEDS WINS

MR. WELLS... WHAT KIND OF STATEMENT ARE YOU TRYING TO MAKE HERE?
--DOES ANYONE CALL YOU "TITAN" ANYMORE--?
ONE AT A TIME, PLEASE...
I'M FROM FOX NEWS-- ARE YOU GETTING PAID FOR YOUR APPEARANCE HERE?

...I THINK, IF THERE'S ANY KIND OF "STATEMENT" TO BE MADE, IT'S FOR EVERYONE ON THE PLANET TO TAKE A GOOD, HARD LOOK AT THINGS.
EVERY DAY I ASK MYSELF, "AM I REALLY NEEDED?" BUT IF YOU'D SEEN WHAT I'VE SEEN THESE PAST FEW WEEKS...

THEN WHY THE MEDIA SPECTACLE?
I GUESS I'VE FINALLY FIGURED OUT WHAT KIND OF WORLD WE LIVE IN THESE DAYS...

...AND I WANT TO MAKE SURE THE MESSAGE GETS THROUGH UNFILTERED.
LIVE
GENTLEMEN, I NEED SOMEONE TO TELL ME--

ARE YOU SERIOUS?
DESPITE APPEARANCES, THE REDLINE PILOTS WERE DESIGNED FOR MORE...COVERT OPERATIONS, SIR. ANTITERRORIST OPS AND THE LIKE...
BUT THIS IS A GOOD SIGN, MR. PRESIDENT. FOR NOW, LET'S JUST SEE WHAT TRANSPIRES...

I KNOW I'VE PROBABLY BEEN SEEN--BY THE REST OF THE WORLD--AS SOME SORT OF FASCIST SYMBOL OF AMERICAN POWER.
I'M HERE TO TELL YOU... IT'S NOT TRUE.

SO, YOU SERVE THE WORLD...HOW DOES THAT ATTITUDE MANIFEST ITSELF?
AND DOES THAT VIEWPOINT PUT YOU AT ODDS WITH YOUR HOME COUNTRY...?

ACTUALLY, I DON'T SEE MYSELF AS HAVING A "HOME COUNTRY" ANYMORE. TO ME, IT'S JUST ONE BIG PLANET.
HOW MY FRIENDS IN AMERICA FEEL ABOUT ME... I REALLY CAN'T SAY.
THEIR APPROVAL ISN'T REALLY A PRIORITY...
PEACE

I'VE GOT IT ON DEEP BACKGROUND THAT THE AMERICAN MILITARY IS, IN FACT, QUITE CONCERNED ABOUT YOUR RECENT ACTIONS...
...IN MEXICO... IN SOUTH SUDAN... RUMORS OF NORTH KOREAN ACTIVITY...

OKAY, I CAN CONFIRM THOSE RUMORS...BUT IT'S NOT LIKE I WAS SEEKING PUBLICITY OR EVEN CREDIT...
MY GOALS ARE SIMPLY TO HELP...TO GO WHERE I'M NEEDED...
KANT
POWER

YOU WANNA HELP?!
THAT'S WHAT YOU WANNA DO?!
HUH?
WHO SAID THAT...?

Y'KNOW, WHEN I HEARD ABOUT YOUR LITTLE BED-IN HERE, I HAD TO SEE FOR MYSELF!
AND NOW THAT I'M HERE--NOW THAT I'VE HAD TO LISTEN TO YOU RAMBLE ON WITH YOUR STUPID SPEECHES--
--IT'S TIME SOMEONE REMINDED YOU WHAT YOU REALLY ARE!
SO STAND AND DELIVER, SUPERHERO!
SIGH
IT NEVER ENDS...!
EXCUSE ME! WHAT DID I TELL YOU OUT IN THE HALLWAY?!
WE PUT SAFETY AT A PREMIUM IN HERE!
OWER
IS THAT SO...?
THE NEXT MOMENT-- EVERYTHING CHANGES!
TWO PARTS HYDROGEN! ONE PART OXYGEN!
MULTIPLIED BY BILLIONS AND BILLIONS IN THE BLINK OF AN EYE! REACTIVITY ON A GRAND SCALE! A HYDROEXPLOSIVE OCCURRENCE THAT DEFIES NATURE--

--BUT EPITOMIZES SUPERVILLAIN RAGE IN ALL ITS RIGHTEOUS FURY!
AND THAT'S WHY THEY CALL ME "FLOOD," BEE-YOTCHES!
PEACE
LUCKILY, FRANK WELLS IS ON THE CASE!
HOPE I DIDN'T MISS ANYONE IN THE CONFUSION--THINK I GOT THEM ALL!
AND THE HEROIC RESULTS SPEAK FOR THEMSELVES--
YOU...YOU SAVED US...!
COUGH!
SPUTTER!
UHHH... REMEMBER... THAT LAST NAME IS SPELLED W-E-L-L-S...!
I'LL WASH AWAY EVERYONE'S SINS BEFORE I'M DONE--
THAT'S ENOUGH--
--ENDANGERING THE LIVES OF INNOCENT PRESS!
THAT'S A STEP TOO FAR, FLOOD!
POWER

TIME TO JUMP BACK INTO YOUR LIFE, FRANK--
?!
--THIS IS WHERE YOU BELONG!
...EVERYONE WANTS WHAT THEY CAN'T HAVE.
GAH--!
YOU ALL SEEM TO WANT THE SAME THING--
IT'S SIMPLY HUMAN NATURE, FRANK...
I KNOW YOU WANT TO RISE ABOVE SUCH ANTIQUATED HOO-HAH. IT'S THE EXISTENTIAL THAT INTERESTS YOU NOW.
BUT I CAN'T FIGHT YOUR BATTLES FOR YOU. NO ONE CAN.
SO GET ON WITH IT, SON!

HEADACHES...THE HAPPENSTANCE...THE HELLACIOUSNESS OF...
Amazing Grace
GRACE-- ALL I WANT IS FOR YOU TO UNDERSTAND WHERE I'M COMING FROM!
I'M SORRY, MR. SEAVER... I'LL NEVER UNDERSTAND!
BUT THIS IS SO WRONG!
TWO SOULS DANCING ON THE BRINK OF THE APOCALYPSE-- BUT EVEN MORE HEARTBREAKING-- THEY'RE ON A DESPERATE DESCENT INTO NOTHING LESS THAN
LOVE ENTROPY!

AH, THE BIRDS AND THE BEES...!
GIVE IT UP FOR COLE PORTER. CALLED ON HIS IGNORANCE (I.E., RACISM), HE REWROTE LYRICS THAT COINED A PHRASE THAT FOREVER ALLOWED FOR SOCIAL DELICACY WHEN IT COMES TO DISCUSSING THE TENETS OF MALE-FEMALE INTERACTION.
SO LET'S DO IT--
--LET'S FALL IN LOVE!
AND THIS...
...IS NO EDUCATED FLEA.
SIGH
SOMETIMES PASSION CANNOT BE CONTAINED.
A SYMBOLIC VICTORY CARRIES MUCH WEIGHT. IT SENDS THE RIGHT SIGNALS TO THE REST OF THE UNIVERSE.
BUT I NEVER THOUGHT RESORTING TO VIOLENCE WOULD BRING THIS TO SUCH A SWIFT END.
THEN AGAIN, I'VE ALWAYS BEEN--
EH--?

THUNDER CRACK TO THE JAW!
FOR HUMANITY!
GRACE IS THE WORD--

--IT'S GOT GROOVE! IT'S GOT MEANING!

THE BELL HAS BEEN RUNG!
THIS IS ONLY ROUND ONE--

--AND SHE'S READY TO RUMBLE!

AND BACK IN GOLDEN CITY, THERE'S ALSO NO SHORTAGE OF ACTIVITY...
SHE'S ON THE MOVE--

--MAKE SURE WE DON'T LOSE HER!
LOCKING ONTO HER SIGNAL...
IF IT'S GETTING PHYSICAL, I HOPE SHE CAN KEEP IT AWAY FROM ALL CIVILIZATION--

"--SOMEWHERE THERE WON'T BE ANY COLLATERAL DAMAGE!"
SUCH... FEISTINESS...
B-BUT THE FIRST RULE OF GALACTIC COMBAT...
...IS TO NEVER LET YOUR OPPONENT BREATHE--
AMAZING GRACE IS WELL AWARE OF THE RULES OF GALACTIC COMBAT!
WHOA--!
SEISMIC MONITORS JUST JUMPED--!
ARCTIC CIRCLE-- IT'S ON!
LET'S NOT PROLONG THIS, SEAVER.
YOUR ALIEN ORIGINS HAVE BEEN UNCOVERED... YOUR INTENT OF CONQUEST TOO.
YOU WANTED TO GET PHYSICAL--
INDEED I DID--

--AND SO IT SHALL!
I TOLD THEM I KNEW WHAT I WAS DOING!
BUT THE SEPTENARIUS WILL NOT BE DENIED!
"SEPTENARIUS"...?!
GOT IT.

THERE THEY GO--
--SHE'S KNOCKING HIM ALL OVER CREATION!
TRACKING TO NEXT LOCATION...

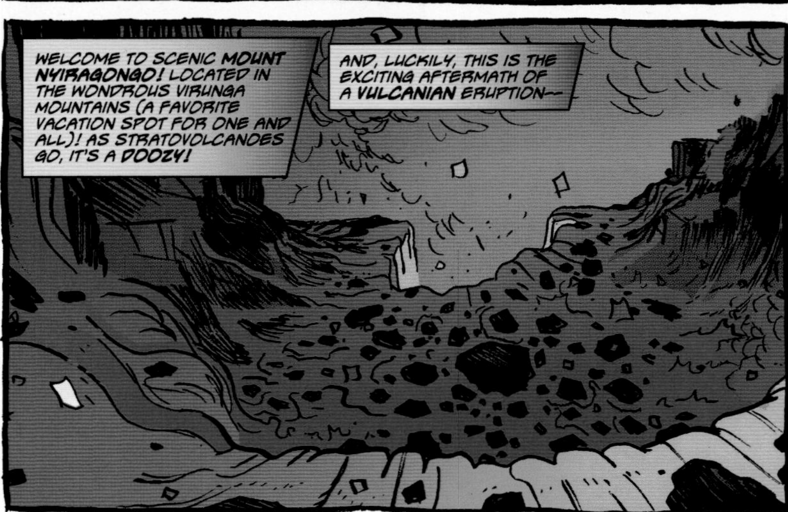
WELCOME TO SCENIC MOUNT NYIRAGONGO! LOCATED IN THE WONDROUS VIRUNGA MOUNTAINS (A FAVORITE VACATION SPOT FOR ONE AND ALL)! AS STRATOVOLCANOES GO, IT'S A DOOZY!
AND, LUCKILY, THIS IS THE EXCITING AFTERMATH OF A VULCANIAN ERUPTION--

--A PERFECT SETTING FOR LIVING, BREATHING ROMANCE!

HAD ENOUGH?
I CAN DO THIS ALL DAY...

...BUT I'M PRETTY SURE THERE'S A TICKING CLOCK INVOLVED.
ISN'T THERE...?
YOU... HAVE NO IDEA...

...I GAVE YOU THE GREATEST OPPORTUNITY IN THE KNOWN UNIVERSE!
YOU DON'T KNOW WHAT HORRORS YOU HAVE INVITED BY SPURNING MY AFFECTIONS!

ONE WOMAN'S AFFECTIONS ARE ANOTHER WOMAN'S AFFLICTIONS...
...AND AS FAR AS ALIEN INVASIONS GO, THIS WORLD IS OFF LIMITS.

THERE IS NO SUCH THING!
YOU WILL BE MINE!
SEAVER RALLIES HIS FINELY TUNED MOJO--

--AND FROM ACTION COMES RESULT!
Y-YOU... CAN'T MAKE ME WANT YOU...
I'M... STRONGER THAN...

...THAT...

UH-OH... WE'RE MONITORING GRACE'S PHYSIOLOGY--
--SOMETHING STRANGE IS HAPPENING!
PICKING UP FLUCTUATIONS IN HER HYPOTHALAMIC-PITUITARY SYSTEM! DEFINITE HORMONE ACTIVITY!

Y-YOU... BASTARD...
...I CAN FEEL YOU... INSIDE ME...
I'M SURE YOU CAN...

...THIS IS HOW IT WAS ALWAYS MEANT TO BE!
DOMINATION IS THE WILL OF EXISTENCE!
MANIFEST DESTINY ON THE GRANDEST SCALE IMAGINABLE!

DO YOU FEEL ME, GRACE...?
NO...?

HOW 'BOUT NOW?!
PERHAPS YOU'RE A LITTLE MORE SUSCEPTIBLE TO WHAT I'VE COME ALL THIS WAY TO DO...!

OH DAMN...
...CAN'T GET A LOCK ON HER VITALS NOW--!
WHAT THE HELL'S HE DOING TO HER?!

I WANT YOU TO KNOW SOMETHING...
...THIS WAS NOT WHAT I WANTED. IT COULD'VE BEEN SO SIMPLE.
BUT THOSE I'VE SWORN TO SERVE--

--THEY'LL BE ECSTATIC THAT IT WENT DOWN THIS WAY!

THEY VALUE BRUTALITY AS AN EFFECTIVE POLITICAL PRINCIPLE.
AND SINCE I'VE FAILED TO ADEQUATELY CHARM YOU...
SEAVER TIGHTENS HIS GRIP, BOTH LITERALLY AND FIGURATIVELY--

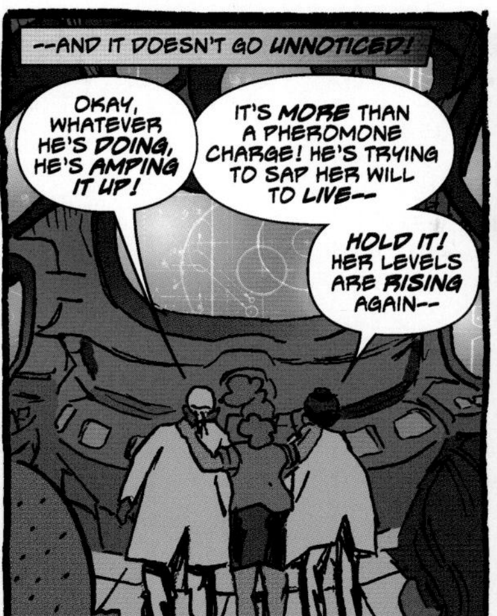
--AND IT DOESN'T GO UNNOTICED!
OKAY, WHATEVER HE'S DOING, HE'S AMPING IT UP!
IT'S MORE THAN A PHEROMONE CHARGE! HE'S TRYING TO SAP HER WILL TO LIVE--
HOLD IT! HER LEVELS ARE RISING AGAIN--

"--LOOKS LIKE GRACE'S GOTTEN HER SECOND WIND."
YOU KNOW WHAT YOUR PROBLEM IS, SEAVER--

--YOU TALK WAY TOO MUCH!

NOW...YOU WANT TO TALK ABOUT BRUTALITY?
THERE ISN'T EVEN A MOMENT'S HESITATION--

--BUT THERE IS SATISFACTION!

SO...
...GOT ANY MORE PICK-UP LINES YOU'D LIKE TO TRY ON ME?

YEAH.
I DIDN'T THINK SO...

...REALLY WEAK SAUCE, SEAVER.

GRACE! ARE YOU READING ME?
THERE'S A LITTLE INTERFERENCE... I'M INSIDE A VOLCANO, Y'KNOW...
WE KNOW...

...WE'VE BEEN TRACKING YOU AND YOUR OPPONENT THIS ENTIRE TIME!
DON'T ASSUME YOU CAN ADMINISTER A NORMAL COUP DE GRACE...
...NO PUN INTENDED...

LISTEN, I DON'T HAVE TIME FOR--
HOW RIGHT YOU ARE...

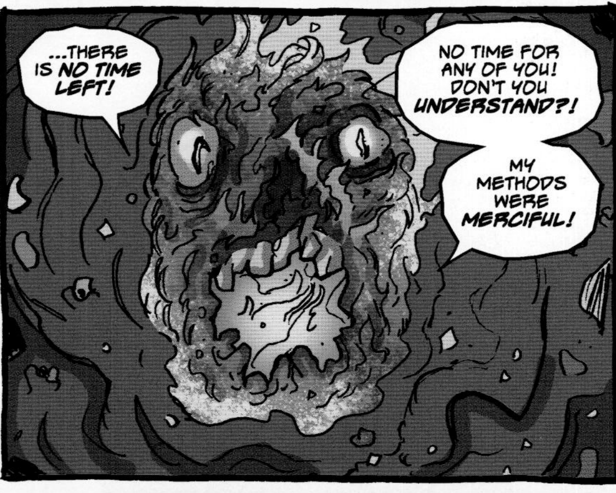
...THERE IS NO TIME LEFT!
NO TIME FOR ANY OF YOU! DON'T YOU UNDERSTAND?!
MY METHODS WERE MERCIFUL!

SURE THEY WERE.
ENJOY THE BURN, ROMEO.
WAIT!
P-PLEASE... DO NOT MAKE LIGHT OF MY DILEMMA...!

THIS PHYSICAL VESSEL MAY BE OBLITERATED... BUT MY ESSENCE LIVES ON...
>SOB!<
...IT WILL BE SENT BACK TO MY POINT OF ORIGIN...

...WHERE THE PRICE OF MY FAILURE WILL BE UNIMAGINABLE HORRORS!
YOU HEAR THAT--?
IS HE... CRYING...?!

AND THAT'S MY PROBLEM... HOW...?
YOU MADE YOUR BED, SEAVER...NOW YOU GET TO LIE IN IT.
SO TO SPEAK.
>SNFF<
YOUR NAIVETÉ IS YOUR LEAST APPEALING QUALITY...

...IT WAS NEVER GOING TO END WITH ME! I WAS MERELY THE ADVANCE MAN!
HAD I PLANTED MY RIGHTEOUS SEED IN YOU--
>HGL!<
--AN ENTIRE LEGION OF MY BRETHREN WOULD'VE FOLLOWED...TO COMMENCE WORLDWIDE COPULATION...!

AN ENTIRE GENERATION OF ALIEN NEWBORNS...
EXACTLY! WHAT BETTER WAY TO DOMINATE?!
NOW PLEASE--
--DO NOT LET ME RETURN IN SHAME!

YOU'RE REALLY LOOKING FOR COMPASSION...?
I GUESS THAT'S WHAT HAPPENS WHEN YOUR PRIMARY ABILITIES ARE BASED ON MANIPULATING EMOTIONS...

TELL ME YOU DIDN'T FEEL SOMETHING TOO!
WHO ELSE IS A BETTER MATCH FOR YOU?!

OH, I FELT SOMETHING, ALL RIGHT. BUT CLEARLY...
...I GOT OVER IT.

NOOOO--
--YOU CAN'T HIDE FROM WHAT'S COMING NEXT--
--*

GENTLEMEN...

...THAT'S ONE ALIEN INVADER DOWN.
BUT I'M THINKING... THERE'S SEVERAL BILLION TO GO.

LUCKILY, THE REST OF US CAN!

YOU THINK STEEL HARBOR WAS TOUGH, YO...!

YEAH! DIS PLACE MAKES HUNTER WOODS SEEM LIKE A WI SPA!

YOU READY TO RUMBLE, CHEETA?!

WHENEVER YOU ARE, FAKKA!

AGENTS OF CHANGE: SHOWIN' HOW FUNKY
WARMAKER PLAYHELMET FUN!
--MAYBE WE CAN FIGURE OUT WHAT THE HELL TO DO NEXT!
WELL, THAT DEPENDS, DOESN'T IT? HOW MUCH TROUBLE D'YA THINK WE'RE IN, E...?!
THEY ARE UNQUESTIONABLY HEROES OF A NEW AGE, AREN'T THEY? I MEAN LOOK AT THEM--IT'S SO OBVIOUS...
ELVIS WARMAKER! REBEL! RUBY! WOLFHUNTER! SAY IT LOUD--THEY'RE AGENTS OF CHANGE AND THEY'RE PROUD
I MEAN, WE GOT A GUY SLEEPING ON THE JOB...AND ANOTHER ONE WHO JUST CHARBROILED ONE OF OUR SPARRING PARTNERS...!
RUBY...?
I DON'T NEED THE REMINDER, MORRISETTE...
...I KNOW WHAT I DID.
AND SO DO YOU, IF YOU READ LAST ISSUE--
--A COUNTERSTRIKE SECURITY AGENT... MELTED INTO SLAG...
...COURTESY OF RUBY'S DEADLY TOUCH!
BUT HOW HAUNTED IS SHE?
SCUMBAG PROBABLY DESERVED IT...!

HEY, I'M NOT THE ONE WHO'S GONNA ARGUE *ETHICS* WITH *ANYBODY.* YOU DO WHAT YOU *GOTTA* DO WHEN YOU'RE UNDER THE GUN.

BUT THERE'S GONNA BE *REPERCUSSIONS...*

IN LIFE, THERE ARE *MICRO* CONCERNS--

--AND *MACRO* CONCERNS. TAKE A GUESS WHICH IS *WHICH...?*

I CAN'T *WAIT* TO FEEL IT... WHAT *YOU ALL* MUST BE FEELING RIGHT NOW...

...THE ETHEREAL *FOREVER.*

WHAT YOU'RE DOING FOR THE *REST* OF US... IT'S A BEAUTIFUL THING.

ALTHOUGH I'M SURE *ONE* CURRENT RESIDENT DOESN'T APPRECIATE THE VACATION SPOT CREATED JUST FOR *HIM...*

AND I DON'T KNOW *WHY* WE GOT SOMEONE NAPPING ON THE JOB.

I NEVER EVEN SAW HIM GET *HIT--!*

HOLD ON, ELVIS...LET'S GO BACK TO THE "REPERCUSSIONS" YOU MENTIONED...

...Y'KNOW, I'VE GOT MY *CAREER* TO THINK ABOUT! I MEAN--

--I'M THE KIND OF CELEBRITY THAT ALWAYS KEEPS HIS *FANS* IN *MIND...!*

AND IF *THAT* BIT OF DIALOGUE ISN'T AN OBVIOUS *TRANSITION--*

-WOLFHUNTER'S IN THE $%#!*

THIS IS *OUR* HELL! IS IS *YOUR* GHTMARE!

YOU THINK YER *BAD?!*

RIGHT.

THERE'S ONLY *ONE* *WAY* TO SETTLE THIS...!

EVEN LEAVING THE **BRAIN CHAMBER**, THE AIR FEELS **DIFFERENT...**

...ANOTHER GRIM REMINDER OF THE **ROT** THIS WORLD REPRESENTS TO ITS INHABITANTS.

TAR AND NICOTINE SERVE TO **MASK** IT...FOR NOW.

MEANWHILE, WOLFHUNTER HAS TAKEN **LEMONS...** AND MADE SWEET **LEMONADE!**

AIN'T NOTHING LIKE A GOOD DANCE-OFF!

--WHAT ABOUT HIM?
IF THEY ONLY KNEW EXACTLY WHAT MADNESS EXISTS IN THE MIND OF THE MAN--
ULY!
--AND HOW HIS HEARTBEAT PROVIDES THE BACKBEAT FOR A BOMB TRACK! CUE MASS CHOREOGRAPHY!
WOLFHUNTER STEPS FOR HIS LIFE! HIS SANITY! HIS RESPECT! THE DOPPELGÄNGERS ARE FLOORED BY HIS PURE FUNKINESS--
--AND HIS MOVES ARE PURE BANANAS!
BUT WHICH WORLD CONTAINS MORE JEOPARDY FOR THE AVERAGE MEGALOMANIAC?
WHERE TO, SIR?
YOU KNOW SOMETHING, TED...IT DOESN'T EVEN MATTER.
HOW 'BOUT A LEISURELY DRIVE THROUGH THE PARK...?
SO, DOES THIS MEAN WE'RE FUGITIVES--OR WHAT?!
AND IF WE'RE GONNA VACATE THIS JOINT--CAN I GET THE CAMERAS IN HERE FIRST? JUST TO GRAB SOME B-ROLL STUFF--
JEEZ--IS YOUR WHOLE LIFE A T.V. SHOW?!

OH YEAH! YOU'RE ONE TO JUDGE! COME ON--!
I'VE WATCHED ENOUGH BAD T.V. TO KNOW IT WHEN I SEE IT--
--AND RIGHT NOW YOU'RE PLAYING FOR AN AUDIENCE OF NO ONE, MORRISETTE!

YOU CALL ME REBEL WHEN I'M IN UNIFORM!
YOU CALL THAT A "UNIFORM"--?!
NORMALLY, WOLFHUNTER MIGHT ENJOY THIS KIND OF PATENTED SUPERTEAM BANTER--

--BUT HE'S STILL SWEATING SOME SEVERE DANCE FEVER!
...DIS SOME SWEET CRUNK, BUT IT CAN'T LAST FOREVER... TOO MANY DISCO BISCUITS...
...I'M FEELIN' THE FREAK-- AND IT'S GETTIN' TWEAKED!
HE'S HITTING THE LIMITS OF THIS FALSE REALITY--

--UNBEKNOWNST TO THE GIGGLY BLACK-OPS EXPERT WHO ENGINEERED THE TRIP.
...OH, IT WAS AMAZING. A LONG DISTANCE TRANSFERENCE THAT THE TARGET IN QUESTION HAD NO PREEXISTING KNOWLEDGE OF...!
EVEN NOW, HE'S STILL LOST IN A VIRTUAL STATE...WITHOUT THE SELF-AWARENESS NEEDED TO COPE WITH HIS NEW SURROUNDINGS...
FAMOUS LAST WORDS--
--BUT NOT AS GOOD AS THESE:
GAWD-DAYAM!

HOLY CRAP--! HE'S FINALLY UP AN' AT 'EM!
FEELING RESTED AFTER YOUR LITTLE TIME-OUT, PAL...?!

WHOA... MY HEAD...
...JUST GIMME A SECOND...TO MAKE SURE I'M BACK IN THE REAL WORLD...

SO...WHAT HAPPENED TO YOU, MAN? YOU JUST CHECKED OUT ON US IN THE MIDDLE OF THE MADNESS...
YOU GOT SOME SORT OF BLOOD SUGAR THING...?

I GOT...SENT SOMEPLACE... YOU WOULDN'T BELIEVE IT...
...BUT I DUNNO WHO THE HELL PUT ME THERE...!
THAT'S PROBABLY... SOMETHING WE NEED T'KNOW...
RIGHT...?

THE PIONEER MINDS HAVE LED THE WAY...AND ITS THEIR GENIUS WE'RE GOING TO PRESERVE.
WE'RE FINALLY GOING TO SAVE HUMANITY ONCE AND FOR ALL--
--WHEN ITS ELITE CAN LIVE FOREVER IN THE ULTIMATE CLOUD STORAGE WORLD!

THIS IS FRANK WELLS. HE WAS TRYING SOMETHING DIFFERENT.
IN A WORLD WHERE MIGHT MAKES RIGHT... THERE IS AN ALTERNATIVE. AN UNEXPLORED PATHWAY COLLECTIVELY LEADING US ALL OUT OF THE DARKNESS...AND INTO ENLIGHTENMENT.
TO THAT END, HIS LATEST ENDEAVOR INVOLVED ENGAGING THE WORLD AT THE MOST PASSIVE LEVEL POSSIBLE--FROM BED.
THAT WORKED OUT ABOUT AS WELL AS YOU'D EXPECT...
SIGH
IT NEVER ENDS...!
NOW...THIS IS THE FABLED BABA LAMA.
HAS HE BEEN THE JIMINY CRICKET TO FRANK'S PINOCCHIO? THE McMAHON TO HIS CARSON? THE BARUCHEL TO HIS ROGEN? OR SOMETHING EVEN MORE SIGNIFICANT...?
THIS IS NOTHING MORE THAN A DISTRACTION, FRANK.
BY ALL MEANS, DON'T GIVE THIS CLEARWATER SPORT MORE CREDENCE THAN IT DESERVES. DO NOT ENGAGE IN A REVIVAL OF THE PAST!
EVEN THOUGH YOU FOOL YOUR SOUL--STAND AND DELIVER!
AND DON'T FORGET FLOOD.
HER ABILITIES ARE BASED ON THE SIMPLISTIC CONTROL OF A CHEMICAL SUBSTANCE IN WHICH EACH MOLECULE CONTAINS TWO HYDROGEN ATOMS COVALENTLY BONDED TO ONE OXYGEN ATOM.
AND SHE STILL WANTS RESPECT!
OKAY, LET'S LAY DOWN THE LAWS OF THE RELATIONSHIP RIGHT AT THE TOP.
"SUPERHERO"--
--MEET "SUPER-VILLAIN"!
POWER
THE BALLAD OF FRANK WELLS:
HOT-TUB TIME OUT

SHE PACKS A PUNCH, THAT'S FOR SURE...
PAIN IS ETHEREAL! WE ARE BORN WITH A CHANCE!
SHE WANTS TO DRAW THE BLOOD FROM YOUR LOINS!
DOWN ON THE SIDEWALK BELOW, THE ATTENDANT PRESS ARE DRAWING THEIR OWN BLOOD...
--I'M TELLING YOU! HE SAVED ALL OF US! PLUCKED US RIGHT OUT OF THE AIR!
THEY'RE STILL UP THERE! GET THE NEWS COPTER OVER HERE--
EMT
EMT
EMT
WHUPWHUP WHUPWHUP
--YOU'LL GET A GREAT VIEW OF THE ACTION!
ROGER THAT. WE'RE GOING IN LOW--AND LIVE--LOOKING FOR THE BEST SHOT...
NO MATTER WHAT MANNER OF ARTILLERY IS THROWN YOUR WAY--YOU MUST ENDURE!
THIS ENDEAVOR WAS ANOTHER STEP UP JACOB'S LADDER...BUT YOU MISCONSTRUE MY O-MIKUJI...
...THE DIRECT APPROACH IS THE ONLY SHORTCUT WORTH CONSIDERING.
OH YEAH! I'VE DEALT WITH MY SHARE OF COSTUMED CARPETBAGGERS!
THOSE VULTURES HAVE NO IDEA HOW MUCH SURFACE TENSION I HOLD ONTO!
I NEED RELEASE!

TRYING TO GET THE GHT **ANGLE** SO YOU CAN WITNESS THE ACTION AS **IT HAPPENS!**

WHAT BEGAN AS SOME ORT OF BIZARRE **PRESS CONFERENCE** HAS PLODED INTO **VIOLENCE!** WE CANNOT POSITIVELY DENTIFY THE **ASSAILANT,** T WE CAN **CONFIRM** THE TEMPTED MURDER OF AN ENTIRE GROUP OF REPORTERS, NEWSMEN, LOGGERS...ALL OF THEM SAVED FROM CERTAIN DEATH BY ONE **FRANK WELLS!**

MONTREAL HAS NEVER EXPERIENCED THIS KIND OF COSTUMED **CHAOS**--A STARK CONTRAST TO THE KIND OF **EVOLUTION** THAT WELLS WAS ESPOUSING JUST MINUTES EARLIER!

AS WE ALL WATCH THIS DRAMA PLAY OUT **LIVE**--THE **WORLDVIEW** HE TRIED TO PRESENT TO US DEMANDS **CONSIDERATION...**

LIVE MONTREAL

...ARE WE REALLY **"ONE WORLD,"** AS HE SO ELOQUENTLY CLAIMS?

AND DOES HIS **INVOLVEMENT** IN SEVERAL **PROBLEM AREAS** AROUND THE WORLD SUGGEST THAT WE'RE IN NEED OF THIS KIND OF **GUIDANCE...?**

UNITED KINGDOM

GHANA

AS **WORLD CITIZENS,** HOW DO WE **RESPOND** TO WELLS'S **SUCCESS** IN HIS ACTIONS...?

IS FRANK WELLS MAKING OUR OWN LEADERS **OBSOLETE...?**

OH MY GOD.

THIS ISN'T HAPPENING...

SONY

FRANK! THIS ISN'T EVEN A **WORTHWHILE** DISTRACTION!

YOU NEED TO GET YOUR MIND, BODY, AND SPIRIT BACK IN THE GAME!

I'M TRYING!

EVEN I CAN ADMIT THERE ARE SOME THINGS YOU CANNOT EVOLVE YOUR WAY OUT OF...
...SO, IN THAT SPIRIT, FEEL FREE TO PROVE YOUR BONA FIDES.
YOU WANNA SEE ME DEAL WITH THIS OLD SCHOOL?!
FINE!
SKASH
ARCTIC BLAST BLOW!
DEFINITELY A TACTIC THAT FLOOD CANNOT DEFEND AGAINST IN TIME!
NOOOOOO--
--*
SEE? THIS IS AN INTERESTING PROGRESSION...OUT OF SUCH NONSENSE, YOU'VE CREATED ART.
I'M SURE SHE'LL DEFROST EVENTUALLY.
IN THE MEANTIME, LET'S GET BACK TO THE ENLIGHTENMENT AT HAND. IT'S TIME YOU TOOK THAT FINAL STEP IN THE UNKNOWN...
SPLING!
TINKLE
...IT'S TIME FOR THE HERO TO FACE THE TRUE ENEMY.
OKAY.
I'M READY.
AND SO, FROM LA BELLE VILLE...

O THE HUB OF THE IVERSE. THE WALKING TY. THE CRADLE OF ODERN AMERICA.
IAT WOULD BOSTON, ASSACHUSETTS, THE WAY.)
THIS IS THE CORPORATE HEADQUARTERS OF A MULTINATIONAL NUTRITIONAL, SNACK FOOD, AND HEALTH-RELATED CONSUMER GOODS COMPANY...NAMED NASTIE.
ND INSIDE THE OFFICE OF ASTIE C.E.O. CURTIS HAYNES, HERE IS ALWAYS BUSINESS O BE DONE.
THE REPORTS YOU ASKED FOR ARE ON YOUR DESK, MR. HAYNES... BUT ISN'T IT A BIT LATE FOR--
MONEY NEVER SLEEPS, ROSE. I'LL SEE YOU BRIGHT AND EARLY IN THE MORNING.
CLICKETY
CLICKETY
CLICKETY
ARE YOU HAPPY, MR. HAYNES?
GAH--!
WHO THE HELL ARE YOU?! HOW DID YOU GET IN HERE?!
IT DOESN'T MATTER WHO I AM.
I'M HERE TO TALK ABOUT THE CANDY BARS YOU MAKE BILLIONS SELLING...
...THEY COME AT A MUCH HIGHER PRICE, DON'T THEY?
DON'T ACT LIKE YOU DON'T KNOW WHAT I MEAN.
UHHH...
WHU... WHAT IS THAT...?

FIGURES YOU WOULDN'T KNOW A ***COCOA POD*** WHEN YOU SEE ONE.
BUT YOU KNOW HOW TO ***GET*** THEM--
--DON'T YOU?!

--YOU ARE NOW ORDERED TO CEASE ANY AND ALL HOSTILITIES AND SURRENDER YOURSELF TO OUR AUTHORITY!
WE ARE THE REDLINE SQUADRON AIRBORNE DIVISION AND--IF YOU REFUSE TO COMPLY--WE HAVE BEEN DULY AUTHORIZED TO ENGAGE!
ACKNOWLEDGE IMMEDIATELY!
ONCE AGAIN, FRANK WELLS IS FACED WITH THE VERY THING THAT HE'S BEEN TRYING TO ESCAPE FROM--
--ANOTHER SHOWDOWN. ANOTHER MEANINGLESS CONFLICT. MORE PRO WRESTLING SHENANIGANS FOR THE COUCH POTATO BRIGADE.
IN A MOMENT LIKE THIS, IT TAKES EVERYTHING INSIDE OF HIM TO STAY FOCUSED ON EXACTLY WHAT HE WANTS TO BE...
...VERSUS WHAT HE TRULY IS.
JUST WHEN I THOUGHT I WAS OUT...
...THEY PULL ME BACK IN!

QUESTION: HOW MANY YEARS CAN SOME AGENTS EXIST BEFORE THEY'RE ALLOWED TO BE FREE? OR SOMETHING LIKE THAT...
THEN AGAIN, THERE'S FREEDOM... AND THEN THERE'S WHAT YOU'RE WILLING TO DO TO ACHIEVE IT. (AND WHO YOU'RE WILLING TO EXPLOIT TO ACHIEVE IT...!)
MEANWHILE...CALL THEM ELVIS WARMAKER! REBEL! RUBY! WOLFHUNTER! THESE HEROES DON'T BORE US--THEY GET TO THE CHORUS!
WANNA MAKE SOMETHIN' OF IT?
AGENTS OF CH-CH-CHANGE: UNO
BUT THESE THINGS TAKE TIME AND PLANNING... NOT TO MENTION A DEGREE OF INSPIRATION...
...WHICH IS WHAT BRINGS US TO SUCH AN IDYLLIC SETTING. SURELY A SPOT AS BEAUTIFUL AS THIS HAS MANAGED TO KEEP OUT THE WORLD'S CORROSION, RIGHT...?
RIGHT?!

THINK AGAIN.
GAZER.
HARD TO BELIEVE THEY FINALLY CAUGHT UP WITH YOU.
NO KIDDING. NOW QUIT BOTHERING ME, WHOEVER YOU ARE...

OH, YOU DEFINITELY DON'T KNOW ME. BUT I CAN GUARANTEE THAT YOU WANT TO.
UNLESS YOU'D RATHER HANG AROUND HERE FOR THE NEXT FIFTY YEARS...

IS THIS SOME KINDA NEW WORK RELEASE PROGRAM...?
LET'S JUST SAY... WE BOTH GET SOMETHING OUT OF IT.
AND YOU CAN REALLY GET ME OUT OF HERE? WHO THE HELL ARE YOU, MAN--
--SOME KIND OF GOVERNMENT SPOOK?!

JUST CALL ME BERT.
AND "GOVERNMENT SPOO DOESN'T BEGIN TO COVE MY AREA OF EXPERTISE.
IN THE MEANTIME, LET GET YOU BACK DOING WHAT YO DO BEST...

...KNOW WHAT I MEAN?
DON'T PUSH ME, 'CAUSE I'M CLOSE TO THE EDGE...

...BUT I'LL DO WHATEVER IT TAKES TO GET OUT OF THIS PEN...!
LEAD THE WAY.
HOLD ON.
SO SOME SUIT WITH A NICOTINE HABIT JUST WALTZES IN...AND THAT SICKO GETS SOME SHORE LEAVE...

...HOW'S THAT WORK?!
DON'T EVEN THINK ABOUT IT.
YOU'RE DOIN' FORTY TO LIFE, SCUMBAG. NOW GET BACK TO YER GARDENING AND SHUT IT--!

BUT JUST BEFORE THE DAWN...I REMEMBER THAT YOU SAID GOODBYE TO END ALL THESE THINGS...
DON'T LOOK TOO CLOSELY AT THE WORLD AROUND YOU...
WHO WILL YOU HAVE TO FETCH HER AWAY ON A COLD AND FROSTY MORNING...
...OR AT WHAT MAY BE HIDING IN THE SHADOWS--
THE DEMON OF YOUR OWN DISCONTENT!
DON'T TOUCH ME!!!
THE PAST FEW NIGHTS, IT'S BEEN THE SAME THING...
...THE SAME VISIONS IN MY HEAD.
NOT A NIGHTMARE... IT ACTUALLY FEELS LIKE SOMETHING HAS INFECTED MY BRAIN...
IT'S LIKE THEY'RE ON REPEAT OR SOMETHING...
SORRY, KID... I LEFT MY Ph.D. IN PSYCHOLOGY IN ONE OF MY OTHER SAFE HOUSES...
BACK OFF, ELVIS. I GET WHERE SHE'S COMIN' FROM.
SOMEONE'S OBVIOUSLY EFFIN' WITH US, BIG TIME...

THIS IS STANDARD COUNTER-INTELLIGENCE TACTICS...!
UNLESS SOMETHING ELSE IS HAUNTING YOU, KID...
...LIKE THE WAY YOU FRIED THAT COUNTERSTRIKE AGENT--

HEY!
I DON'T DO "GUILTY CONSCIENCE," OKAY?!
AND DON'T CALL ME "KID," FERRELL-- UNLESS YOU WANT TO GET PIMP SLAPPED TOO!
I'D HATE TO MESS UP YOUR PRETTY FACE--!

WHOA, WHOA, WHOA-- HOLD ON, GIRL!
I'M JUST RULING OUT ANY AND ALL POSSIBILITIES! THEY GOT IN MY HEAD TOO, REMEMBER?!

JEEZUS...
...FEELS LIKE WE'RE BACK IN GROUP THERAPY...!

LISTEN, I GOT NO BACKGROUND IN DEALING WITH TELEPATHIC ATTACKS...
ME NEITHER.
I GUESS NONE OF US ARE IMMUNE, ARE WE?

MAYBE SOMEONE'S TRYING TO SMOKE US OUT OF HIDING...
GENIUS DEDUCTION, WOLF. OF COURSE SOMEONE'S TRYING TO SMOKE US OUT...

...ONE WEAK SPOT AT A TIME!
ELVIS WARMAKER SPEAKS MACHO TRUTH!

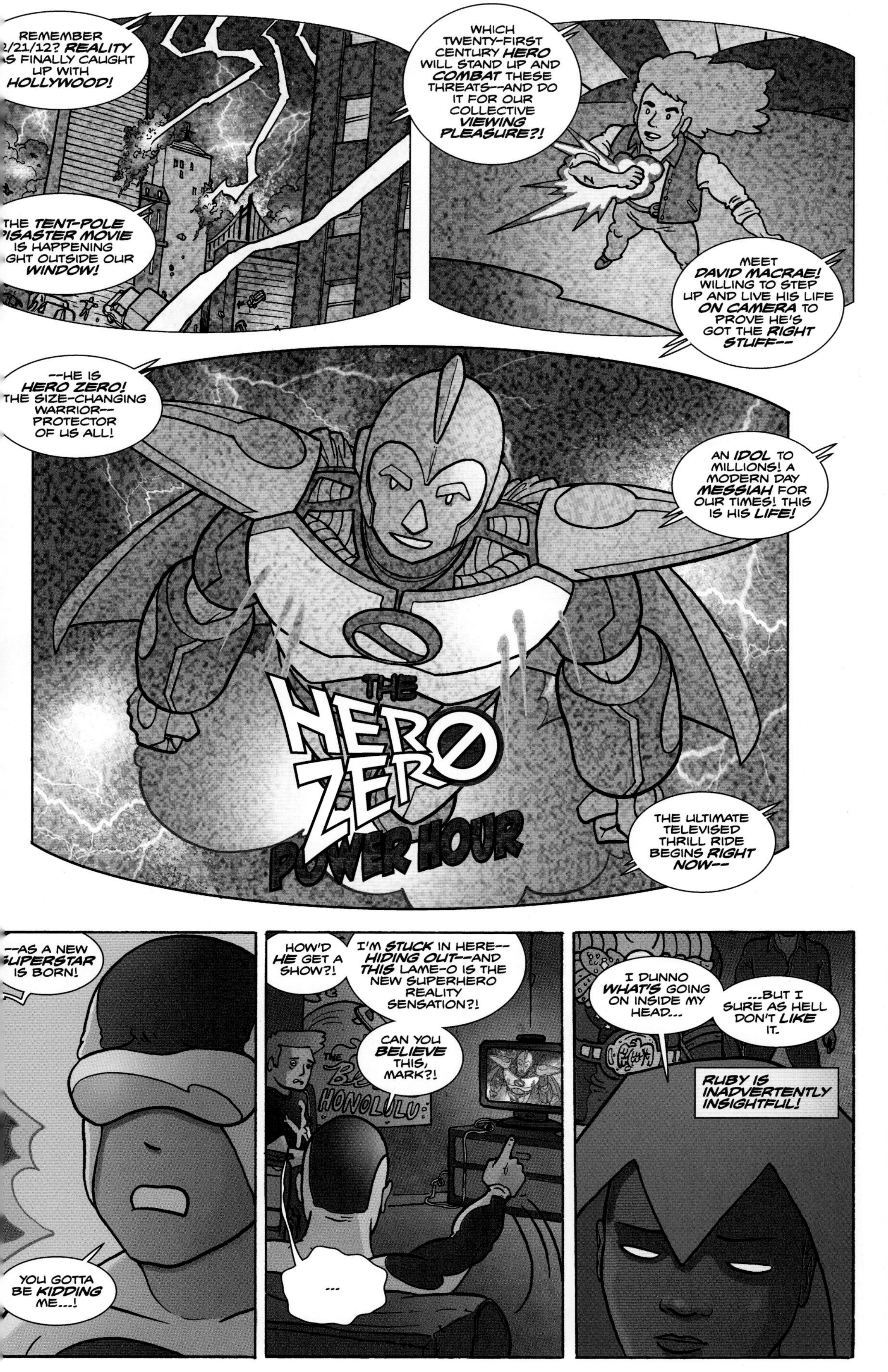

REMEMBER 2/21/12? *REALITY* AS FINALLY CAUGHT UP WITH *HOLLYWOOD!*

THE *TENT-POLE DISASTER MOVIE* IS HAPPENING IGHT OUTSIDE OUR *WINDOW!*

WHICH TWENTY-FIRST CENTURY *HERO* WILL STAND UP AND *COMBAT* THESE THREATS--AND DO IT FOR OUR COLLECTIVE *VIEWING PLEASURE?!*

MEET *DAVID MACRAE!* WILLING TO STEP UP AND LIVE HIS LIFE *ON CAMERA* TO PROVE HE'S GOT THE *RIGHT STUFF--*

--HE IS *HERO ZERO!* THE SIZE-CHANGING WARRIOR--PROTECTOR OF US ALL!

AN *IDOL* TO MILLIONS! A MODERN DAY *MESSIAH* FOR OUR TIMES! THIS IS HIS *LIFE!*

THE HERO ZERO POWER HOUR

THE ULTIMATE TELEVISED THRILL RIDE BEGINS *RIGHT NOW--*

DON'T MISS THE ADVENTURES OF HERO ZERO EACH AND EVERY WEEK! HE'S A HERO YOU CAN'T HELP BUT LOVE!
NO WAY! AIN'T GONNA HAPPEN WHILE I'M STILL KICKIN'!
REBEL'S JEALOUSY IS SUPERCHARGED!
WE GOTTA FIGURE OUT WHO'S GOT THE STONES TO BE MESSIN' WITH OUR--
TIME TO ASSEMBLE, AGENTS!
WHAT THE HELL ARE YOU ON ABOUT, MORRISETTE?!
JUST GOT A TEXT!
SOME BIGTIME BADDIE'S HOLDING A HOSPITAL CHILDREN'S WARD HOSTAGE--
LEMME SEE THAT...
FIRST OF ALL, WE'RE SUPPOSED TO BE RADIO SILENT! NO COMMUNICATIONS IN OR OUT OF HERE...!
SECOND... THIS IS FROM YOUR MANAGER!
WHAT...HE'S TRYING TO GET YOUR MUG BACK ON T.V.?!
DON'T FALL FOR IT, PRETTY BOY.
WHOA--!
HEY, MAN! I GOT THAT IN A GIFT BAG AT THE DAYTIME EMMYS!

LOOK--WHO CARES WHERE IT CAME FROM?! THE CRISIS IS LEGIT!
ARE WE STILL OUT TO CHANGE THINGS, OR WHAT?! KIDS ARE IN DANGER...!
KIDS, HUH?
DAMN...

YEAH, I GOTTA ADMIT...WHEN I HEAR THAT IT'S KIDS...
...STAYING PUT SEEMS KINDA PUNK ASS, Y'KNOW...?

SO IT'S QUITE A MOB SCENE OUTSIDE OF ST. FIACRE'S HOSPITAL. AUTHORITIES HAVE SET UP A PERIMETER. POLICE TAPE HAS BEEN APPLIED. BYSTANDERS ARE GAWKING.
THE BUZZWORDS ARE FLYING: "CRISIS MODE"..."HIGH ALERT"...
SPECIAL TOUCHES CHILDREN'S HOSPITAL
S.W.A.T.

..."HOSTAGE SITUATION."
YOU KNOW WHAT I LIKE BEST...?

I LIKE SOFT SKIN.
I LIKE THE SMELL OF INNOCENCE.
I REALLY SHOULD BE HOSTING MY OWN KIDS' SHOW. I SHOULD BE INTRODUCING CARTOONS AND PLAYING WITH PUPPETS.
GAZER--BACK IN ALL HIS DEMENTED GLORY!

THEY CALL ME A CHILD KILLER. CONSIDERING MY PERSONAL HISTORY... IT'S HARD TO ARGUE.
BUT IS A BIRD SHOWING OFF WHEN IT FLIES?
ANYWAY--
--I GUESS YOU'RE FIRST.
DON'T BE AFRAID. THE END ALWAYS COMES QUICKLY.
I DON'T KNOW WHY I NEVER THOUGHT OF GOING THIS ROUTE--
--BEFORE...?
THUNDER IN THE NIGHT!
THE WORLD ENDING UNDERNEATH OUR FEET--

--AND A MODERN GOD OF WAR TAKING STOCK OF OUR FRAGILITY.
CAN YOU SMELL IT? THE WHOLE GODDAMN SPECTRUM. TRINITROTOLUENE... UREA NITRATE... TRIACETONE TRIPEROXIDE...
SMELLS LIKE VICTORY.
QUIT POSIN' AND START HOSIN', E!
HEY! HAVEN'T I SEEN YOU ON T.V.--?!
THE AGENTS PERFORM A SURGICAL STRIKE--ALL IN THE NAME OF CHANGE!
HEY, KID...
...WHILE THEY'RE KNEE DEEP IN THEIR VERSION OF WRESTLEMANIA, LET ME GET YOU--
--OUTTA HERE...?!
OH DAMN...!

SUDDEN FIBRILLATION VIA EXTERNAL ELECTROCUTION. THAT $#!% HURTS.
MUCH TOO PAINFUL FOR RUBY TO APPRECIATE THE IRONY.

LEAVE SOME FOR ME, YO.
WE'LL HANDLE THIS LIKE WE USED TO BACK IN THE NEIGHBORHOOD...!

WELL, GET IT IN GEAR, WOLF!
LET'S DO WHAT WE DO AND GET MOVIN'!
WARMAKER LETS THE ORDNANCE SING--

--A SONIC BOOM MELODY MAKER!
YEEOOOW!
HEY, MAN--
--WATCH OUT WHO YOU'RE FIRING ON, ELVIS!

NO WORRIES--
WOLFHUNTER--CRACKIN' LIKE KAREEM IN THE GAME OF DEATH!
HUHHN--!
TIMING IS EVERYTHING!
OH JEEEEEEZUS...!
N-NOT NOW--GYUHHNT!
JUST AS THIS MORRISETTE BROTHER LOSES HIS MEGAMOJO...
...THIS MORRISETTE BROTHER IS STILL LOCKED AWAY IN A SAFE HOUSE.
AND FOR THE TRANSFER OF "REBEL POWER," PROXIMITY IS EVERYTHING...!
ELVI
IN SPA
HOWEVER, SOMEONE'S CLOSE BY...
MAYBE "FAME WHORE" WAS TOO HARSH...
...BUT NEVER LET IT BE SAID THAT I DON'T KNOW YOU, MATTHEW.
OR IS IT MARK...?
DOES THAT EVEN MATTER AT THIS POINT?
OH C'MON, KID--
--THIS AIN'T THE TIME FOR THIS!
...UUUHHH...
...NEED TO... TRANSFER... POWER...

WH-WHU...?
N-NO...
...NO AUTOGRAPHS...
...NOT R-RIGHT NOW, ANYWAY...
YOU KNOW KIDS... THEY WANT WHAT THEY WANT--
--AND, RIGHT NOW, THEY SEEM TO WANT SUPERHERO BLOOD!
WHAT A BEAT DOWN!
NOT SO TOUGH WHEN YOUR OPPONENT'S GOT PUBES, EH?
YOU TRYIN' TO SAY SOMETHING THERE...?
MMFFGLLL...!
THAT'S WHAT I'M TALKING ABOUT--!
TALK INTO THE MIKE--!
OUCH! SOMEONE SHOULD'VE STAYED IN PRISON!
WELL, THAT WORKED. NOW WE SHOULD--
YO, E...
...WHAT HAPPENED TO THE REST OF OUR PEEPS--?!

DAMN! LOOKS LIKE REBEL GOT PUNKED--!

HE'S OUT LIKE ELLEN DE-GEE!

AND WHERE'S RUBY?!

WATCH IT, WOLF--

--BEHIND YOU!

IT HAPPENS FAST. A MOTION BLUR OF GARANIMAL SPIRIT AND MUZZLE FLASH VIOLENCE!

DOUBLE-TAP ATTACK!

WHA--?!
GYEEAHHH--!
RESPONSE TIME: SIX POINT FOUR FEMTOSECONDS!
CONTROL METHOD: CYANOCARBON PLUS!

DIZZINESS...RESTRICTED BREATHING...DISORIENTATION...
...AND, ULTIMATELY-- IN WARMAKER'S CASE-- A DEEP, DARK NOTHINGNESS--!
...S-SON OF A... BIIIIITTTCHHHH...
ELVIS

ALL IN A DAY'S WORK...
COMMENCING CHECK-IN...
SCRAMBLE CODE: GAMMA-SEVEN-GISH. INITIATE.

...AS REQUESTED, AGENTS HAVE BEEN EFFECTIVELY NEUTRALIZED VIA MULTIPLE ENGAGEMENT SCENARIOS.
ALL AGENTS ARE INTACT, ALSO AS REQUESTED.
SIR? ARE YOU READING ME...?
I AM INDEED. WELL DONE...

...IT'S ALWAYS GRATIFYING WHEN A SIMPLE TRAP IS SPRUNG WITH SUCH EFFECTIVENESS.
NOW WE CAN FINALLY GET ON WITH THINGS...
...AND SEE IF THESE AGENT ARE TRULY UP FOR THE CHANGES I HAVE IN STORE.

WHEN YOU STOP AND THINK ABOUT IT...BOSTON IS THE LAST PLACE ON EARTH YOU'D EXPECT THIS KIND OF SHOWDOWN...
FRANK WELLS!
YOU ARE ORDERED TO EVACUATE NASTIE CORPORATE HEADQUARTERS AND SURRENDER YOURSELF IMMEDIATELY--
--AVOIDING CONFLICT IS COMPLETELY UP TO YOU!
FREE WILL: A DANGEROUS THING WHEN PLACED IN THE HANDS OF A SUPERHERO.
FOR CURTIS HAYNES, CURRENT C.E.O. OF NASTIE, THERE IS ONLY ONE CHOICE...
DON'T WORRY, MR. HAYNES...
...WHEN I'M DONE WITH THEM, WE'LL CONTINUE OUR CONVERSATION.
THE BALLAD OF FRANK WELLS: LESTER BANG BANG
DELICIOUS!

HOW LONG DO WE GIVE HIM, SIR?
AS LONG AS IT TAKES, REDLINE FIVE.
REDLINE LEADER! SIX O'CLOCK POSITION--

FRANK WELLS, AKA TITAN
ABILITIES:
STRENGTH, FLIGHT, HEIGHTENED SPEED AND STAMINA IMPERVIOUS TO PAIN.
KNOWN ADVERSARIES:
KING TIGER, VORTEX, WARMAKER
WEAKNESSES:
UNKNOWN
--TARGET HAS GONE EXTERIOR!
HE MOVES WITH PURPOSE AND DIGNITY...

...THIS TIME, THINGS WILL BE DIFFERENT.

REDLINE SEVEN!
EXECUTE HAWKWIND ACTION!

THE REDLINE SQUADRON IS A STATE-OF-THE-ART AIR COMBAT UNIT. GOD HELP YOU IF YOU END UP IN THEIR CROSSHAIRS.
BUT THIS IS NEW-MODEL FRANK--

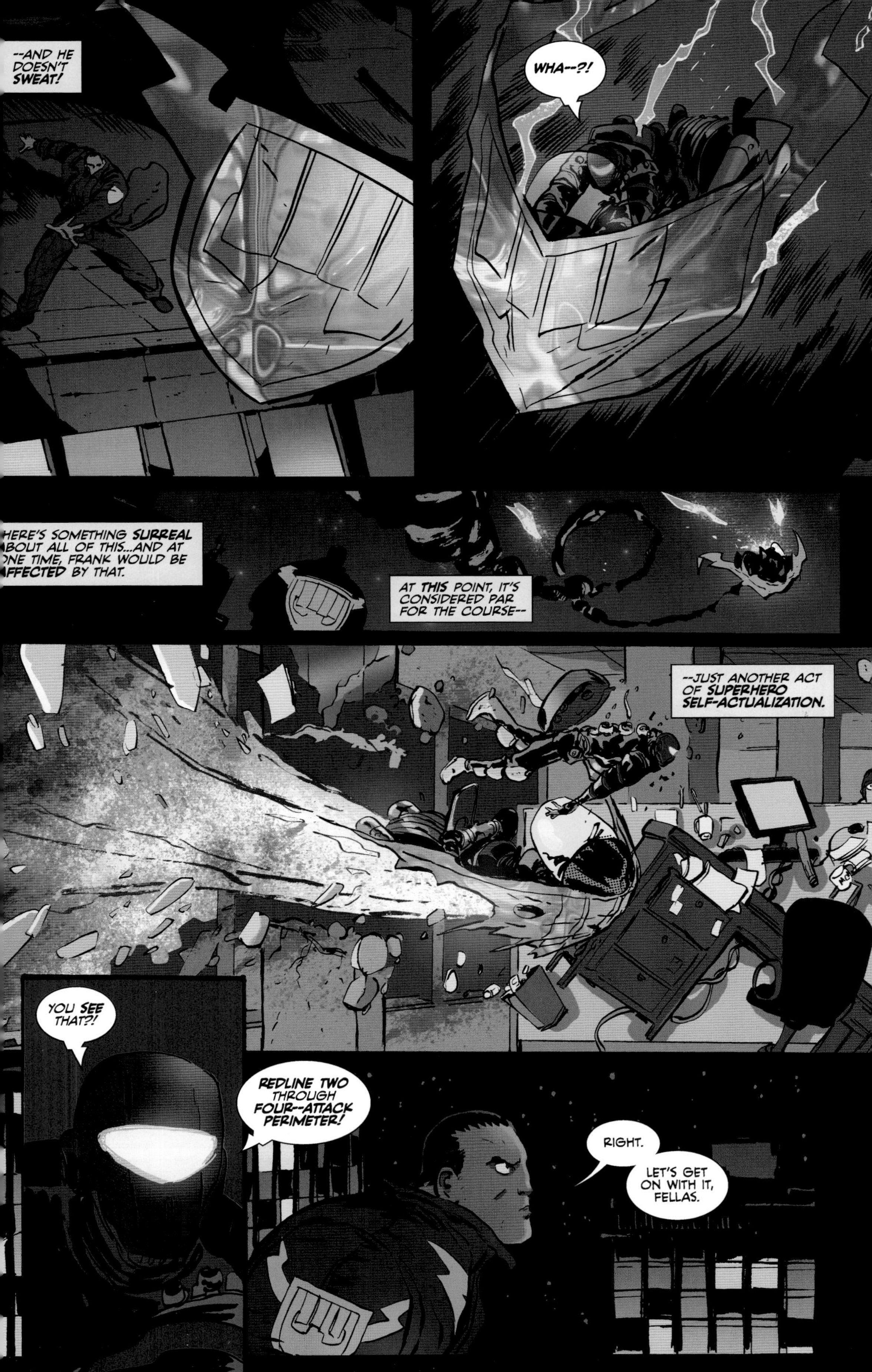
--AND HE DOESN'T SWEAT!
WHA--?!
HERE'S SOMETHING SURREAL ABOUT ALL OF THIS...AND AT ONE TIME, FRANK WOULD BE AFFECTED BY THAT.
AT THIS POINT, IT'S CONSIDERED PAR FOR THE COURSE--
--JUST ANOTHER ACT OF SUPERHERO SELF-ACTUALIZATION.
YOU SEE THAT?!
REDLINE TWO THROUGH FOUR--ATTACK PERIMETER!
RIGHT.
LET'S GET ON WITH IT, FELLAS.

HE RECALLS ALL THAT HE HAS LEARNED.
VIIPPP
WHOA--!
WE'VE GOT MULTIPLE TARGETS! HOW THE HELL--?!
VIIIP
VIIPP
ENGAGE YOUR OPPONENTS WITH WHAT THEY EXPECT...TO CONFIRM THEIR PROJECTIONS--

I GOT THIS ONE--!

--AND ALL WAR IS BASED ON DECEPTION!

THIS ONE'S MINE--
--GYYYUUHH--!
IN THE MIDST OF CHAOS, THERE IS OPPORTUNITY.

HE'S PLAYING SOME SORT OF GAME WITH US!
HOW MANY OF THESE THINGS ARE--
OPPORTUNITIES MULTIPLY AS THEY ARE SEIZED.

--HUUHHHTT--!
SORRY. THIS IS NO GAME.
JUST DEMONSTRATING A REAL PROBLEM WITH FOLKS IN OUR LINE OF WORK--
--WE DON'T PAY CLOSE ENOUGH ATTENTION, DO WE?
MOVE SWIFT AS THE WIND AND CLOSELY FORMED AS THE WOOD--
--ATTACK LIKE THE FIRE AND BE STILL AS THE MOUNTAIN!
THE GREATEST VICTORY IS THAT WHICH REQUIRES NO BATTLE.
THINK I READ THAT IN A GUM WRAPPER WHEN I WAS A KID...
FOOM
THERE ARE NO ENEMIES ANYMORE.
ONLY OPPONENTS.
ONLY OBSTACLES.

STRATEGY WITHOUT TACTICS IS THE SLOWEST ROUTE TO VICTORY.
TACTICS WITHOUT STRATEGY IS THE NOISE BEFORE DEFEAT.
REDLINE LEADER! HE'S BACK ON THE BUILDING!
ALL UNITS-- GO TO ULTRA-VULTURE!
THIS IS IT!
SURROUND AND CONTAIN!
CONFRONT THEM WITH ANNIHILATION, AND THEY WILL THEN SURVIVE...
...PLUNGE THEM INTO A DEADLY SITUATION, AND THEY WILL THEN LIVE.
TO REPEAT: THE GREATEST VICTORY IS THAT WHICH REQUIRES NO BATTLE.
I WISH...!
KNOW THYSELF, KNOW THY OBSTACLES.
HE WHO IS PRUDENT AND LIES IN WAIT FOR AN OPPONENT WHO IS NOT--

--WILL BE VICTORIOUS!
CHAIN REACTION!
TUSKEGEE
ALERT! ALERT! ALERT! REDLINE SQUADRON STATUS: OFFLINE.
COLLATING CURRENT KEYHOLE SAT DATA--
DAMMIT--!
GENERAL! I THOUGHT THESE PILOTS WERE TRAINED FOR THIS!
HE'S CLEARLY GOT SOME SORT OF POLITICAL AGENDA. AND I DON'T KNOW ABOUT YOU...
BUT LET'S PUT THAT ASIDE FOR NOW. CONSIDER HIS TARGET, SIR.
MR. PRESIDENT... I CAN'T SPEAK DIRECTLY TO THEIR LEVEL OF EXPERTISE, BUT MAY I POINT OUT THAT WE DID ADVISE AGAINST THIS ACTION--
...BUT WHEN SUPERHEROES GET POLITICAL, I TEND TO GET VERY NERVOUS.

THIRTY DAYS FOR YOU... ONE SECOND FOR THEM: THE HARD-WORKING LAB TECHS OF GOLDEN CITY--
DID YOU JUST SAY...
...SEVERAL BILLION ALIEN INVADERS...?!
WELL, TO BE PERFECTLY HONEST, GUYS...

...I'M THINKING THAT'S A PRETTY CONSERVATIVE ESTIMATE.
BUT... WHATEVER THE NUMBER IS...THEY'RE DEFINITELY COMING...
SHE IS EARTH'S GREATEST PROTECTOR! SHE IS THE ULTIMATE ROLE MODEL FOR OUR AGE! SHE IS THE PROVERBIAL UNSUNG HERO--
--YOU DON'T MESS WITH THIS MEASURE OF GRACE!
AMAZING GRACE: THE HARDEST PART

W-WE NEED TO... TO...
UHHHNN...
WHOA!
DAMMIT! SOMEONE CALL AHEAD TO THE MED LAB--

--TELL 'EM WE'RE ON OUR WAY!
BY THE WAY, THIS IS ONE OF THOSE TIMES...

...WHEN IT'S SOMETHING MUCH MORE FOREBODING THAN DARKNESS THAT CONFRONTS THE UNCONSCIOUS GRACE.
...NATURE FAVORS WORLDS SUCH AS YOURS--

--EVERY LIVING PLANET IS THE SAME. ONE BY ONE, THE GREAT HORROR SEEKS THEM OUT.

THE REAVER SWARM...CUTTING A BLOODY PATH OF DESTRUCTION ACROSS THE UNIVERSE...ALL IN THE NAME OF THE SEPTENARIUS...

YOU WOULD NOT WISH TO KNOW WHAT ELSE THE SEPTENARIUS HAS IN STORE FOR YOUR WORLD...

YOU WANT TO KNOW EVERYTHING, GRACE...TO CONTROL IT ALL...
STOPPING THE REAVER SWARM IS YOUR RESPONSIBILITY!

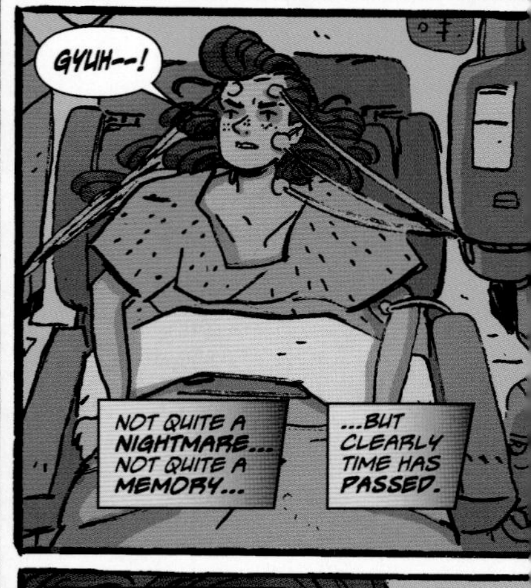

GYUH--!
NOT QUITE A NIGHTMARE... NOT QUITE A MEMORY...
...BUT CLEARLY TIME HAS PASSED.

THAT MEANS... CONVALESCENCE IS OVER.
OH DAMN.
NOT THIS ROOM AGAIN...!

A COUNCIL MEETING IS HASTILY ARRANGED...
SO, ONCE AGAIN... WE'RE ON THE FRONTLINES OF ARMAGEDDON, AND WE'RE THE ONLY ONES WHO KNOW ABOUT IT...!
PAR FOR THE COURSE, TYRONE...

...BUT INFORMATION IS POWER.
DON'T TELL SANTOS THAT. UNLESS WE WANT TO BRING HIM INTO THE LOOP...
WHAT'S THE POINT? IT'S NOT LIKE HE CAN ADEQUATELY DEFEND THE COUNTRY, MUCH LESS THE PLANET...!
IN THAT CASE, CAN WE TALK ABOUT OUR SCIENTIFIC ANALYSIS...?
MODERN POLITICS IN ACTION!

ARE THERE MORE LOCALIZED MEASURES WE CAN TAKE TO ENSURE--
HOLD IT. LET'S ALL JUST CUT THE CHATTER.
I WANT TO HEAR THE TECH ANALYSIS...

WELL, AS YOU KNOW, WE MONITORED BOTH OF YOUR VITALS DURING YOUR...CONFRONTATION. THE DATA WE GLEANED WAS SIGNIFICANT.
SEAVER'S POWERS OF INFLUENCE CARRIED WITH THEM AN INTERLACED SIGNAL OF OBVIOUS ALIEN ORIGIN.
AS YOU CAN SEE...THAT SIGNAL WAS TRACEABLE.

JUST AS WE SEE THE LIGHT OF CERTAIN STARS AFTER THOSE STARS ARE ALREADY DEAD...
OUR PATENTED ECHO TECH PROVIDED A CLEAR PATH BACK TO A POINT OF ORIGIN.
RIGHT.
I KNOW WHERE THIS IS GOING...

HOW SOON CAN WE LOAD TELEMETRY AND READY A NEW LAUNCH CRAFT--
HOLD ON. YOU'RE ASSUMING A LOT HERE.
I JUST DEALT WITH ONE OF THESE THINGS. I KNOW WHAT HE SAID...WE ALL HEARD HIS THREATS...

...BUT I'M NOT SURE I'M READY TO HURL MYSELF INTO THE VOID AGAIN. THIS IS THE END OF SOMETHING THAT STARTED YEARS AGO.
IF IT'S GOING TO BE THE END OF ME TOO... I NEED TO THINK IT OVER.
A RARE MOMENT OF HESITATION...
...LEADING TO A RARE MOMENT OF CONTEMPLATION...
...TAKING IN THE KIND OF VIEW THAT HAS ALWAYS BEEN HER GOOEY CENTER.
BEYOND SIMPLY BEING HOME... THIS PLACE STILL REPRESENTS SOMETHING TO HER.
AN IDEAL FOR THE REST OF HUMANITY TO STRIVE FOR (IN THEORY, AT LEAST...IF NOT IN ACTUAL PRACTICE). A MODEL FOR SOCIETY (AGAIN, IN THEORY)...
AN EXAMPLE OF FIRST-WORLD ARCHITECTURE THAT DOESN'T--
WHAT'S THAT--?
ANYWAY...
...EVEN IN PARADISE, THERE'S ALWAYS SOMEONE WHO NEEDS A HELPING HAND.

CASE IN POINT...
HELL OF A WAY TO GET MY ATTENTION, KIDDO...
I WASN'T WORRIED. I KNEW YOU'D SAVE ME.
YOU KNOW I SAW YOU...IN THE CITY SQUARE.
ONE OF MY FINER MOMENTS, I'M SURE.
YOU LOOKED LIKE CRAP, MA'AM. ABSOLUTE CRAP. IT WAS PRETTY INTENSE...
...BUT YOU DIDN'T QUIT. YOU KEPT GOING.
I'VE LIVED HERE ALL MY LIFE. I NEVER REALIZED HOW LUCKY I WAS...KNOWING YOU WERE HERE, PROTECTING US...
LISTEN...DON'T PUT TOO MUCH FAITH IN YOUR HEROES. YOU'VE GOT A GREATER RESPONSIBILITY, WHETHER YOU KNOW IT OR NOT...
...I'M COUNTING ON YOU TO TAKE YOUR OWN POWER.
AND TO QUESTION AUTHORITY.
I DON'T KNOW...
...I DON'T THINK ANYONE'S GONNA BE ABLE TO DO WHAT YOU DO.
IT'S... AMAZING...

LET ME TELL YOU WHAT'S "AMAZING"...
...FORGET ABOUT THE CONCEPT OF ARMAGEDDON. THE FACT THAT--IN THE FACE OF THE UNKNOWABLE--SOMEONE CAN STILL STAND UP AND MAKE SUCH A LEAP...
...WELL, I'M INSPIRED.
SEE? IN WHAT OTHER CITY CAN SO STUPID AN ACT--LIKE WHAT YOU DID--BE INTERPRETED AS A PROFOUND LEAP OF FAITH...?
C'MON...
...TIME TO GO.
COLLATING IGNITION SYSTEMS//// FUEL CELLS STABILIZED////
BOOSTERS ONLINE//// SILO FEEDS ARE ACTIVE////
AWAITING FINAL COUNTDOWN////
AMAZING GRACE IS BACK ON THE LAUNCH PAD...
...HER EYES CAST TOWARD THE STARS!
CONTROL CENTER!
I THINK I'VE BEEN SITTING HERE LONG ENOUGH--

--LET'S LIGHT THIS CANDLE!
YOU HEARD THE LADY...
COMMENCE COUNTDOWN--!
INITIATE LAUNCH IN 5...4...3...2...1--

--IGNITION////
BLAST OFF////

VEHICLE HAS CLEARED THE SILO////
Y'KNOW, THE LAST TIME SHE TOOK THIS KIND OF TRIP...SHE SAVED THE WORLD.
WELL, DAMN...
...HERE'S HOPING HISTORY REPEATS ITSELF.

AND BENEATH THE BRAVADO, A FLEETING MOMENT OF SELF-REFLECTION--
THE SEPTENARIUS... THEIR SO-CALLED REAVER SWARM... I HAVE NO IDEA WHAT TO EXPECT.
BUT ONE THING'S FOR SURE...

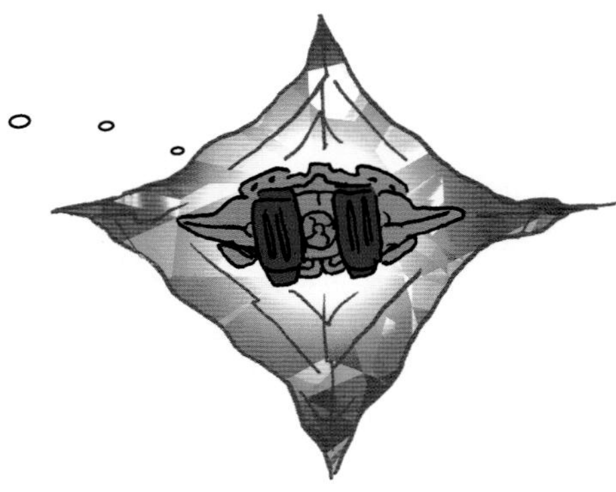
...I DON'T THINK THEY'RE GOING TO BE TOO HAPPY TO SEE ME.

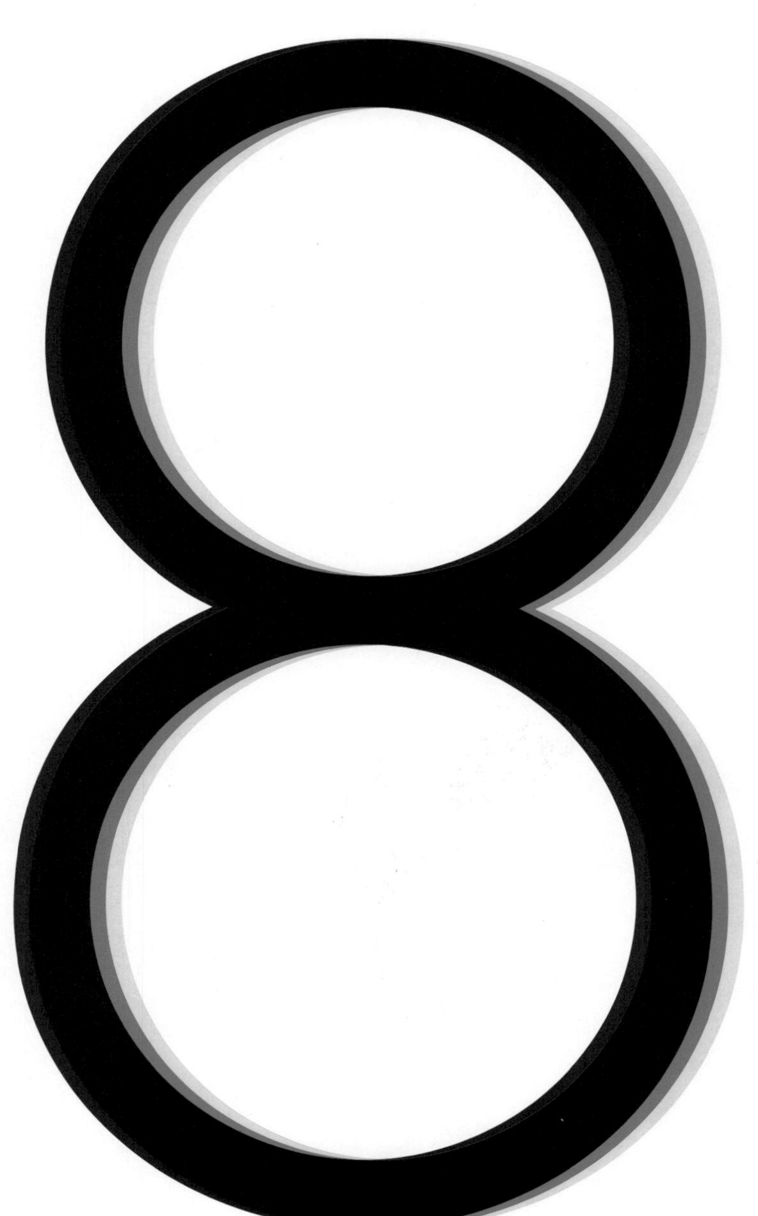

SAD FACT OF LIFE: SOME PEOPLE ARE SATISFIED WITH LESS.
THE REAL TRAGEDY STEMS FROM WHEN THEY DON'T KNOW THEY HAVE LESS...
WELCOME TO MINIMUM WAGE WORLD.
MEGABUGGER
99 VALUE
MEGABUGGER
AGENTS OF CHANGE: THE MORE THEY STAY THE SAME

THEY DON'T EVEN NOTICE THE SMELL OF DESPERATION...
THERE Y'GO. DON'T GET ANY ON YA...
NEXT IN LINE! WHAT'LL YOU HAVE...?
ICE COLD BEVERAGE
SOMETHING OFF THE DOLLAR MENU...

...I HEAR THAT'S THE BEST VALUE.
ON THE OTHER HAND, I HEAR THE MANAGERS GET A BONUS IF THEY CAN KEEP THE TURNOVER RATE DOWN. THAT'S SOME JOB SECURITY--

--EVEN IF YOU DON'T KNOW A FRENCH FRY FROM A MILKSHAKE STRAW.
DID YOU WANT SALT OR NO SALT--
--OOOWWCH!

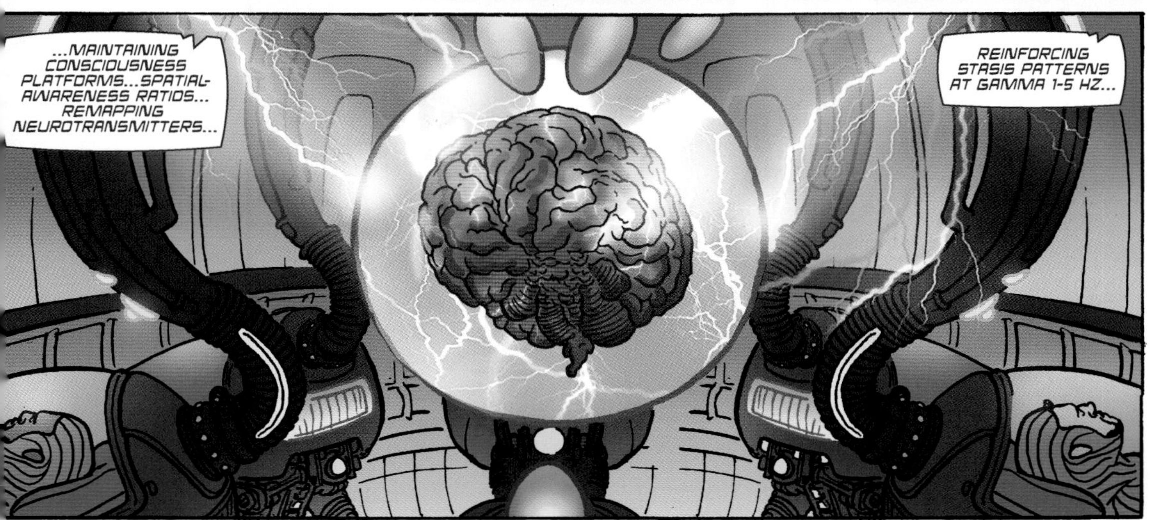
...MAINTAINING CONSCIOUSNESS PLATFORMS...SPATIAL-AWARENESS RATIOS... REMAPPING NEUROTRANSMITTERS...
REINFORCING STASIS PATTERNS AT GAMMA 1-5 HZ...

LISTEN, FORGET ABOUT THE FOOD. IT'S TERRIBLE HERE, ANYWAY.
WHY DON'T YOU GUYS COME OUT AND SIT WITH ME FOR A FEW MINUTES...
...I'LL TELL YOU ABOUT THE FACTS OF LIFE.
YEAH, OKAY. I REALLY DON'T THINK WE'RE ALLOWED TO--
WHAT'S THE HOLD-UP OUT HERE--

--WHO'S TRYING TO GET MY PEOPLE TO LEAVE THEIR STATIONS?!
I'M RUNNING A BUSINESS HERE-- NOT GROUP THERAPY!

WHO THE HELL ARE YOU TO COME IN HERE AND DERAIL MY OPERATION?!
YOU KNOW... I ALMOST FORGOT THAT WE PUT YOU IN HERE TOO.
LOOKS LIKE YOU TOOK TO THIS LIFE LIKE A DUCK TO WATER...

...BUT BY NO MEANS ARE YOU IN CHARGE.
WHAT'RE YOU--
--*

HEY, WHAT AM I MISSING OUT HERE...?
HE JUST... DID SOMETHING TO...
DON'T WORRY, GUYS...

...HE'S JUST TAKING A LITTLE TIME OUT.
NOW, WHERE WERE WE...?
...

SO, TAKE A SEAT. GET COMFORTABLE.
I WOULD SUGGEST WE GET SOME FOOD, BUT I THINK YOU'VE ALL SUFFERED ENOUGH.
Y'KNOW WHAT? HOLD ON A SEC. WE'RE MISSING SOMEONE...

HEY, ELVIS--

--DROP THE MOP AND GET OUT HERE.
EMPLOYEE MEETING IN THE MAIN DINING AREA, ASAP.
UNLESS YOU LIKE THE SMELL OF OLD URINAL CAKES...

...BUT I THINK YOU KNOW YOU WERE MEANT FOR SOMETHING BETTER.

KAY, I WARNED OU. BUT IT'S NOT KE YOU HAVE TO WORRY ABOUT EART DISEASE IN HERE...
FOR THE RECORD, I DON'T TOUCH THIS STUFF...

GOOD TO KNOW, REBEL. IT'S INTERESTING THAT CERTAIN PERSONALITY TRAITS SEEP THROUGH, NO MATTER WHAT THE ENVIRONMENT.
SO LET'S GET RIGHT TO IT. THE TRUTH BEHIND THE LIE.
CLEARLY, WORKING IN THIS DUMP IS NOT WHAT ANY OF YOU ARE REALLY ALL ABOUT.

WE PUT YOU HERE. AND WE MADE SURE THAT YOU DIDN'T QUESTION YOUR EXISTENCE HERE.
AS FAR AS YOU KNOW, THIS IS REALITY. BUT BELIEVE ME...

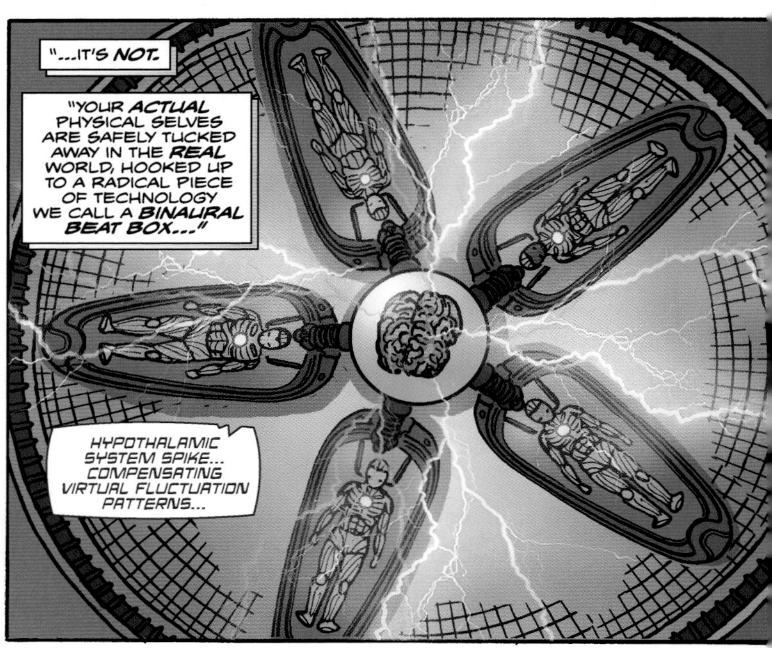
"...IT'S NOT.
"YOUR ACTUAL PHYSICAL SELVES ARE SAFELY TUCKED AWAY IN THE REAL WORLD, HOOKED UP TO A RADICAL PIECE OF TECHNOLOGY WE CALL A BINAURAL BEAT BOX..."
HYPOTHALAMIC SYSTEM SPIKE... COMPENSATING VIRTUAL FLUCTUATION PATTERNS...

...IN OTHER WORDS, THINK OF YOUR EXISTENCE HERE AS SOMETHING AKIN TO A WAKING DREAM.
YOU TALKIN' SOME SMACK THERE, BRUTHA...!
I-I...THINK I NEED TO GET BACK TO MY FRY STATION...

I DON'T... UNDERSTAND WHAT HE MEANS...
HE MEANS... OUR WHOLE LIVES ARE ONE BIG LIE!
HA! BUNCHA BULL, IF YA ASK ME...!

OF COURSE YOU THINK THAT, ELVIS. WE MADE SURE YOU WOULDN'T QUESTION YOUR SURROUNDINGS.
THIS IS ABOUT CONTROL.
I RECRUITED EACH AND EVERY ONE OF YOU TO BE AN AGENT OF CHANGE. I HAD BIG PLANS FOR YOU.
UNFORTUNATELY, YOU WEREN'T EXACTLY PLAYING BALL...SO WE TOOK YOU OFF THE GRID IN HOPES OF RECONDITIONING YOU...

...LET'S HOPE THIS TIME, YOU GET WITH THE PROGRAM.
WHATEVER.
YOU'RE GONNA HAVE TO BE MORE CONVINCING THAN THAT. NOW, I GOTTA GO SWAB THE WOMEN'S HEAD...

LISTEN, I'M JUST EASING YOU ALL IN. IDENTITY REENTRY CAN BE A BIT OF A SHOCK.
I GUESS THERE'S NO SENSE IN DRAGGING IT OUT...

ACCELERATING HIPPOCAMPUS AMPERAGE...
OKAY, THAT'S OUR CUE.
PREPPING INFO LOAD...

...THESE GUYS ARE ABOUT TO REMEMBER EXACTLY WHO THEY ARE.
...UPLOADING SELF-SYSTEM PACKAGES...

"LOOK, AROUND HERE, I'M JUST THE..."
...CLEANUP... GUY...?
JEEZUS.

OH MY GOD...I-I... REMEMBER...
WHAT THE HELL HAPPENED TO ME...?!
TO ALL OF US, WOLF--!
DO YOURSELF A FAVOR. JUST TAKE A MOMENT...

...JUST LET YOUR TRUE IDENTITIES BACK IN.
TAKE IT SLOW.

IT HAPPENS SUDDENLY...THE EMERGING AWARENESS THAT THEY ARE AGENTS OF CHANGE!
WOLFHUNTER! RUBY! ELVIS WARMAKER! REBEL!
THEY DON'T TAKE THE NEWS WELL...
DAMN, BERT--!
YOU'RE THE ONE WHO AMBUSHED US!
AND YOU STUCK US IN FAST FOOD HELL?!
YOU'VE GOT BALLS, SUIT...
...IF I WERE YOU, THERE'S NO WAY I WOULD'VE BROUGHT US BACK!

LISTEN... YOU WENT OFF THE RESERVATION!
I HAVE TO GET YOU BACK ON TRACK FOR YOUR ACTUAL PURPOSE...

...YOU PEOPLE HAVE A SPECIFIC JOB TO DO!
WHATEVER! I AIN'T DOWN WITH BEING ANYONE'S PAWN!
I KNEW THIS WAS A BLACK-BOX JOB--!

CALM DOWN.
I'M OFFERING TO PUT YOU GUYS ON THE FRONT LINES OF A NEW REALITY. A HOME FOR THE BEST AND THE BRIGHTEST THAT HUMANITY HAS TO OFFER.
WE'VE FINALLY BROKEN THROUGH TO THE NEXT PLANE OF EXISTENCE, AND WE NEED GUARDIANS AT THE GATE.

THAT'S YOUR IDEA OF "CHANGE," HUH?!
A VIRTUAL REALITY COUNTRY CLUB?!
YOU REALLY WANT TO FRONT, REBEL...?
SOMEWHERE A BUTTON IS PRESSED--

--WELCOME TO A WORLD OF CAUSE AND EFFECT!
HOLY CHRIST--
--MECHA?!
MEGABUG
NOT AGAIN--!
THIS IS A WEAK PLAY!
MAYBE IT'S THE ONLY ONE HE'S GOT...!
SPEAKING OF WHICH--
--WHERE THE HELL DID BERT DISAPPEAR TO?!
THAT SNEAKY SONUVABITCH--!
ELEVATING MULTIPLE RESPONSE MODES: 38.55%...
THEY'RE BEING INCREDIBLY UNCOOPERATIVE.
DID YOU HAVE SOMETHING ELSE IN MIND, SIR...?
WELL, THEY'VE CLEARLY BONDED AS A TEAM, TO SOME DEGREE.
BUT I MADE THAT TEAM...

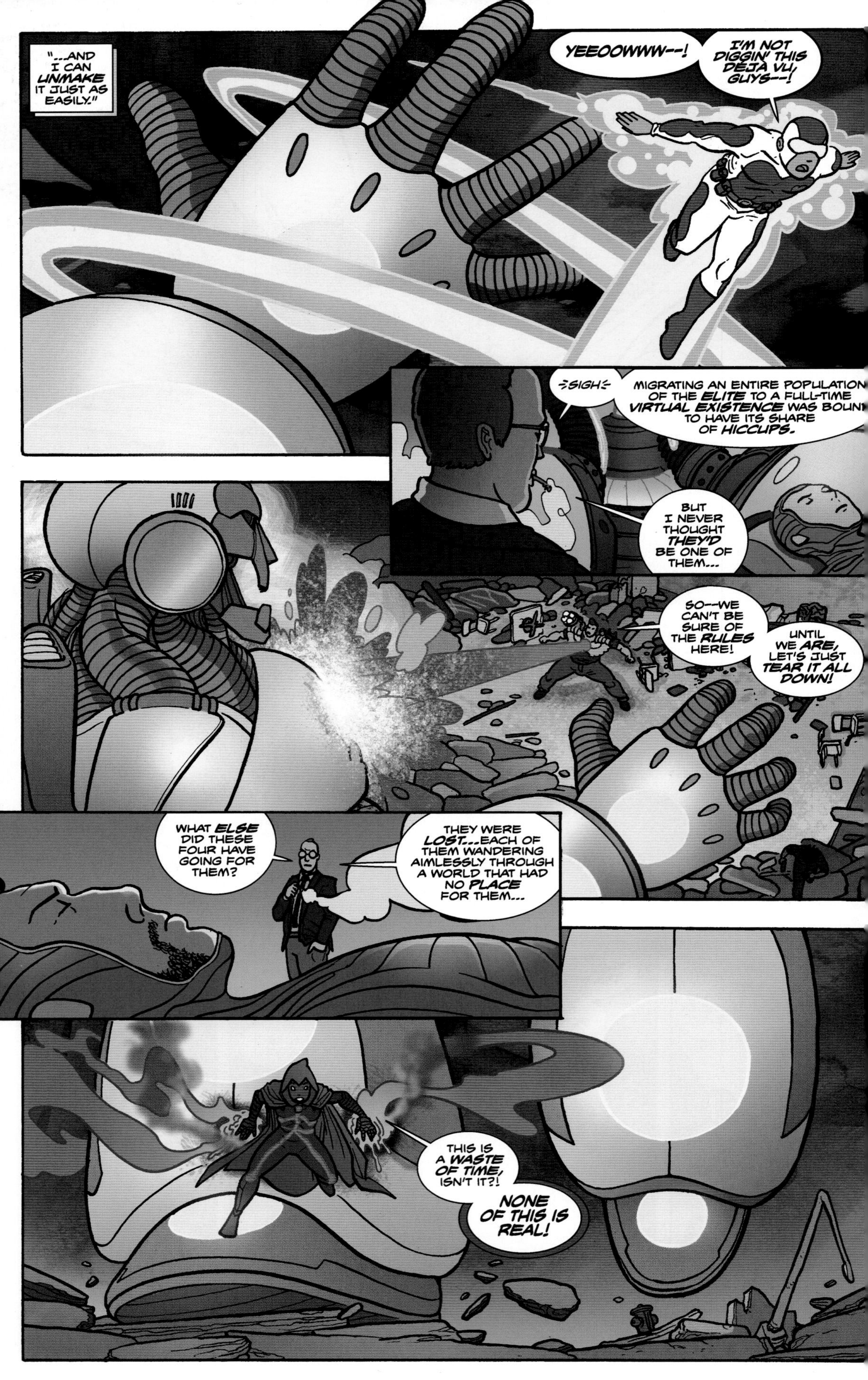
"...AND I CAN UNMAKE IT JUST AS EASILY."
YEEOOWWW--!
I'M NOT DIGGIN' THIS DEJA VU, GUYS--!
=SIGH=
MIGRATING AN ENTIRE POPULATION OF THE ELITE TO A FULL-TIME VIRTUAL EXISTENCE WAS BOUND TO HAVE ITS SHARE OF HICCUPS.
BUT I NEVER THOUGHT THEY'D BE ONE OF THEM...
SO--WE CAN'T BE SURE OF THE RULES HERE!
UNTIL WE ARE, LET'S JUST TEAR IT ALL DOWN!
WHAT ELSE DID THESE FOUR HAVE GOING FOR THEM?
THEY WERE LOST...EACH OF THEM WANDERING AIMLESSLY THROUGH A WORLD THAT HAD NO PLACE FOR THEM...
THIS IS A WASTE OF TIME, ISN'T IT?!
NONE OF THIS IS REAL!

THEY COULD'VE BEEN A NEW TYPE OF HERO...THEY COULD'VE STOOD FOR SOMETHING...
NOW WE HAVE TO SHOW THEM WHAT'S AT STAKE HERE...

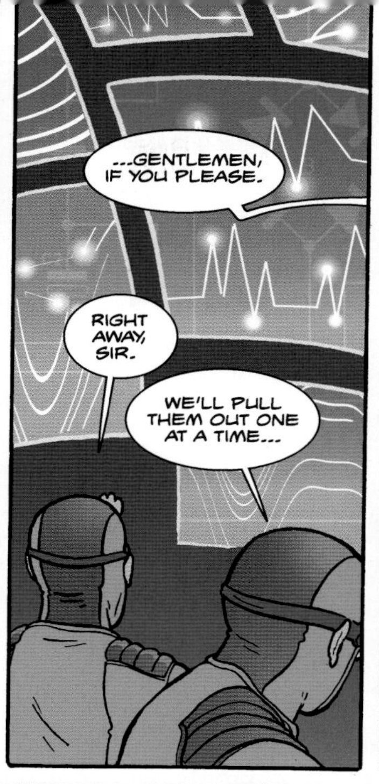
...GENTLEMEN, IF YOU PLEASE.
RIGHT AWAY, SIR.
WE'LL PULL THEM OUT ONE AT A TIME...

WOLFHUNTER-- LOADED FOR BEAR!
AWWW YEAH!
THIS MAY BE WRONG, BUT IT FEELS SO--

--RIGHT...?!
RIGHT AWAY, IT'S A TINGLE OF RECOGNITION--
--FOLLOWED BY ANOTHER HARSH REALITY!
HUHHNDT!

THIS LOOKS JUST LIKE...

...STEEL HARBOR...!

OH DAMN...

HE WAS RAISED ON THESE STREETS. THEY WERE HIS INSPIRATION. HIS WELLSPRING OF SPIRIT.

SEEING IT PLUNGED INTO COMPLETE CHAOS... DESCENDED INTO THE HELL HE ALWAYS FEARED IT MIGHT--

--IS TOO MUCH FOR ANY FAVORITE SON TO TAKE!
NOOOOO--!

SCATTERING SIGNAL RATIOS...
OKAY. WE'VE GOT THEM SEPARATED AND ISOLATED...
NOT TO MENTION, KEYED INTO THEIR INDIVIDUAL PSYCHE PROFILES...
EXCELLENT...

"...NOW LET'S SEE HOW THEY FARE AGAINST THEIR OWN PERSONAL ISSUES."
WHOA.
THIS IS SERIOUSLY DIFFERENT--
TIME TO TAKE YOUR MEDICATIO MR. MORRISETTE

...NOW, IF YOU WON'T TAKE IT ORALLY, WE'LL ADMINISTER IT IN SOME OTHER WAY.
BUT I DON'T THINK YOU'LL LIKE IT.
ARE YOU KIDDING...?!
YOU CAN'T KEEP ME HERE--

--HNNGGG!
T-TOO WEAK...
BUT... WHY...?!
THERE ARE SOME INSTANCES WHERE PUBLIC RELATIONS ARE USELESS!

ONCE I PULL THEM BACK FROM THE ABYSS... MAYBE THEY'LL UNDERSTAND...
...THIS WORLD OF FLESH IS WAY TOO FRAGILE TO LIVE IN.

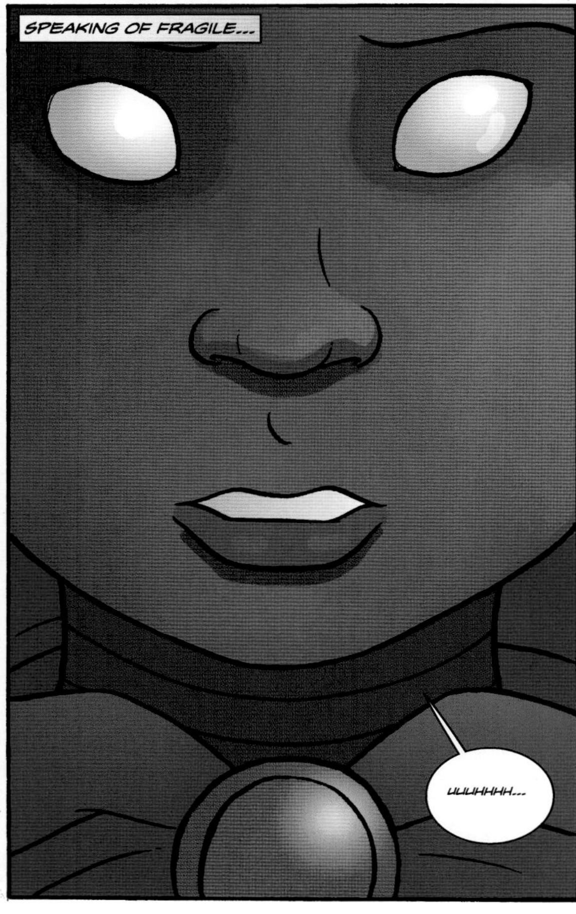
SPEAKING OF FRAGILE...
UUUHHHH...

...HOW DID I GET HERE...?
NO...NO... NO...
I'M... COMPLETELY ALONE...
OH GOD...
HIDDEN NEUROSES ABOUND--

--THE BLADES STAB DEEP!
UH...?
OKAY...

...THIS IS NEW.
SUPER BIG DOPE
THE SMELL OF FRESH-CUT GRASS. THE SOUND OF EARLY EVENING INSECTS. THE GENTLE BREEZE OF SUBURBIA...
IT'S ALL COMPLETELY REAL...

...A SPECIFIC KIND OF HELL...
DAD! DAD! IT WASN'T ME!
DON'T LISTEN TO HIM, DAD--
SUPER

--BILLY TOOK MONEY FROM YOUR WALLET!
HE BOUGHT CIGARETTES--
--SKIPPED SCHOOL AND SMOKED OUT WITH HIS SCUMBAG FRIENDS!
I DID NOT! DAD-- THEY'RE TOTAL LIARS!
?!
WHO THE HELL ARE YOU FUGGIN' PEOPLE?!
DON'T TRY TO WEASEL OUT OF IT, BIG E--

--OUR KIDS ARE HALF YOURS, Y'KNOW...!
NOW WASH YOUR HANDS, WILLYA? YOU SMELL LIKE GARBAGE!
UPSTAIRS TOILET'S CLOGGED, TOO...

...EITHER CALL A PLUMBER OR FIX IT YOURSELF!
BERT!
YOU BASTAAAARRRDDD!

MIGRATING ICONIC... ECHOIC...HAPTIC PLATFORMS...
I'M SURE IT'S NOT EASY FACING YOUR DEEPEST, DARKEST FEARS ABOUT YOURSELF.
BUT YOU'LL DAMN SURE APPRECIATE A LIFE WITHOUT THEM...

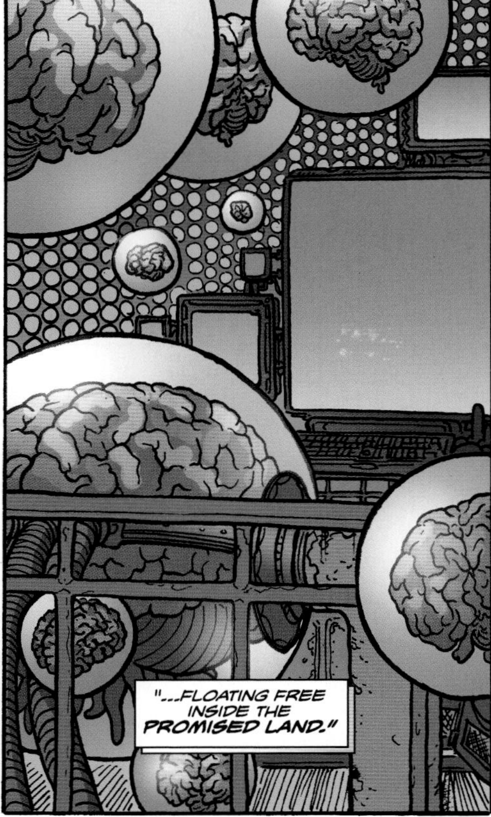
"...FLOATING FREE INSIDE THE PROMISED LAND."

SO LET THEM STEW FOR A WHILE.
I'LL BE BACK WHEN THEIR RESOLVE HAS SOFTENED A LITTLE MORE.
YES, SIR.
SYMPATHY FOR THE DEVIL, EH...?
IN THIS CASE, NOT SO MUCH, NO...
...I WANT TO MAKE SURE I'VE GOT MY SEAT ON THE BIG RIDE TOO.
ALL HAIL THE GRAND SCHEME.
EVERY "I" DOTTED. EVERY "T" CROSSED. ALL PERTINENT DETAILS ACCOUNTED FOR.
CREATED WITH CLOCKWORK PRECISION...EACH OF THE MYRIAD COMPONENTS AIMED TOWARD A SINGLE PURPOSE...
THE OTHER MORRISETTE BROTHER ("NON-REBEL" AT THE MOMENT).
THESE COMPLEXITIES CAN OFTEN OBSCURE A SIMPLE TRUTH...
SOMETIMES, EVEN THE BEST LAID PLANS--
--CAN BE SUBJECT TO UNEXPECTED CHANGE.

YOU MIGHT NOT BE AWARE...THERE IS A DARK SIDE TO CHOCOLATE.
NASTIE MAY BE THE LARGEST FOOD COMPANY IN THE WORLD MEASURED BY REVENUE, BUT THEY ALSO PURCHASE COCOA BEANS FROM IVORIAN PLANTATIONS THAT USE CHILD SLAVE LABOR.

UNTIL NOW, NASTIE C.E.O. CURTIS HAYNES HAD NO REAL OPINION ON THAT FACT...
I GUESS BEING THE BOSS HAS ITS PERKS...
...BUT ACCOUNTABILITY PROBABLY ISN'T ONE OF THEM.
FRANK WELLS USES A BIG WORD!

YOU HAVE KIDS, MR. HAYNES...?
HOW WOULD YOU FEEL IF THEY WERE SOLD INTO SLAVERY?
NFF
GK--!
MAYBE WE SHOULD FIND OUT--
YOU'RE SO GRIM...

...I KNOW I POINTED YOU IN THIS DIRECTION, BUT NOT TO PROVE YOUR TRUE GRIT.
LOOK AT THAT FAT FACE...
BABA LAMA!
THIS IS NASTIE'S CHIEF EXECUTIVE OFFICER! THE MAN IN CHARGE!

HUH.
YOU REALLY BELIEVE THAT...?
ARE YOU GOING TO MENACE EVERY NASTIE STOCKHOLDER NEXT...?
THE BALLAD OF FRANK WELLS: THE MIRROR OF TERRIBLE TRUTHS

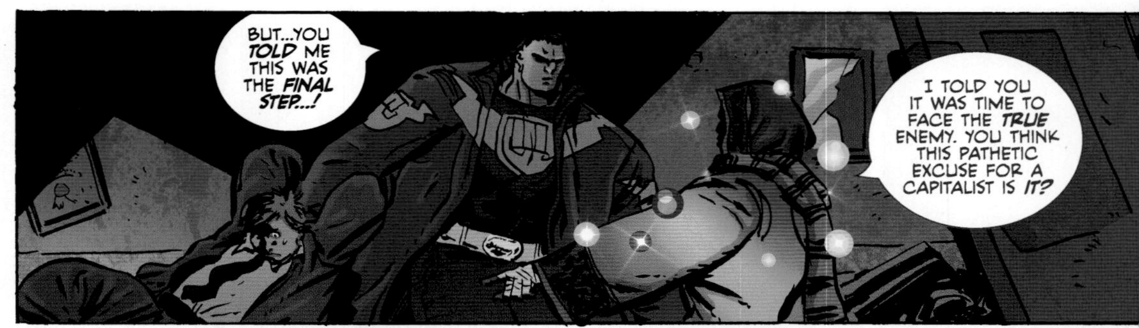
BUT...YOU TOLD ME THIS WAS THE FINAL STEP...!
I TOLD YOU IT WAS TIME TO FACE THE TRUE ENEMY. YOU THINK THIS PATHETIC EXCUSE FOR A CAPITALIST IS IT?

I DON'T UNDERSTAND...
WELL, THAT'S WHY I'M HERE. BUT FIRST THINGS FIRST. THIS VENDETTA AGAINST NASTIE IS STILL A SHORTSIGHTED ENDEAVOR.
BESIDES, THE COCOA IS ONLY ONE ATROCITY. THEY ALSO SELL WATER AT EXORBITANT PRICES...

...THEIR FROZEN DINNERS CONTAIN HORSE MEAT...
THOSE ALLEGATIONS...ARE C-COMPLETELY BASELESS! NASTIE VALUES CORPORATE RESPONSIBILITY!
J-JUST... LOOK AT OUR WEBSITE...!

BUT IT SEEMS SO SIMPLE! IF I JUST TAKE THIS WASTE OF SPACE AND--
AND WHAT?
GYAH--!
YOU WANT MORE BLOOD ON YOUR HANDS? AND THERE'D ONLY BE A LINE OF WEASELS SCURRYING UP BEHIND HIM TO TAKE HIS PLACE...!

THIS IS NOT BEING ENLIGHTENED...!
YOU'VE BEEN SO CONCERNED WITH THE EXTERNAL FORCES THAT SHAPE YOUR WORLD, SO MUCH SO THAT IT'S COME TO THIS...

...BUT THE DEEPER TRUTH CAN ONLY BE FOUND FIRST WITHIN ONESELF.
NOW LET'S BAIL.
BUT LEAVE THE CORPORATE FAT CAT.
IT DOESN'T TAKE MUCH CONVINCING...

...TO RETURN TO THE FABLED TIBETAN PLATEAU.

BUT THIS IS NO SIMPLE RECAPITULATION OF WHAT YOU MIGHT'VE READ BEFORE...
I'M NOT HERE TO LEAD YOU DOWN A PRIMROSE PATH, FRANK. NOR DO I BELIEVE YOU WANT TO WALK ONE.

I WANT... TO BE EFFECTIVE. TO MAKE A REAL DIFFERENCE.
THINGS AREN'T TOO FAR GONE, ARE THEY...?
THAT'S NOT FOR ME TO SAY...

...I CAN ONLY TRY TO PROVIDE PERSPECTIVE. FROM THAT, YOU MAY GLEAN A BIT OF WISDOM.
IN ANY CASE, THIS HAS PROVED TO BE AN EFFECTIVE TECHNIQUE TO ACHIEVE BOTH GOALS.

IT'S...JUST A MIRROR...
I-I DON'T SEE HOW THIS IS GOING TO--
LOOK INTO IT, FRANK.
LOOK LONG AND HARD...

OKAY, BUT I DON'T REALLY SEE THE POINT...
I MEAN, IT'S ME.
JUST ME...

PERHAPS YOU'RE NOT SEEING WHAT'S ACTUALLY BEING REFLECTED BACK AT YOU.
BUT I GUARANTEE YOU... IF YOU DON'T LOOK AWAY, THINGS WILL EVENTUALLY BE REVEALED TO YOU.

FINE. THEN I'LL KEEP...
...LOOKING...
AND THEN IT HAPPENS...

...YOU TRAVEL ALONG THE THREADS OF YOUR OWN JOURNEY, SKIPPING **SIDEWAYS** THROUGH TIME WITHIN YOUR MIND LIKE A POLISHED STONE ACROSS A TRANQUIL SEA. BUT NEVER COMING TO A COMPLETE **REST.**

AND IT DOESN'T TAKE LONG TO ENCOUNTER THAT SAME OL' **TURBULENCE,** DOES IT? THE SAME KIND YOU'VE EXPERIENCED YOUR ENTIRE LIFE (SUCH AS IT IS)...

...YOU'VE NEVER FELT REAL **FREEDOM,** HAVE YOU? EVEN THE SENSATION OF **FLIGHT** IS NOT ENOUGH TO BREAK THE BONDS THAT HAVE HELD YOU CAPTIVE FOR SO LONG. THERE WAS ALWAYS A CERTAIN **WEIGHT** YOU CARRIED AROUND WITH YOU IN ALL OF YOUR TRAVELS...PRESSING DOWN...**CRUSHING** YOU...

...STAMPING OUT ANY SENSE OF **PURITY** YOU MIGHT'VE HOPED FOR IN YOUR LIFE. YOUR GREAT STRENGTH WAS **USELESS** AGAINST IT. AND THERE HAS BEEN **NO ESCAPING** IT...IT HAS BECOME SUCH AN INTEGRAL PART OF WHO YOU **ARE...**

...IT HAS **HYPNOTIZED** YOU. IT HAS REDUCED YOU TO SOMETHING MUCH **LESS** THAN YOUR FULL POTENTIAL. IT HAS TRICKED YOU INTO **THINKING** YOU ARE **ONE** THING...AND NOT **ANOTHER...**

...IT HAS MADE YOU A **VICTIM.** IT HAS CREATED A **REALITY** IN YOUR MIND WHERE YOU FOUGHT THE **DRAGON--** AND **LOST.** ONCE AND FOR ALL, THE **VORTEX** CHURNING UP EACH AND EVERY **INSECURITY** LOCKED INSIDE OF YOU...

ACCEPT THE RESPONSIBILITY FOR YOUR ACTIONS--AS I HAVE.

IT WAS YOUR FEAR THAT CAUSED YOUR PAIN.

IT'S ALL YOUR FAULT.

YOU KNOW ALL ABOUT **PAIN,** DON'T YOU? FOR SO LONG...IT'S WHAT **DEFINED** YOU. IT'S WHAT YOU CARRIED WITHIN YOUR OWN, FIERY **HEART...**

...AND THEN THERE WAS THE **END OF THE WORLD**. NOT A **RANDOM** OCCURRENCE...NOT COMPLETELY **UNEXPECTED**...BUT STILL TERRIFYING IN ITS **SUDDENNESS**...

THERE WAS A MOMENT OF **PARALYSIS**, WASN'T THERE? HIDDEN FROM THE WORLD, BUT YOU CERTAINLY **FELT** IT.

ULTIMATELY, YOU DON'T KNOW **WHAT** DROVE YOU TO CONFRONT THE MADNESS THAT HAD DESCENDED UPON YOUR WORLD...

...MAYBE YOU **KNEW** THAT YOU WERE **DESTINED** TO ENGAGE THIS UNENDING, UNHOLY SPAWN--**NIBIRU**--AND, IN **FACING** THIS BEAST, YOUR KNOWLEDGE OF **SELF** WOULD SOMEHOW BENEFIT.

INSTEAD, YOU WERE PRESENTED WITH **MORE** NIGHTMARES...SUDDEN, PARALLEL DIMENSIONS OF DEEP DEMENTIA THAT ARE MEANT TO PERMANENTLY SCAR YOUR PSYCHE. SO MANY **MULTIVERSAL VISIONS**...

CAR WAS

YET, YOU SAW AN **OPENING**...AND YOU **TOOK** IT...

A FULL-TILT **POWER DIVE** INTO **INSANITY'S** GAPING MAW. A FLEETING MOMENT OF **HEROIC SACRIFICE**...

...BUT WITHIN THE FIERY BLOODSTREAM OF THE BEAST, FENDING OFF THE PRIMAL MADNESS LOCATED THERE AND FIGHTING HIS OWN, PRIVATE WAR, HE WAS SURE HE FELT AN ECHO OF SOMETHING STRANGELY FAMILIAR...
...IT WAS NO VISION THIS TIME. IT HAD THE DISTINCTLY RESONANT RING OF REALITY TO IT. IT HAD FORM...IT SUGGESTED FUNCTION...
...NOW, WITHIN THIS REFLECTION--THIS REPEAT OF EVENTS LONG PAST--HE DOES WHAT HE DIDN'T DO THEN...HE LOOKS MORE CLOSELY AT WHAT THIS SUDDEN VARIABLE COULD POSSIBLY BE...
...AND THE ANSWER AMAZES HIM!
THERE IS NO RATIONAL RESPONSE TO THE FACTS! THERE IS ONLY THE REACTION OF SOMEONE WHO HAS UNAVOIDABLY CRASHED INTO HIMSELF...AND HAS FINALLY SEEN HIMSELF FOR WHAT HE TRULY IS IN THIS CONTEXT...
...JUST ANOTHER PATHETIC CREATURE, DEVOID OF GRACE!

SALVATION REPLAYS ITSELF... ONLY HIS ROLE HAS CHANGED.
HE IS NO LONGER A CATALYST.
MERELY A WITNESS.
SO NOW YOU KNOW THE TERRIBLE TRUTH.
BUT WHAT DOES IT MATTER...?
DO YOU SOMEHOW FEEL DIFFERENTLY...?
Y-YOU DON'T UNDERSTAND...IT WASN'T ME...IT WAS NEVER ME...
...I DIDN'T... SAVE ANYTHING...
...SHE DID...!
THERE ARE HEROES ON ALL SIDES OF THE EQUATION, FRANK.
THE END OF THE WORLD WAS CANCELED. SO BE IT. YOU STILL REMAIN TO TAKE IT FORWARD.
NOW GET UP.
THAT WAS THE LAST TIME YOU'LL EVER BE ON YOUR KNEES.
YOUR FINAL TEST STILL AWAITS YOU. ONE MORE THRESHOLD TO CROSS. STEP OUTSIDE OF THE BOUNDARIES THAT HAVE ALWAYS BOXED YOU IN.
NO MORE PRO WRESTLING. NO MORE HOT SPOT HOPSCOTCH. THE TRUE POLITICS OF SUPERHEROES IS READY TO ROLL...
...AND, UNLIKE BEFORE, THE OUTCOME IS ENTIRELY UP TO YOU.
OKAY...
...I THINK I'M READY TO MOVE THE NEEDLE.
FOR REAL THIS TIME.

THIS TRIP IS WAY BEYOND DÉJÀ VU.

IT DIDN'T FEEL LIKE THIS BEFORE.

AND THE ARRIVAL WASN'T NEARLY THIS VIOLENT...!

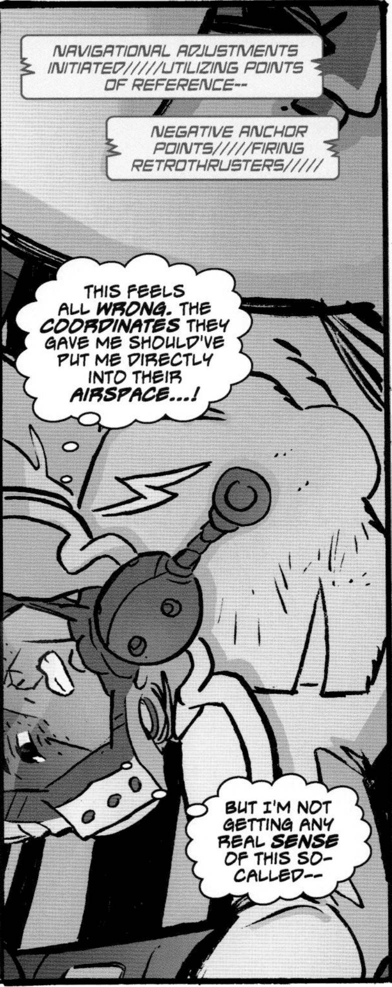
NAVIGATIONAL ADJUSTMENTS INITIATED/////UTILIZING POINTS OF REFERENCE--
NEGATIVE ANCHOR POINTS/////FIRING RETROTHRUSTERS/////
THIS FEELS ALL WRONG. THE COORDINATES THEY GAVE ME SHOULD'VE PUT ME DIRECTLY INTO THEIR AIRSPACE...!
BUT I'M NOT GETTING ANY REAL SENSE OF THIS SO-CALLED--

--"SEPTENARIUS"...

HER QUADRILATERAL TELEPORTATION ABILITIES--GENERATED FROM SOMEWHERE DEEP AND MYSTERIOUS WITHIN HER OWN AMAZING D.N.A.--HAVE ONCE AGAIN BROUGHT HER TO THE OUTER REACHES OF THE UNIVERSE! ONCE AGAIN SHE HAS ARRIVED TO BRING THE FIGHT TO THE ENEMY!
THIS IS WHERE SHE MAKES HER STAND AGAINST THE REAVER SWARM!
FOR EARTH! FOR HUMANITY! FOR THE FUTURE!
AMAZING GRACE: SWARM IF YOU WANT TO

OKAY...WHAT THE HELL AM I DEALING WITH HERE...?
SCANNING LOCALIZED QUADRANTS//////

SYSTEM FAILURE//////
CROSS-REFERENCING////// LIFE FORMS RESISTANT TO ANALYSIS//////
OFFENSIVE OPTIONS: UNABLE TO COLLATE//////

ACHILLES PROGRAM: FAILED//////
SO MUCH FOR TRYING TO KEEP MY DISTANCE...!

THEY SAY THERE IS NO SOUND IN SPACE.
BUT SHE WOULD SWEAR SHE HEARS SOMETHING...

...THE SOUND OF THE UNKNOWN.
A SCREAMING CHORUS OF DEATH.

SHE CAME HERE TO ESTABLISH A **BEACHHEAD**... HOPING TO NEUTRALIZE AN ALIEN THREAT **BEFORE** IT REACHED HER PLANET...

...BUT **THIS** THREAT ATTACKS ON **MULTIPLE FRONTS**. THE **PHYSICAL**... THE **PSYCHOLOGICAL**...

...THE **SPIRITUAL**...

STUCK IN THE PRIMORDIAL SOUP OF THE COSMOS...

...SHE IS, HERSELF, INVADED BY THE SWARM...

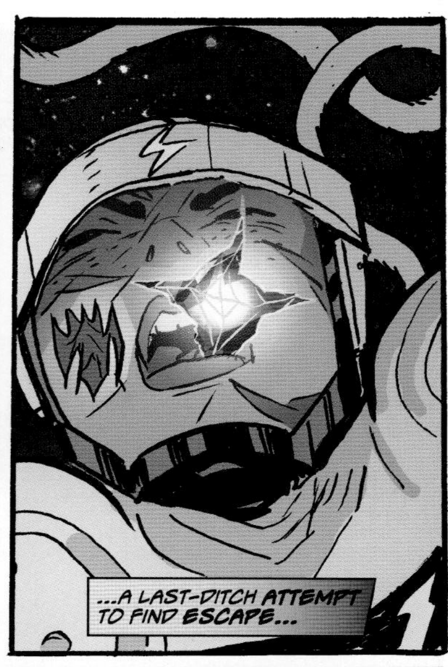
...A LAST-DITCH ATTEMPT TO FIND ESCAPE...

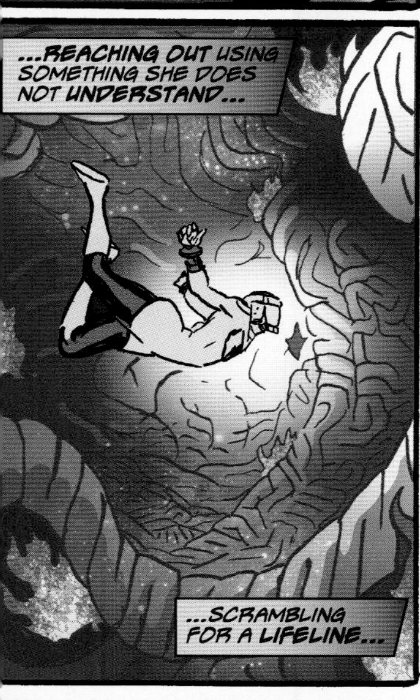
...REACHING OUT USING SOMETHING SHE DOES NOT UNDERSTAND...
...SCRAMBLING FOR A LIFELINE...

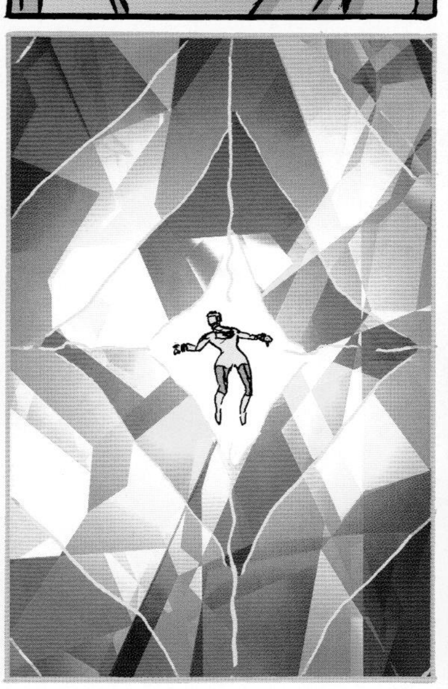

...THOUGHTS OF HOME ARE A MOMENTARY SOLACE...
...THE NOTION THAT SOMEWHERE, LIFE IS STILL NORMAL...

THE POPULATION OF GOLDEN CITY HAS NOT OFTEN INVOLVED ITSELF IN THE AFFAIRS OF THEIR GUARDIAN...

...UNTIL NOW.
OH, WOW...

...IS THAT...?
SHE DOESN'T DARE SPEAK THE NAME OUT LOUD.
JUST IN CASE...

I SEE HER! I DO!
RIGHT THERE!
HOLY CRAP...!
I KNEW SHE HADN'T ABANDONED US...

HOW MANY ECHOES DID SHE SEND OUT INTO THE VOID... A LAST-DITCH ATTEMPT AT HUMAN CONNECTION--
--BUT TO WHAT END?
UUHHH--!

BUT THAT'S HAPPENING ACROSS THE UNIVERSE. WHILE, HERE AT HOME...
I'D LIKE TO THINK WE'RE ALL IN AGREEMENT HERE...

...SHE'S BEEN GONE FOR MONTHS NOW. NO SIGNAL... NO SIGN...
WELL, WHAT EXACTLY WERE YOU EXPECTING, TYRONE?! IT'S NOT LIKE SHE'S OUT OF THE COUNTRY--!
WE'VE HAD OUR TECHS MONITORING HER TELEMETRY AS BEST THEY CAN, AND EVEN THEY SAY--
WE GOT SOMETHING--

--NOT ACCOUNTING FOR SUBSPACE DISTANCING... MEANING WE DON'T KNOW WHEN IT HAPPENED, BUT WE CAN CONFIRM--
--HER TRANSPORT'S GONE COMPLETELY OFFLINE!
OUR CONSENSUS: IT WAS DESTROYED!

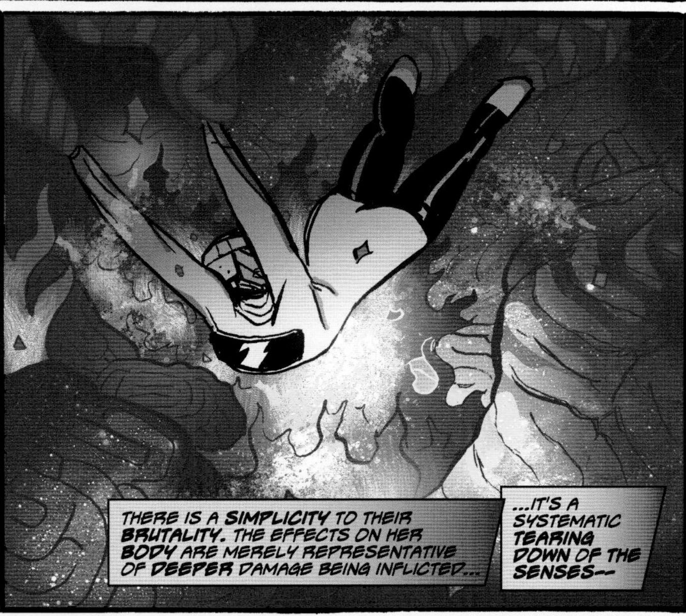
THERE IS A SIMPLICITY TO THEIR BRUTALITY. THE EFFECTS ON HER BODY ARE MERELY REPRESENTATIVE OF DEEPER DAMAGE BEING INFLICTED...
...IT'S A SYSTEMATIC TEARING DOWN OF THE SENSES--

--LEAVING NOTHING BUT PURE TERROR!

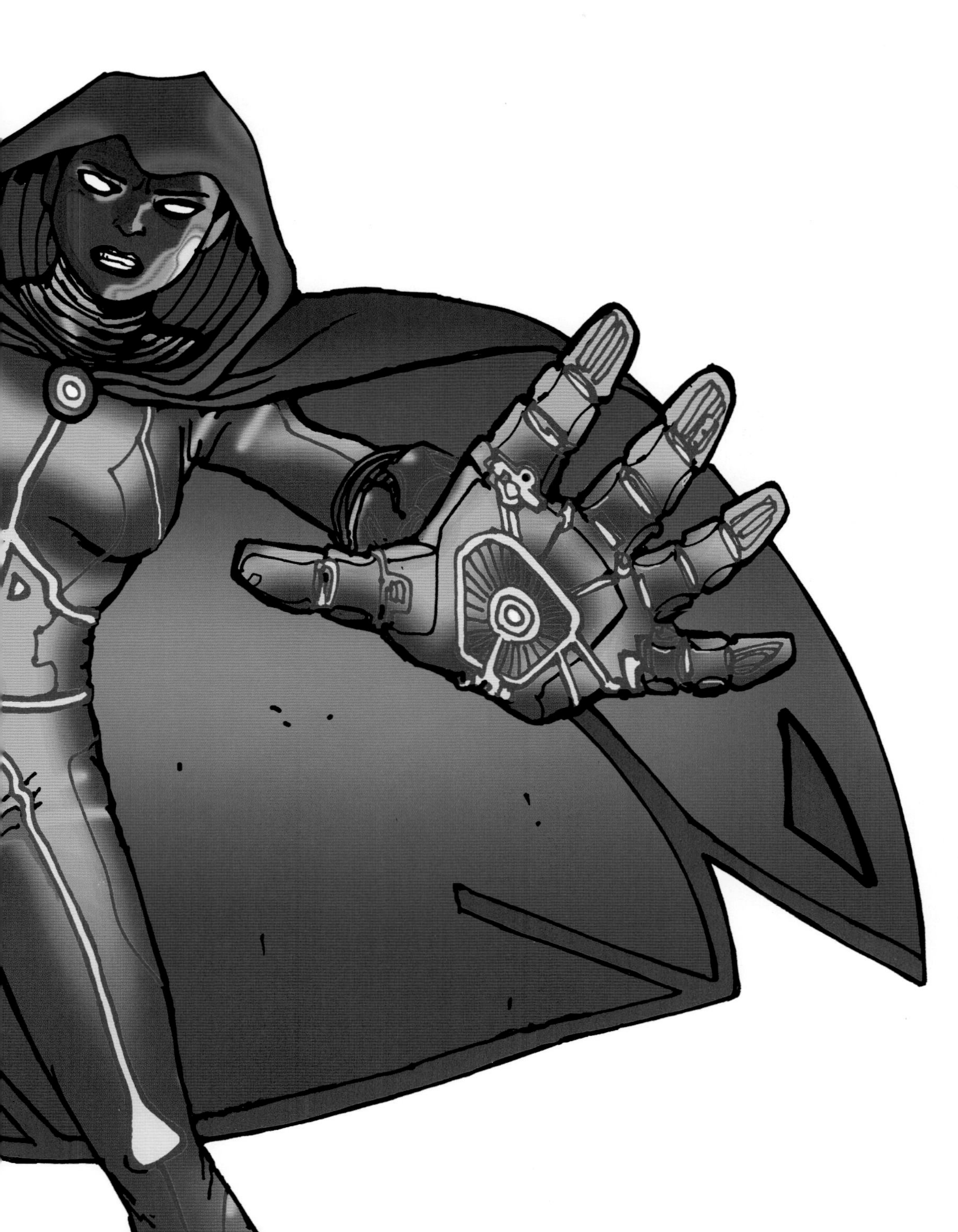

WAS THERE EVER ANY DOUBT THAT A GUY LIKE BERT WOULD EXCEL AT PUBLIC SPEAKING...?

TECHNOLOGY, ENTERTAINMENT, AND DESIGN...THERE'S ONLY ONE PLACE WHERE THESE ALL TRULY CONVERGE.

NOW, I WANT YOU ALL TO KNOW... THIS TALK IS NOT GOING OUT OVER THE INTERNET.

IN OTHER WORDS, THIS INFORMATION IS NOT MEANT FOR EVERYONE.

TED

I'M HERE TO TALK ABOUT A UNIQUE OPPORTUNITY... ONE THAT APPLIES ONLY TO THE MOST ELITE OF WORLD CITIZENS.
WE ALL REMEMBER WHAT HAPPENED IN NEW YORK, DON'T WE? BUT WHAT YOU WEREN'T TOLD ABOUT THAT HORRIFIC EVENT...

...WAS THAT THE ENTIRE PLANET WAS ON THE BRINK OF THE APOCALYPSE.
WHO KNOWS HOW OR WHY WE PULLED OURSELVES AWAY FROM THAT BRINK...

...BUT IT'S NOT SOMETHING I'D WANT TO RISK AGAIN.
NOW, I'M SURE YOU'RE ALL SAYING TO YOURSELVES, "LIFE ON EARTH IS RISK. IT'S UNAVOIDABLE."
UP UNTIL NOW, THAT WAS TRUE.

BUT WHAT IF I TOLD YOU THE REAL TRUTH OF OUR COLLECTIVE EXISTENCE HAD LESS TO DO WITH THE PHYSICAL WORLD YOU EXPERIENCE EVERY DAY...

"...AND MORE WITH A NEW WORLD THAT CAN BE CREATED USING THE ENERGY OF OUR OWN MINDS?"

AGENTS OF CHANGE: LEVEL UP

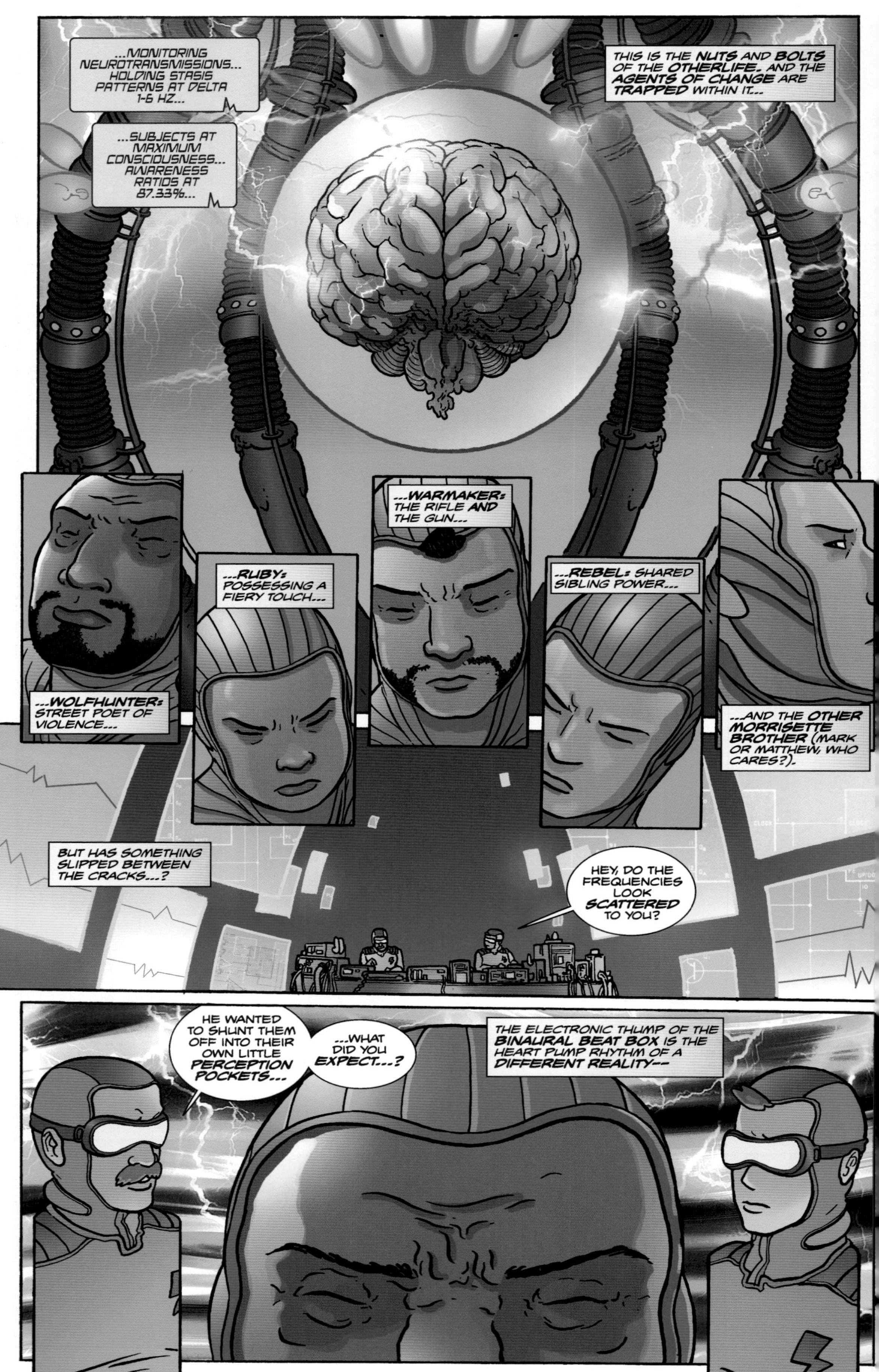

...MONITORING NEUROTRANSMISSIONS... HOLDING STASIS PATTERNS AT DELTA 1-6 HZ...
...SUBJECTS AT MAXIMUM CONSCIOUSNESS... AWARENESS RATIOS AT 87.33%...
THIS IS THE NUTS AND BOLTS OF THE OTHERLIFE. AND THE AGENTS OF CHANGE ARE TRAPPED WITHIN IT...
...WOLFHUNTER: STREET POET OF VIOLENCE...
...RUBY: POSSESSING A FIERY TOUCH...
...WARMAKER: THE RIFLE AND THE GUN...
...REBEL: SHARED SIBLING POWER...
...AND THE OTHER MORRISETTE BROTHER (MARK OR MATTHEW, WHO CARES?).
BUT HAS SOMETHING SLIPPED BETWEEN THE CRACKS...?
HEY, DO THE FREQUENCIES LOOK SCATTERED TO YOU?
HE WANTED TO SHUNT THEM OFF INTO THEIR OWN LITTLE PERCEPTION POCKETS...
...WHAT DID YOU EXPECT...?
THE ELECTRONIC THUMP OF THE BINAURAL BEAT BOX IS THE HEART PUMP RHYTHM OF A DIFFERENT REALITY--

--AND WOLFHUNTER'S BEEN DROPPED INTO ONE!
NO WAY...

THE SIGHTS, THE SOUNDS, THE SMELLS... IT'S ALL TOO REAL!
...THIS AIN'T THE STEEL HARBOR I KNOW!
THIS IS... SOME KINDA NIGHTMARE...!

YO, REV! IT'S ME--WOLF! WE GREW UP TOGETHER!
WHAT'RE YOU DOIN', MAN?! YOU DON'T DISRESPECT THE NEIGHBORHOOD--!

DON'T MAKE ME--
--BUST YOU...?
SOMETIMES ALL IT TAKES--

--IS A MOMENT OF PURE UNREALITY!
THE INCONGRUOUS NATURE OF HIS PRESENCE HAS IMMEDIATE EFFECTS.
IT'S MORE THAN A MOMENTARY RIPPLE. THE SUBCONSCIOUS IS STRONG...

...BUT NOT STRONG ENOUGH.

AWWW DAMN...

...AIN'T THIS A BITCH?!

C'MON, NOW--!

THE BIG SWEEP! IT'S QUICK AND (RELATIVELY) PAINLESS...

...WHAT ARE YOU DOING HERE?!

EVERY AGENT HAS HIS OWN EMOTIONAL BEACHHEAD...
BUY ME A NASTIE'S CRUNCH BAR, DADDY!
FOR CHRISSAKES-- DON'T TAKE TOO LONG! I WANNA GET BACK ON THE ROAD!
BUY ME TWO!
YEAH, YEAH, YEAH...
...KILL ME NOW.

THIS IS HELL, ISN'T IT...?
NO WAY OUT...
Jesus saves

SUPER BIG DOPE

HEY, BUDDY...
I DON'T KNOW WHERE YOU'RE HEADED, BUT I WAS WONDERING IF I COULD CATCH A RIDE WITH--
THERE'S AN EASIER WAY OUT, ELVIS...

...LET ME POINT THE WAY.
OH, JEEZUS...!
NOW I KNOW NONE OF THIS IS REAL...!
JACK

FINALLY, ONE LAST PIECE ON THE MINDSCAPE CHESSBOARD...
DAMMIT--!
LEMME GO! LEMME OUTTA THIS NUTHOUSE!
YOU BASTARDS CAN'T DO THIS!
I'M A FAMOUS SUPERHERO!
I DON'T WANT TO HAVE MY BRAIN--
--FRIED...?
IT'S LIKE FINDING RELIGION...
YOU'RE LOOKING WEAK, BROTHER...
...SO LET'S RIDE THIS ROLLER COASTER RIGHT OUT OF HERE.
YOU'RE... NOT...
I AM HE AS YOU ARE HE AS YOU ARE ME AND WE ARE ALL TOGETHER.
T. S. ELIOT SAID THAT...
I'LL LET YOU BE IN MY DREAMS IF I CAN BE IN YOURS...

...I SAID THAT.
AND SOMEONE SAID, "LET THERE BE LIGHT..."

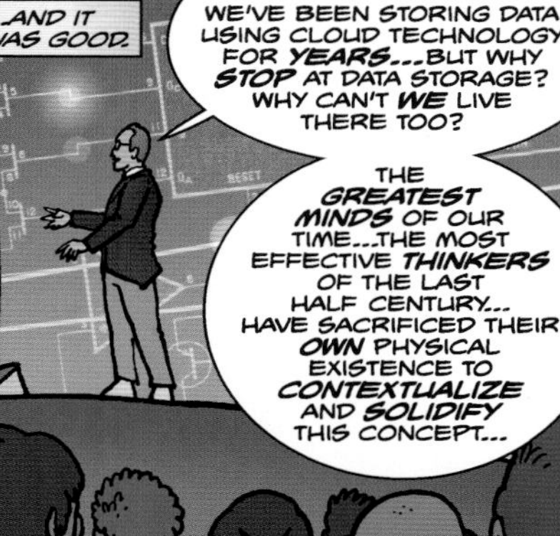
...AND IT WAS GOOD.
WE'VE BEEN STORING DATA USING CLOUD TECHNOLOGY FOR YEARS... BUT WHY STOP AT DATA STORAGE? WHY CAN'T WE LIVE THERE TOO?
THE GREATEST MINDS OF OUR TIME... THE MOST EFFECTIVE THINKERS OF THE LAST HALF CENTURY... HAVE SACRIFICED THEIR OWN PHYSICAL EXISTENCE TO CONTEXTUALIZE AND SOLIDIFY THIS CONCEPT...

...WHICH IS BEING BETA TESTED EVEN AS WE SPEAK.
OCCIPITAL AND TEMPORAL LOBE FUNCTIONS, MANIPULATED BASED ON INDIVIDUALIZED NEEDS AND ORGANIZED VIA OUR PATENTED BINAURAL MECHANISM...

ALERT: GRID FLUCTUATIONS... TRACKING NEOCORTEX PATTERNS...
WHAT THE HELL--?!
I THOUGHT WE HAD A GOOD GRIP ON THESE SUBJECTS...!

THINK AGAIN, TECH HEAD--
--YOU GOT A LOT BIGGER PROBLEMS THAN MEASURIN' OUR BIORHYTHMS OR WHATEVER BERT'S GOT YOU DOIN' HERE...!
OUR TWO-WHEELED TEAMMATE HERE HAS ALREADY CONVINCED US NOT TO SMASH YOUR LITTLE ERECTOR SET...
...MEANWHILE, YOU TWO ARE CLEARLY EXPENDABLE.

BUT BEFORE WE GET TO THAT...
...WHERE IS BERT?
MAKE NO MISTAKE... THIS NEW WORLD EXISTS. WE ARE WORKING TO POPULATE IT RIGHT NOW.
A WORLD SAFE FROM ANY AND ALL THREATS WHICH PLAGUE THIS ONE.
AND FOR A MODEST FEE, YOU CAN LIVE THERE TOO.
CONSIDERING WHAT YOU PAID TO ATTEND THIS FUNCTION, YOU'D BE FIRST ON THE WAITING LIST.
I PROMISE YOU WON'T REGRET IT.
AND THAT'S MY TIME. THANKS FOR LISTENING.
PERHAPS THIS IS AN IDEA WHOSE TIME HAS COME...
...THE ROAR OF THE CROWD FOLLOWS HIM BACKSTAGE.
AS DOES THE SELF-SATISFACTION.
BUT FAME CAN BE FLEETING...
QUITE A PLAN, BERT...

...SOUNDS LIKE THERE'S GONNA BE A LOTTA MONEY IN IT.
WERE YOU PLANNING ON CUTTING US IN ON SOME OF THAT ACTION?
START TALKING, SUIT.
OKAY.
IT'S OBVIOUS YOU HAVE AN ISSUE WITH THE WAY I'VE BEEN IMPLEMENTING THIS ENDEAVOR.
BUT CERTAINLY YOU CAN'T ARGUE WITH THE NEED FOR A SAFE HAVEN FOR--
Thanks Joe! ULY FAR!
FOR ANYONE THAT CAN AFFORD IT-- THE RICH AND THE PRIVILEGED?!
IT'S TOUGH TO OFFEND ME--BUT THAT DOES IT!
HEY-- WATCH IT!
YO--!
LISTEN TO ME. I TRIED TO EXPLAIN IT ALL TO YOU.
YOU SERVED A VERY IMPORTANT FUNCTION. EVERY WORLD NEEDS ITS OWN SUPERHEROES... IT MAKES PEOPLE FEEL SAFE...
...YOU WERE GOOD MARKETING.

SUPER CO
WELL, I CAN'T ARGUE WITH THAT... BUT YOU DIDN'T TAKE SOMETHING INTO ACCOUNT, BERTY-BOY.
MY OTHER HALF IS UNIQUELY QUALIFIED TO BUST YOUR BRAIN BOX WIDE OPEN. GOT US RIGHT OUT.

OH, YEAH-- WE'RE OUT, ALL RIGHT...!
CLEARLY, YOU'RE NOT SEEING THE BIGGER PICTURE...

...THIS IS THE FUTURE. AND, CONSIDERING THE FACT THAT NONE OF YOU SEEMED TO HAVE ONE OF YOUR OWN LINED UP, I FIGURED YOU'D JUMP AT THE CHANGE OF SCENERY.
DON'T YOU REMEMBER HOW PATHETIC YOU ALL WERE?!

RUBY...?
I...
...WAS NEVER PATHETIC.

CLEARLY, YOU DON'T KNOW HOW TO DANCE, BERT.
BUT IT'S OUR TURN NOW, Y'DIG?
AND LESS THAN A MINUTE LATER...

--GIVE IT UP FOR THE ***AGENTS OF CHANGE!***

NOW, SOME OF YOU MIGHT'VE SEEN ME ON MY OWN REALITY SHOW.
LET ME BE THE FIRST TO TELL YOU...THERE WASN'T A LOT OF "REALITY" INVOLVED THERE...
YOU THINK THAT'S HIS OWN PERSONAL EPIPHANY...?

MEANWHILE-- A RECKONING IN THE DRESSING ROOM!
L-LISTEN... WHICHEVER ONE YOU ARE...
...I DON'T FEEL GOOD ABOUT HAVING TO TAKE DOWN SOMEONE WHO'S...WELL...IN YOUR CONDITION...

BUT YOU CAN'T POSSIBLY HOPE TO KEEP ME...
NEVER UNDERESTIMATE THE LESS FORTUNATE--

...HERE...
--ESPECIALLY SINCE THEY MIGHT NOT BE LESS FORTUNATE!

WHILE ONE MORRISETTE BROTHER WEARS THE TIGHTS...

S.POSTAL
...THE OTHER CAN INDULGE THE ART OF REMOTE REALITY CREATION!
NEXT UP IN LINE--
WAIT A MINUTE...
...I'M A... POSTAL WORKER...

NOOOOOO--!

DON'T WORRY ABOUT BERT. WE'RE KEEPING HIM SOMEPLACE SAFE... SOMEPLACE WHERE HE CAN'T CAUSE TROUBLE.
IN THE MEANTIME, WE'LL BE IN CHARGE OF THE TECHNOLOGY HE WAS TRYING TO SELL YOU ON...

...WE'LL MAKE SURE IT DOESN'T FALL INTO THE WRONG HANDS.
STRONG WORDS PROVOKE A STRONG CROWD RESPONSE--

--AND THOSE WORDS SOON GO VIRAL!
...AMATEUR VIDEO OF THE EVENT HAS SPREAD WORLDWIDE, AND WE'RE LEFT TO WONDER ABOUT THESE "AGENTS OF CHANGE"...
...AND WHAT THEIR TRUE AGENDA MIGHT BE.
CHANGE IS GOOD, PEOPLE. GET USED TO IT.
PUBLIC OPINION IS STILL DIVIDED ON WHETHER THIS GROUP IS MORE SUPERHEROIC OR MORE SUBVERSIVE.
TIME WILL TELL WHOSE INTERESTS THEY'RE ACTUALLY SERVING...
CN NEWS 12

...BUT I AIN'T LEAVING UNTIL THIS ONE'S DONE.
ONE THING I LEARNED FROM BERT'S SHENANIGANS... SOMETIMES YOU JUST GOTTA PLANT YOUR FLAG.
MAKE YOUR MARK.
BUT AS LONG AS SOMETHING'S REAL--
--THEN WE CAN STILL CHANGE IT, RIGHT?
WARMAKER DROPPIN' SCIENCE!
TRUER WORDS WERE NEVER SPOKEN. TRUER INK NEVER ETCHED IN FLESH.
AGENTS of CHANGE
ORIGINS BE DAMNED...
SEE YA REAL SOON!
WHY? BECAUSE WE LIKE YOU!
THE BEGINNING

DURING THE BURNING OF WASHINGTON IN THE EARLY YEARS OF THE NINETEENTH CENTURY, EVEN THE WHITE HOUSE WASN'T SPARED.
THAT DESTRUCTION OCCURRED A LONG TIME AGO...
...MAYBE IT'S PAST DUE.
ALTHOUGH FRANK WELLS DOESN'T NEED HISTORY TO MAKE HIS POINT.
HE'S OUT THERE, MR. PRESIDENT.
HE'S BEEN CRISSCROSSING THE GLOBE, BUT HE'S FINALLY ENDED UP HERE--
I'VE BEEN FOLLOWING THE DATA, JOSH. SO WE KNOW WHERE HE IS...
...BUT NONE OF US KNOWS WHAT HE WANTS.
DO WE...?
THE BALLAD OF FRANK WELLS: ROCKING CHAIR

HE SAVED NEW YORK. HE SAVED THE WORLD. AND NO ONE KNEW IT.
WE HAD OUR CHANCE TO RECOGNIZE WHAT HE'D DONE, TO BRING HIM IN FROM THE COLD... AND WE BLEW IT.
NOT ONLY THAT, WE TRIED TO FORCE THE ISSUE WITH THE REDLINE SQUADRON...

"...ANYONE THINK THERE'S A CHANCE HE MIGHT ACTUALLY HOLD A GRUDGE...?"

WELL...WHO CAN SAY WHEN IT COMES TO THEIR KIND, MR. PRESIDENT? SUPERHEROES ARE TYPICALLY UNPREDICTABLE.
WE'VE ALL READ FRANK'S PSYCH FILE. IT DOESN'T PAINT A VERY PROMISING PICTURE REGARDING HIS ABILITY TO BE REASONABLE...

J-JUST... SIGN HERE... P-PLEASE...
OF COURSE.

FRANK WELLS

THIS HAS GOTTEN WAY OUT OF HAND...
WHAT ARE YOU WHINING ABOUT?! YOU'RE THE PRESIDENT! YOU MADE YOUR DECISION--NOW STAND BY IT!
HE COMES IN HERE...YOU SHOW HIM WHY YOU WERE ELECTED WITH FIFTY-ONE PERCENT OF THE POPULAR VOTE...!

I REALLY DON'T THINK THAT MY--
MR. PRESIDENT...
...WE NEED TO TALK.
YOU WANT...TO TALK...?
IT'S NICE TO SEE YOU ALLOWED ME IN WITHOUT INCITING SOME UNNECESSARY CONFLICT...
I NEVER ASSUMED THAT WE WERE ADVERSARIES...
...NOT TO MENTION, THEIR "SHOOT FIRST, ASK QUESTIONS LATER" POLICY.
...I THINK WE'RE BOTH PAST THAT, DON'T YOU...?
I KNOW I AM.
REALLY? I DON'T THINK THE REDLINES WOULD CORROBORATE THAT SENTIMENT...
BUT, LIKE I SAID, WE SHOULD TRY TO MOVE PAST ANY AND ALL MISUNDERSTANDINGS.
I'M HERE TO MAKE A DEAL.

Y'KNOW, I'VE SEEN A **LOT** RECENTLY. BEEN ALL **OVER.**
THIS WORLD HAS A LOT OF **PROBLEMS** THAT NEED **SOLVING.** I DID MY **BEST,** BUT I JUST COULDN'T GET TO THE **ROOT** OF THINGS...
...AND THEN I REALIZED, I NEEDED TO TAKE THE FIGHT TO THE **TOP** OF THE TREE.
CHIEF
THE FIGHT...?
YOU **REALIZE...** THE WORLD IS BUILT ON A **COMPLEX** SYSTEM OF POLITICAL MECHANISMS...
OH, I'M AWARE BUT WE'RE GOING TO **CUT THROUGH** ALL OF THAT NONSENSE.
I'VE DECIDED TO SET YOU STRAIGHT... **OLD SCHOOL** STYLE...
<"...YOU'VE **SEEN** WHAT I CAN DO. YOU KNOW WHAT I'M **CAPABLE** OF. YOU **DON'T** WANT TO BE ON MY BAD SIDE...">
<TRANSLATED FROM RUSSIA
<...WHAT YOU NEED, MORE THAN ANYTHING, IS **PROTECTION...**>
<TRANSLATED FROM FARSI>
<...FORTUNATELY, THIS IS A SERVICE I AM UNIQUELY QUALIFIED TO **PROVIDE...**>
<TRANSLATED FROM CHINES

<...YOU'LL HAVE NO NEED TO FEAR YOUR ENEMIES, BECAUSE I'LL BE KEEPING A CLOSE EYE ON ALL OF THEM...>
<TRANSLATED FROM HINDI>
<...YOU'LL FINALLY BE ABLE TO FIND YOUR TRUE PLACE IN THE WORLD, ENACTING POLICIES BASED MORE ON COMPASSION THAN IMPERIALISTIC GREED...>
<TRANSLATED FROM KOREAN>
...YOU CAN EFFECTIVELY WATCHDOG WHATEVER INJUSTICES ARE HAPPENING IN YOUR OWN BACKYARD...
<...BECAUSE I KNOW DAMN WELL THEY'RE HAPPENING, AND I WANT IT ALL TO STOP...>
<TRANSLATED FROM PORTUGUESE>
...IT'S FINALLY TIME FOR YOU TO PUT YOUR HOUSE-- THIS COUNTRY-- IN ORDER, MR. PRESIDENT. YOU'RE FINALLY OUT OF EXCUSES NOT TO.
SOUNDS A LOT LIKE...
...GLOBAL RACKETEERING...
CHIEF
CALL IT WHATEVER YOU WANT, SIR. BUT WE'RE GOING TO TRY IT FOR A WHILE AND SEE HOW IT WORKS.
KEEP IN MIND, I DON'T TAKE MY RESPONSIBILITIES LIGHTLY. AND I SEE EVERYTHING.
THINK OF IT AS AN OPPORTUNITY-- FOR ALL OF YOU-- TO BE THE LEADERS THE WORLD NEEDS YOU TO BE.

I...DON'T KNOW HOW WELL I RESPOND TO VEILED THREATS.
THEN DON'T THINK OF IT AS A VEILED THREAT...
...THINK OF IT AS A PROMISE. FROM ME TO YOU.
START FIXING THINGS. NOW.
OR I'LL COME BACK FOR ANOTHER LITTLE CHAT. MAYBE NOT SO FRIENDLY NEXT TIME...
SO YOU FEEL YOU ADEQUATELY OUTFLANKED THEM...?
WHO KNOWS? BUT AT LEAST I WAS FINALLY TALKING TO THE RIGHT PEOPLE.
AT LEAST, I THINK I WAS...
PROTECTING THE WORLD FROM ITSELF...
WHEN I THOUGHT I'D PREVENTED THE APOCALYPSE, I WASN'T SURE IF THERE WAS ANYTHING LEFT TO DO...
NOW I KNOW THE TRUTH. NOW I KNOW THE THREAT ISN'T OUT THERE.
IT'S RIGHT HERE. IT'S WHAT WE DO TO OURSELVES.
I CAN'T GIVE THEM A CONSCIENCE. BUT I CAN GIVE THEM A REASON.
...THERE ARE WORSE ENDEAVORS FOR A HERO TO UNDERTAKE.
TIME WILL TELL IF YOUR METHODOLOGY IS TRULY EFFECTIVE.

INDEED. AND FROM THERE...PERHAPS EVEN ENLIGHTENMENT.
AS YOUR EXAMPLE HAS UNDOUBTEDLY PROVED... ANYTHING IS POSSIBLE.
RIGHT...
...IT'S ABOUT HAVING A NEW PERSPECTIVE. LIKE YOU SAID, WHAT HAPPENS NOW... CAN BE FREE OF CLICHÉ.
YOU JUST WATCH.
BUT BEYOND THAT, I FEEL LIKE I LEARNED SOMETHING EVEN MORE IMPORTANT. MAYBE THE MOST IMPORTANT THING...
...I FINALLY REALIZED THAT--
--EH?
SO...
...IT WAS THE END OF THE WORLD... AND IT WAS EVERYTHING OUR COLLECTIVE NIGHTMARES PROMISED US IT WOULD BE! AND MORE!
LUCKILY, SOMEONE HAD THE BIG BALLS TO STAND UP TO TOTAL ANNIHILATION...
...AND HIS NAME WAS FRANK WELLS.
NOT A BAD DAY'S WORK FOR A SUPERHERO.
NOT AN ENDING, BUT A FRESH START

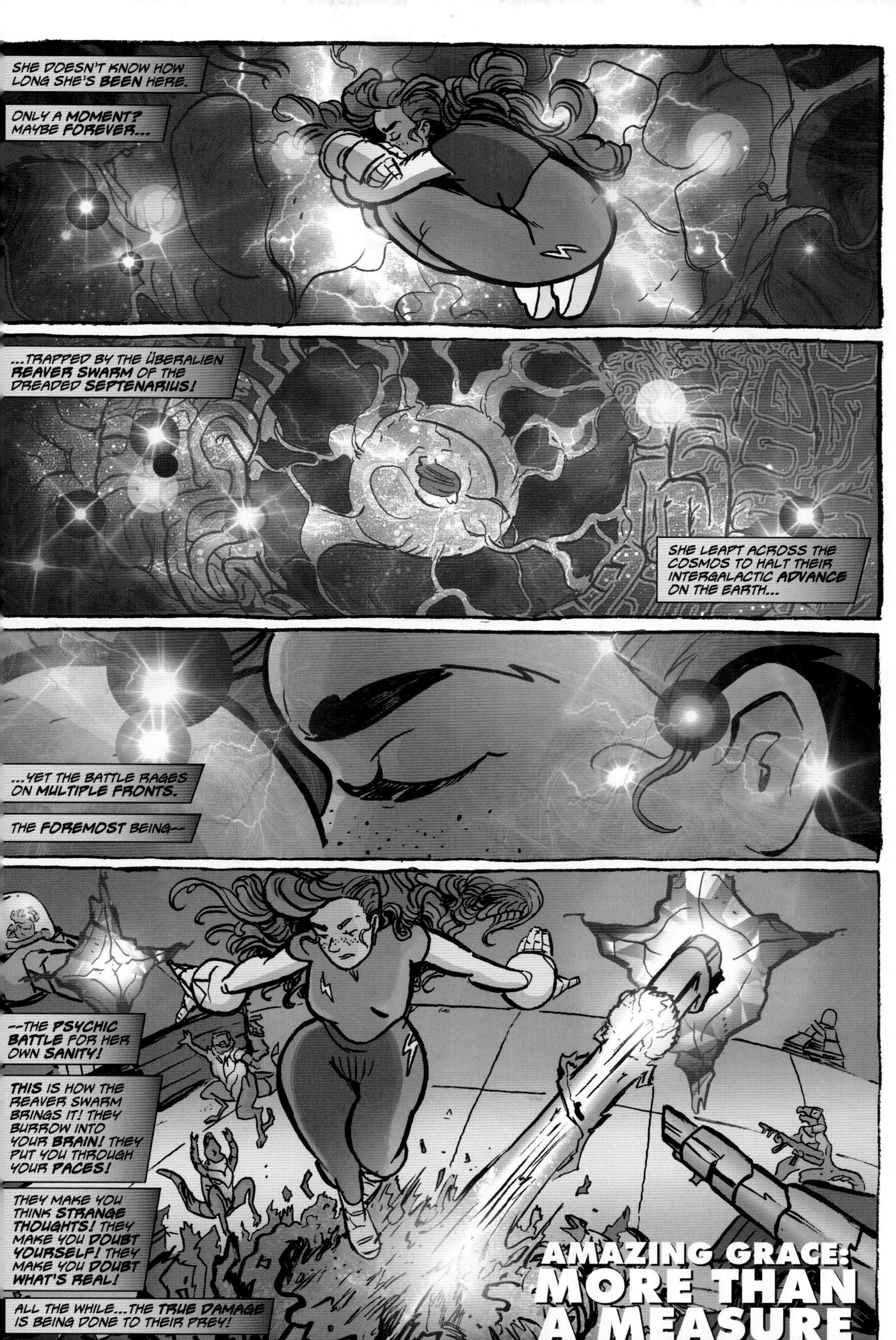
SHE DOESN'T KNOW HOW LONG SHE'S BEEN HERE.
ONLY A MOMENT? MAYBE FOREVER...
...TRAPPED BY THE ÜBERALIEN REAVER SWARM OF THE DREADED SEPTENARIUS!
SHE LEAPT ACROSS THE COSMOS TO HALT THEIR INTERGALACTIC ADVANCE ON THE EARTH...
...YET THE BATTLE RAGES ON MULTIPLE FRONTS.
THE FOREMOST BEING--
--THE PSYCHIC BATTLE FOR HER OWN SANITY!
THIS IS HOW THE REAVER SWARM BRINGS IT! THEY BURROW INTO YOUR BRAIN! THEY PUT YOU THROUGH YOUR PACES!
THEY MAKE YOU THINK STRANGE THOUGHTS! THEY MAKE YOU DOUBT YOURSELF! THEY MAKE YOU DOUBT WHAT'S REAL!
ALL THE WHILE...THE TRUE DAMAGE IS BEING DONE TO THEIR PREY!
AMAZING GRACE:
MORE THAN A MEASURE

BUT GRACE IS NEVER HELPLESS...

...SHE CAN ALWAYS BE HEARD.
UMMM...
...ANYONE ELSE SEE THAT...?

OKAY...
...E-EVERYONE STAY CALM...
...I'M SURE THERE'S...SOME EXPLANATION FOR THIS...
EVEN IF THE MESSAGE IS MISUNDERSTOOD--

--THE ECHOES OF HER PRESENCE CANNOT BE FULLY EXORCISED FROM THE CITY SHE HERSELF BUILT!
HERS IS THE UNDENIABLE SPIRIT OF GOLDEN CITY...

...THOUGHTS OF HOME HAVE TANGIBLE CONSEQUENCES...

...EVEN IF THOSE CONSEQUENCES CANNOT HELP HER HERE.
BUT THERE IS STRENGTH... THERE IS WILLPOWER...

...AND THE FIGHT FOR SURVIVAL CONTINUES!

HUMANITY'S SURVIVAL!

THE STAKES HAVE NEVER BEEN GREATER!

RUMBLE IN THE COSMOPSYCHIC JUNGLE!

REAL IS UNREAL! AND VICE VERSA!

IT TAKES ALL SHE'S GOT!

ALL HER LOVE! ALL HER TERROR!

EVERYTHING SHE IS! AND HAS EVER BEEN!

MEANWHILE, A UNIVERSE AWAY...
THE HOME FIRES CHURN...
WHAT DO WE TELL PEOPLE...?
NO POINT IN HIDING THE TRUTH. THEY KNOW SHE'S GONE. WITH ALL THE DATA RECEIVED PROVIDING CONFIRMATION...

I JUST... DON'T WANT TO ACCEPT IT.
THERE'S A REASON FOR THAT. NONE OF THIS FEELS RIGHT...

...THERE'S A BIG PART OF ME THAT'S STILL HOLDING ONTO SOME SLIM HOPE THAT SHE WAS ABLE TO--
EVERYONE! COME QUICK!

SOMETHING'S HAPPENING IN THE MAIN CITY SQUARE!
YOU'RE NOT GOING TO BELIEVE THIS!

THERE WAS NEVER A PLAN. THERE WAS NEVER A PROCEDURE. IT WAS NOT TALKED ABOUT.
PEOPLE JUST STARTED SHOWING UP.

SHE WASN'T EVEN THE FIRST.
BUT SHE FEELS IT. THEY ALL DO.

IS IT... SOME KIND OF MEMORIAL...?
I REALLY DON'T THINK SO...

"...MORE LIKE A MASS VIGIL."

AND FOR WHAT? THE TRUE SHOWDOWN IS STILL IN PROGRESS!
BUT SOMEHOW... SHE KNOWS.

AND PERHAPS THEIR STRENGTH... CAN BECOME HERS.

THEY ALL HAVE THEIR OWN STORIES... THEY ALL HAVE THEIR OPINIONS OF THE CHAMPION THAT BUILT THIS CITY...
...THE GOLDEN CITY THEY CALL HOME.

BUT THEY SHARE ONE THING TONIGHT...
YOU'LL MAKE IT...
...I HAVE FAITH.

SOMETIMES FAITH IS ALL IT TAKES--

--AMAZING GRACE MAKES HER MOVE!
IT TAKES GREAT STRENGTH TO FINALLY LET GO...

...TO CONFOUND YOUR ADVERSARY WITH A CHANGE IN TACTICS...

...TO DRAW UPON THAT WHICH HAS ALWAYS BEEN WITHIN YOU...

...TO TAKE THE BELIEF OTHERS HAVE IN YOU AND TURN IT INTO PURE POWER...

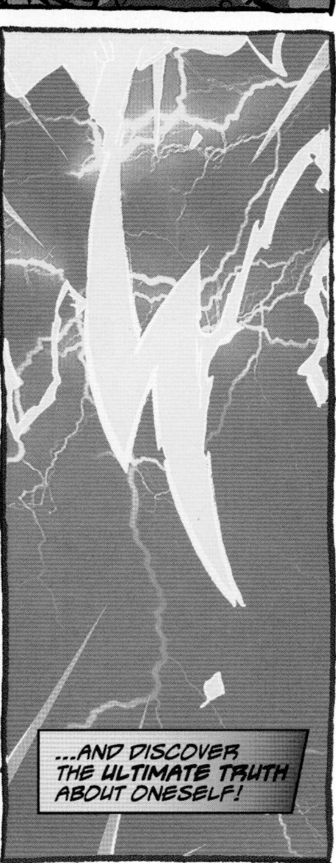
...AND DISCOVER THE ULTIMATE TRUTH ABOUT ONESELF!

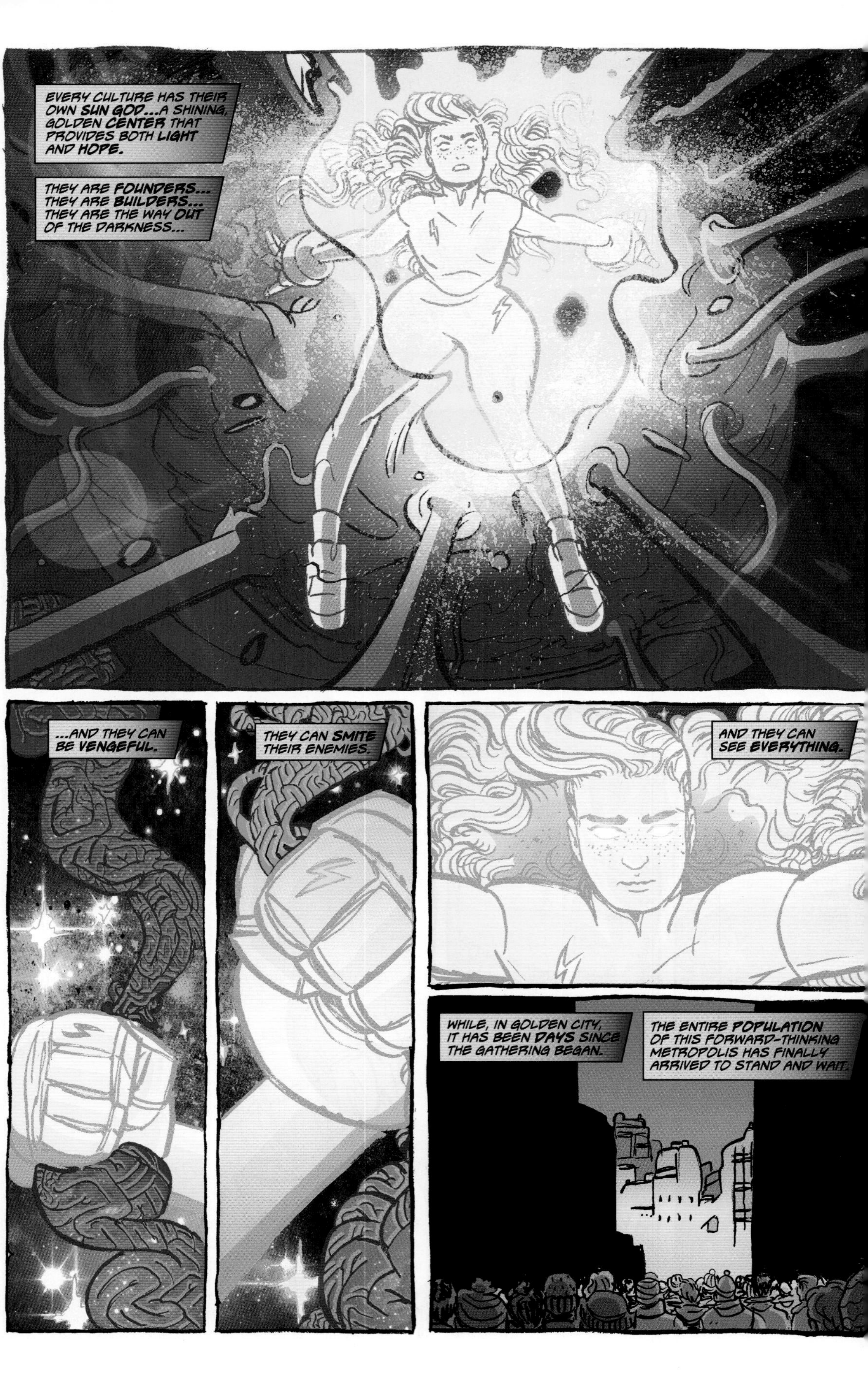

EVERY CULTURE HAS THEIR OWN SUN GOD...A SHINING, GOLDEN CENTER THAT PROVIDES BOTH LIGHT AND HOPE.

THEY ARE FOUNDERS... THEY ARE BUILDERS... THEY ARE THE WAY OUT OF THE DARKNESS...

...AND THEY CAN BE VENGEFUL.

THEY CAN SMITE THEIR ENEMIES.

AND THEY CAN SEE EVERYTHING.

WHILE, IN GOLDEN CITY, IT HAS BEEN DAYS SINCE THE GATHERING BEGAN.
THE ENTIRE POPULATION OF THIS FORWARD-THINKING METROPOLIS HAS FINALLY ARRIVED TO STAND AND WAIT.

SHE NO LONGER NEEDS **ASSISTANCE** TO MAKE THIS TRIP. SHE MERELY **STEPS THROUGH** THE VERY FABRIC OF EXISTENCE AS ONE MIGHT STEP OUT OF THE **SHOWER**.

FOR **HER**, THE UNIVERSE IS SUDDENLY A MUCH **SMALLER** PLACE...BUT NO LESS **IMPRESSIVE**.

BUT SHE **UNDERSTANDS** NOW...IN A WAY SHE NEVER HAD TO **BEFORE**.

ISSUE #1 SAN DIEGO COMIC-CON 2013 EXCLUSIVE JAM COVER

BATTLE BUS

CHARACTER DESIGNS

The heroes of *Catalyst Comix* originate in the Comics' Greatest World universe. Their histories still include all of their nineties adventures, but the characters themselves have been updated by Casey and the artists. This cover from *Will to Power* features Titan in battle with Grace, Warmaker, Ruby, and Rebel (along with Catalyst teammates Mecha and Madison) and shows their original designs.

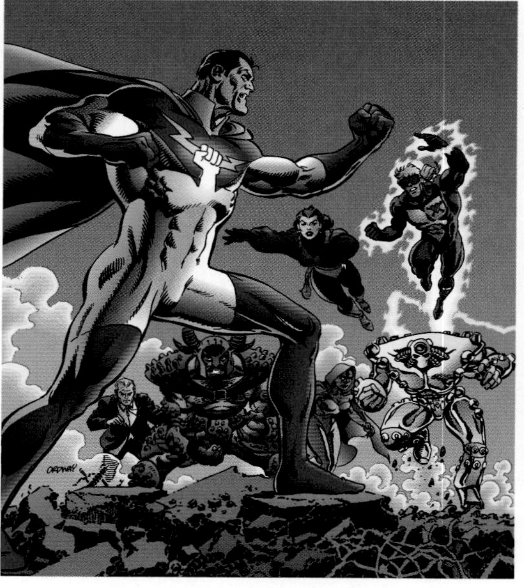

Will to Power #8 cover by Jerry Ordway with Matthew Hollingsworth

Comics' Greatest World: Wolf Gang cover by Chris Warner with Matthew Hollingsworth

Wolf Ferrell is imported into *Catalyst*'s Agents of Change from his origins in the Wolf Gang, a team on which he went simply by the name Hunter (also pictured: Breaker, Cutter, Bomber, and Burner).

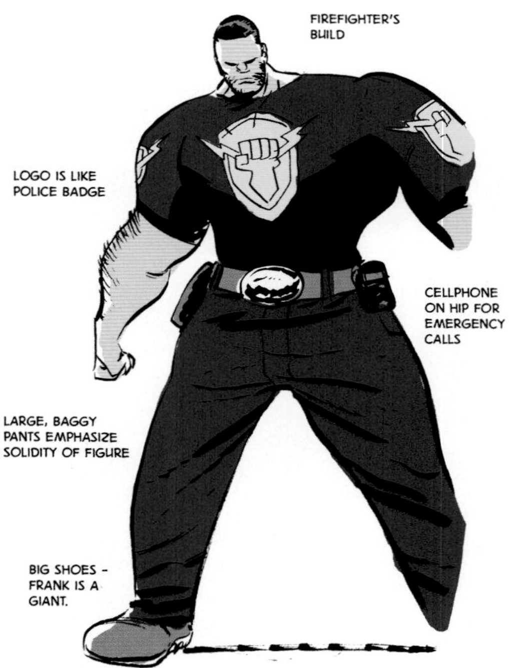

FIREFIGHTER'S BUILD
LOGO IS LIKE POLICE BADGE
CELLPHONE ON HIP FOR EMERGENCY CALLS
LARGE, BAGGY PANTS EMPHASIZE SOLIDITY OF FIGURE
BIG SHOES - FRANK IS A GIANT.

BIG BLUE TRENCHCOAT ECHOES ORIGINAL CAPE.

Early versions of McDaid's Titan redesign used his original logo, but the updated color scheme and the coat replacing his cape were introduced early in the process.

skin shirt badge hair/shoes belt phone coat

Once the new logo was added and extended onto the front of the coat, Titan's design was in place.

NIBIRU [COLOUR CONCEPT]

CROSS BETWEEN A SPIDER, A GNARLED, ANCIENT TREE, AND A STORMCLOUD
LIGHTNING FLICKERS CONSTANTLY ACROSS NIBIRU'S SHOULDERS
CLOUD TRAILS OFF THE MONSTER...
...AND GATHER ROUND THE BASE, OBSCURING IT.

McDaid's ideas for the cosmic threat that opens the series.

WEATHERED SKULL. SMOKE TRAILS FROM SLATTED EYES/MOUTH
CHEST CONTAINS POWER SOURCE. AREA AROUND CAVITY IS MOTTLED, LIKE UNDERSIDE OF TURTLE.
CLEAR BUBBLES, LIKE SPIDER EGGS/EYES
MAIN BODY COMPOSED OF "MEATY", OILY, INTERLOCKING PLATES. PLATES INTERLOCK HAPHAZARDLY.
ARMS ARE LIKE BLACK WOOD, COVERED IN BARBS

Vortex was dramatically reenvisioned, while the Guru is a new character. The Redline pilots were created for the original Comics' Greatest World, but never made it into a story until *Catalyst Comix*.

Maybury's update of Grace retains her original color scheme and iconography, but strips the bodysuit to its minimalist essence while highlighting the boots and gloves.

Farinas tried several approaches to the Agents of Change (in pencil) before settling on the final designs. One version of Ruby imagined her as a being composed of raw energy, with a costume closer to her original look.

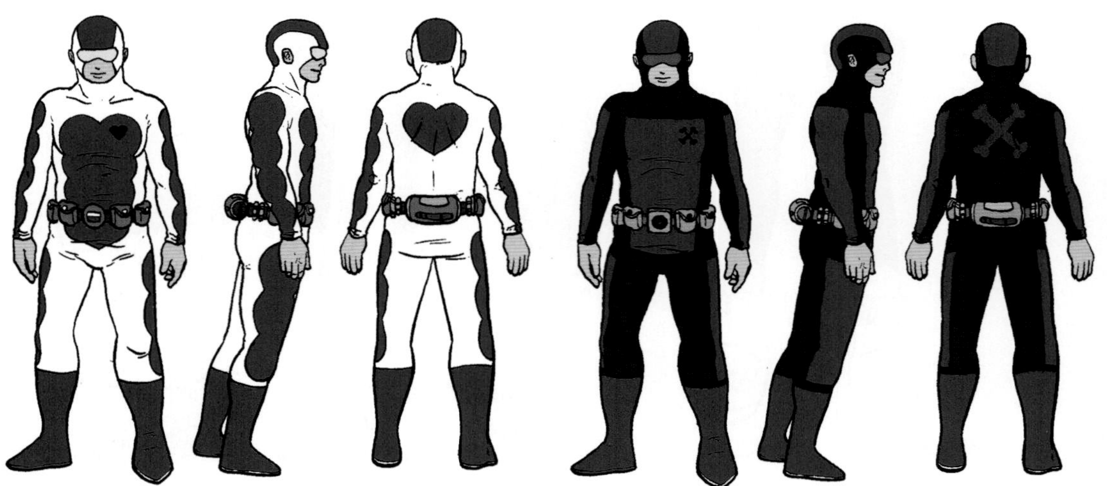

The Rebel twins' look was completely revamped, with two complementary costumes in place of the original single design.

Some concepts for Wolfhunter's fashion sense.

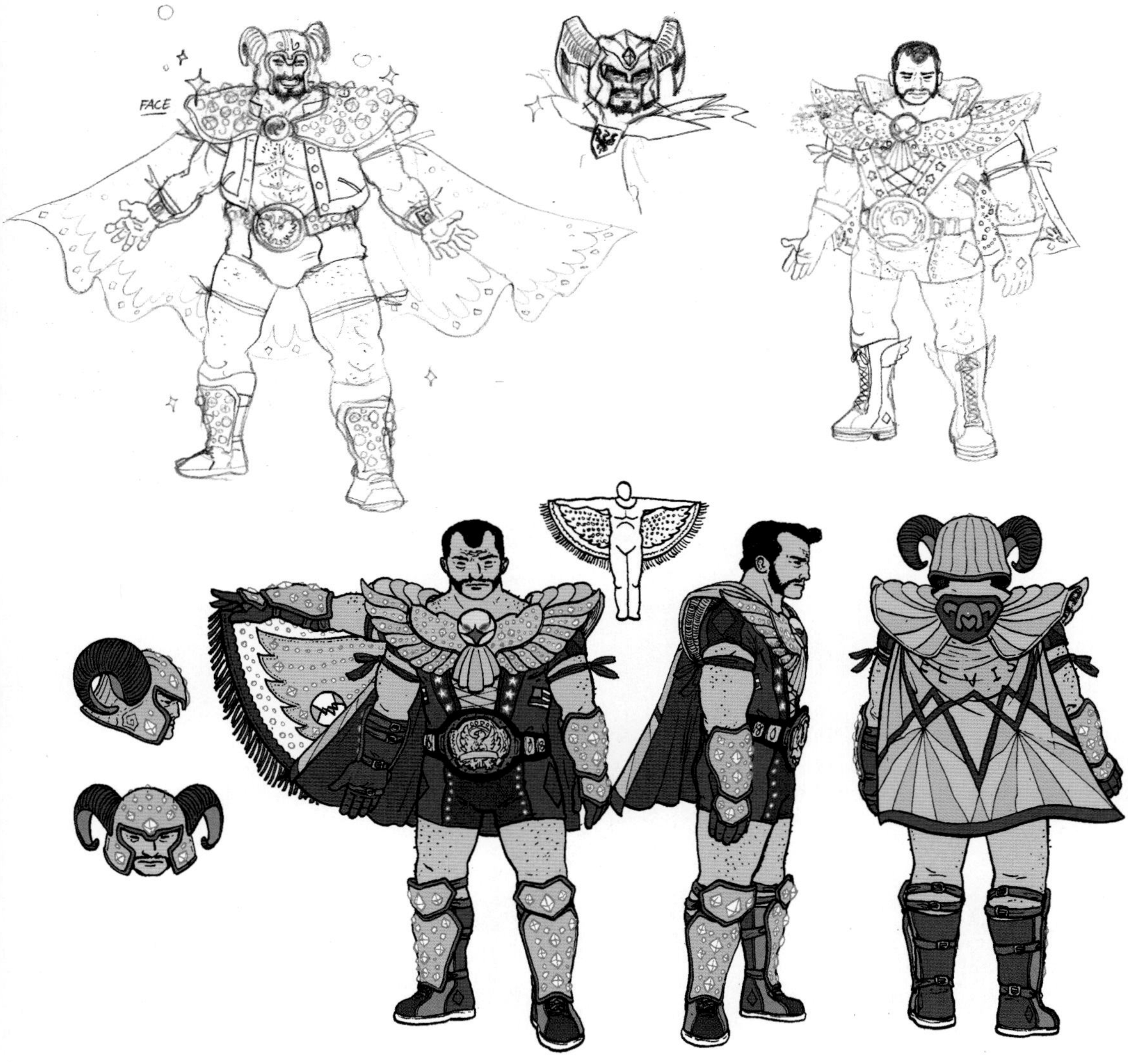

Farinas played with the notion of wrestling-style face and heel personas for Warmaker. The final design is louder and showier than the nineties version, befitting Warmaker's *Catalyst Comix* personality.